S0-BCI-950

The Jewish Literary Treasures of England and America

By the same author:

The Slave Who Saved the City (1960)

A Guide to Hassidism (1961)

The Jewish Literary Treasures of England and America

BY HARRY M. RABINOWICZ

THOMAS YOSELOFF
New York • London • Toronto

Library of Congress Catalog Card Number: 62-14964

Thomas Yoseloff, *Publisher*
11 East 36th Street
New York 16, N. Y.

Thomas Yoseloff Ltd.
123 New Bond Street
London W. 1, England

9790

Printed in the United States of America

In Loving Memory of

ANNE FREEMAN

a great-granddaughter of Solomon Kluger (1783–1869)

Contents

List of Illustrations

The following illustrations appear as a group after page 96.

Preface

"The *Shekhinah* accompanied Israel into exile," says the Talmud picturesquely.[1] Wherever they settled, the "People of the Book," as Mohammed called them, established spiritual citadels, libraries, academies, schools. These were armories that strengthened and protected the Jew against the slings and arrows of outrageous fortune. Books were his constant companions during the unholy wars that crimsoned the Rhine and the Moselle with Jewish blood. They accompanied him through centuries of exile and wanderings, through the perilous passes of the Pyrenees, during the Chmielnicki massacres of 1648, during the pogroms of Eastern Europe, and during the Nazi holocaust.

In many instances the books shared the fate of their homeless, harassed owners. They too had no resting place beneath the sun. They too went through the furnace of affliction. The art of book-burning, born in 1242, was a favorite pastime of mediaeval bigots and was perfected with Teutonic thoroughness during World War II. Hundreds of Jewish libraries were demolished in vast orgies of vandalism that made the flames of the autos da fé pale into insignificance.

England has long been the home of priceless Hebrew treasures. Over 10,000 Hebrew manuscripts and 100,000 Geniza fragments are scattered through the public and private collections of Great Britain. Yet the eclipse of East European Jewry saw the rise of American Jewry as the largest Jewish community in the world. The torch that had illumined Jewish life in the Old World with the fires of Chassidism, Haskalah, and *Jüdische Wissenschaft* was rekindled in the New World. The development there was spectacular. Within half a dozen decades the Jewish and non-Jewish repositories of the New World amassed collections which now outshine the celebrated libraries that Britain took six centuries to build. Today the New World is exceptionally equipped for Jewish research and Jewish studies.

Bibliophiles are not necessarily bibliographers. It is now more than half a century since Steinschneider died, yet his place has not been filled. Catalogues have not kept pace with book collections. Many famous libraries have no catalogue, descriptive or otherwise. Little has been done by the libraries to draw attention to the gems for which they are the setting.

It was not possible within the compass of one small volume to deal with all the collections of England and America. Nor was it possible to include any of the private collections.

I am grateful to the Jewish War Memorial Council for the award of the 1960 Sir Robert Waley Cohen Memorial Scholarship, which enabled me to study some of the libraries in the United States. It is a pleasure to express sincere gratitude for much help most willingly given by librarians on both sides of the Atlantic. I am glad to acknowledge my indebtedness to my sister Rachel, who has not only given me informed and invaluable help at all times but generously gave up much of her scanty leisure to read through the typescript in all its stages. To my wife, who typed the manuscript for me, I am grateful not only for that service but for her unfailing encouragement.

The writer will be richly rewarded if this book makes the reader mindful of the paternal advice of Judah Ibn Tibbon of Lunel (1120–1190): "My son, make thy books thy companions. Let thy bookcase and shelves be thy pleasure grounds and gardens. Bask in their paradise, gather their fruit, pluck their roses, take their spices and their myrrh. If thy soul be satiate and weary, change from garden to garden, from furrow to furrow, from prospect to prospect."

London, September 1961/5722 H. R.

Acknowledgments

Special acknowledgments for valuable assistance, for helpful suggestions, and for permission to reproduce illustrations are due to the following: Dr. J. Rosenwasser and the Trustees of the British Museum; the curators of the Bodleian Library; the librarian of the University Library, Cambridge; Basil Blackwell Publishers Limited; Miss Ruth P. Lehmann, A.L.A., librarian of Jews' College; Mr. Hillier Wise, B.A.; Mr. Raphael Loewe, M.C., M.A.; Mr. Sol Cohen, secretary of the Jewish War Memorial Council, London; Mr. Norman M. Cohen; Mr. Marcus Carr; Dr. Nahum Sarna, librarian of the Jewish Theological Seminary of America; Mr. Ezekiel Lifschutz and Dr. S. Noble of YIVO, New York; Mr. Abraham Berger, chief of the Jewish Division of the New York Public Library; Mr. Jacob I. Dienstag, librarian of the Mendel Gottesman Library of the Yeshiva University; Rabbi I. Edward Kiev, librarian of the Jewish Institute of Religion, New York; Mr. Herbert C. Zafren and Mrs. Dorothy Millstone of the Hebrew Union College Library, Cincinnati; Mr. Maxwell Whiteman of Dropsie College; Mr. F. M. Palmer of Harvard College Library; Dr. A. Katsh of the New York University Jewish Culture Foundation; Dr. Leon Nemoy of Yale University; Mr. Lawrence Marwick, head of the Hebraic Section of the Library of Congress; Pictorial Enquirer, Cincinnati; Mr. Kazik Pazovski; Mr. David J. Hill, M.A.

PART I

The Jewish Literary Treasures of England

Chapter I

The British Museum

The magnificent dome of the British Museum Reading Room is one hundred years old; but infinitely older are many of the 6,000,000 printed books, 75,000 manuscripts, and 9,000 incunabula in this far-famed library, the greatest collection of valuable manuscripts that the world has ever known. Scholars and bibliophiles journey from every corner of the literate globe to this Mecca of the mind. And how rich the variety, how wide the scope of this fabled world of words! Subjects both obscure and commonplace are so clearly catalogued as to make access almost incredibly easy. The masterpieces of the past are at the reader's fingertips as readily as the products of the present—ranging all the way from a Mazarin Bible, the Codex Sinaiticus, or a Caxton first edition to the most recent pamphlet on ritual slaughter.

The Biblical verse "And though thy beginnings were small, yet thy end shall greatly increase," [2] applies aptly to the history of the Museum's Hebrew collection. Two hundred years ago it simply did not exist. Yet Jewry today can take special pride in this renowned repository of Hebraic treasures.

HEBREW MANUSCRIPTS

During the second half of the eighteenth century there were merely a handful of Hebrew manuscripts in the Museum's possession. The wealthy physician, Sir Hans Sloane (1660–1753), bequeathed his library to the Crown, "that it may be visible and seen by all persons provided that the sum of £20,000 be paid to my two daughters, the Lady Cadogan and Mrs. Stanley." [3] George II received the news with considerable skepticism. He doubted whether the country was in a position to spend so large a sum of money. In fact he doubted whether there was £20,000 in the Treasury of England. Happily the country's finances were rather more stable than the King had supposed. The Preamble to an Act of Parliament of 1753 tells the story:

Sir Hans Sloane of Chelsea, in the County of Middlesex, Baronet, having, through the Course of many years with great labor and expense, gathered together whatever could be procured either in our own or in foreign countries, that was rare and curious . . . these shall remain and be preserved for public use, to all posterity . . . and free access is given not only for the inspection and entertainment of the learned and the curious, but for the general use and benefit of the public.

In this manner Parliament acquired 40,000 printed books and 3,500 manuscripts including thirteen works in Hebrew.

The first Earl of Oxford, Robert Harley (1661–1724), was the next major benefactor. His wife had brought him a dowry of a quarter of a million pounds sterling, so Harley was able to follow his bent as a bibliophile. He was assisted by Humfrey Wanley (1672–1726) who was paid an annual salary of £12.

A conscientious book collector, Harley conceived "as part of a Library's Keeper's duty to know what books are extant in other Libraries besides his own." In 1753 the Duchess of Portland sold the Harley collection to Parliament for £10,000. Among its 8,000 items were 130 Hebrew manuscripts.

Three manuscripts were presented by the broker Solomon da Costa Athias (1690–1769), accompanied by the following letter:

Thus saith Solomon, son of the humble, pious and honored Isaac da Costa, surnamed Athias, late of the City of Amsterdam, deceased, one of the people called Jews which are scattered among the nations and from among that part of the captives of Jerusalem which settled in Spain. I have already dwelt 54 years and upwards, with security, advantage and ease of mind in this renowned metropolis, eminent above all others for the number, valor, freedom, commerce, knowledge, ingenuity, politeness and humility of its inhabitants . . . whereas a most stately monument hath been lately erected and endowed by the wisdom and munificence of the British legislature . . . an house abounding in books, old and new, written and printed, and in the choicest curiosities both natural and artificial, with intent to preserve the same to succeeding generations in benefit to the people of these nations and of the whole earth . . . as a small token of my esteem, love, reverence, and gratitude, to this magnanimous nation and as a thanksgiving offering in part, for the generous protection and numberless blessings which I have enjoyed under it.[4]

During the first four decades of the nineteenth century the library acquired manuscripts from the Orientalist and Irish Wesleyan minister Adam Clarke (1762–1832), from the Reina Library of Milan, and from the library of the Duke of Sussex (1774–1843), sixth son of George III. By mid-century Leopold Dukes (1810–1891), the Hungarian historian, who spent thirty-nine years in London, listed three hundred Hebrew manuscripts in the British Museum.

The library was fortunate in its staff. In 1846 the bookseller Asher recommended a scholarly candidate, and at the age of forty-one Joseph Zedner (1804–1871) was appointed assistant in the Department of Printed Books. Zedner was born in Gross-Glogau, birthplace of Joseph Lehmann of Berlin and of Solomon Munk of Paris. A pupil of Rabbi Akiba Eger, he eventually became a tutor in the house of the bookseller Asher. In 1848 he published *Auswahl Historischer Stücke,* a collection of historical authors from the second century to the present day, containing punctuated text, German translation, and explanatory notes. A practicing Jew, Zedner accepted the position at the Museum on the express condition that he was to be free to observe Sabbaths and festivals. Under Zedner's care the collection flourished. In 1859 he compiled a list of 1,000 desiderata, and his 891-page catalogue published in 1867 received the highest praise. Steinschneider constantly acknowledged his indebtedness to Zedner. "The accuracy and trustworthiness which characterize the author, . . . he observed, render his work the best guide in the field."

In 1865 the Museum paid Asher & Company £1,000 for the library of the scholarly collector Joseph Almanzi (1801–1860), secretary of the congregation of Trieste, who had died at the age of fifty-nine. Many of the 332 manuscripts in the collection were of Italian origin, and many had belonged to Chayyim Joseph David Azulai (1724–1800), author of *Shem Hagedolim,* the standard dictionary of literary history. Acquisition of the Almanzi collection, sponsored by Sir Anthony Panizzi (1797–1879), principal librarian of the British Museum, placed the Museum among the world's foremost collectors of Hebraica.

The manuscripts included the first Hebrew dictionary, *Machberet,* by the tenth-century Spanish philologist Menachem ben Saruk, and an autograph copy of Joseph ben Joshua ha-Kohen's martyrology, *Emek ha-Bachah* ("The Vale of Weeping").

Of great beauty are the illuminated manuscripts in this collection. Illustrations in an Italian *siddur* by Feibusch Reiner of Bonn show the current styles in ladies' headgear and men's hats. A Spanish Haggadah consisting of 101 leaves and 56 miniatures has "peculiar value in illustrative art," according to connoisseurs. A decade later that controversial globe-trotter, W.M. Shapira (1830–1884), entered the scene with some spectacular contributions. Born in Poland, he was a colorful character, a baptized Jew and an active missionary who had made his home in Jerusalem. Shapira enriched the British Museum with 300 manuscripts, including 40 from Yemen purchased between 1877 and 1882, and a collection of 145 Karaite works purchased in July 1882. In respect to Karaite literature the Museum became second in importance only to the Firkowitch collection in Leningrad. In the words of the London *Times,*[5] "Mr. Bond, the Principal Librarian, and the Trustees are heartily to be congratulated on this boon which they have conferred upon the nation."

In July 1883 Shapira offered the British Museum a manuscript of Deuteronomy, consisting of fifteen leather strips on which forty columns of Hebrew were inscribed in Old Phoenician characters. These black leather strips were impregnated with the odor of funeral spices. Each piece was six or seven inches long by three-and-a-half inches broad and contained ten lines. The manuscript followed the order of the Book of Deuteronomy, but with singular variations. Remarkably enough certain incidents not recorded in Deuteronomy were imported from the Book of Numbers, as if to fill in lacunae. Omitted, for instance, were the descriptions of the various Israelite conflicts. The Tetragrammaton was never used: *Elohim* was substituted throughout. Each of the Ten Commandments ended with the refrain: "I am God, thy God." The last Commandment reads: "Thou shalt not hate thy brother in thy heart; I am God, thy God."

Shapira prized his treasure highly and demanded one million pounds sterling, a very considerable fortune in those days. He sketched the manuscript's background for the Museum authorities. He told how word concerning these antiquities had first reached him in July 1878. A sheikh had come with an Arab entourage to his place of business in Jerusalem. They spoke in passing of some little black pieces of writing found in the neighborhood of the Arnon. On the following day Shapira dined with the sheikh and gleaned fresh information. He learned that in the year 1865, during a period of persecution, certain Arabs had hidden themselves among the rocks. There, in the shade of a cavern, they had found several bundles wrapped in linen. Peeling off the covering, they had found only black fragments, which they had thrown away in contempt. One of the Arabs, however, had picked them up, believing them to be talismans. He had kept them in his possession and had prospered in consequence, or so he thought. For Shapira the dinner was in every sense a satisfying one. Several days later an Arab of the Ajayah tribe brought him a sample fragment containing four columns. Several such visitations brought Shapira a total of fifteen of these history-steeped fragments.

The "discovery" caused a great stir in London. It was exhibited to the public and attracted great crowds of scholars and laymen. Even the Prime Minister, William Ewart Gladstone (1809–1898), was moved to appear at the British Museum on August 13, 1883, and "Mr. Shapira was closely questioned by Mr. Gladstone, who carefully examined the rolls."

Another distinguished visitor, the French Orientalist Clermont Ganneau (1848–1923), a former consul at Jerusalem, was specially commissioned by the Minister of Public Instruction in France to examine the Shapira manuscript. Clermont Ganneau, who had previously denounced as forgeries a collection of Moabite pottery sold by Shapira to the Prussian Government and who was obviously prejudiced in his disfavor, arrived in England on August 15, 1883. In a letter that appeared in the London *Times* on August 21, 1883, he described his experiences: "As soon as I arrived I went to the British Museum, where my learned and obliging friend Dr. S. Birch was kind enough to introduce me to Dr. Ginsburg, whom I found in the Manuscript Department, engaged in studying the fragments in company with Mr. Shapira. Dr. Ginsburg was good enough to allow me to glance at two or three of the fragments which were before him, and postponed until the next day but one (Friday) a more extended examination. On Friday I went again to the British Museum and Mr. Bond, the principal librarian, informed me in the presence of my distinguished friend Mr. Newton that he could not, to his great regret, submit the fragments to me; their owner, Mr. Shapira, having expressly refused his consent. . . . In these circumstances the object of my mission became extremely difficult to attain and I almost despaired of it. I did not, however, lose courage and I set to work with the meagre means of information which were at my disposal. . . . The fragments are the work of a modern forger."

Christian David Ginsburg (1831–1914), the Biblical scholar consulted by the Museum, reached the same damning decision. In a report dated August 22, 1883 and addressed to Sir Edward Bond, the chief librarian, Dr. Ginsburg stated categorically: "The Manuscript of Deuteronomy which Mr. Shapira submitted to us for examination is a forgery. As the interest which it has excited is so great, and as the public are waiting to hear the result of our investigation, I shall endeavor to give my reasons for the conclusions I arrived at in as popular a manner as the essentially technical nature of the subject will admit. . . . The compiler of the text was a Jew from the north of Europe. . . . [and] from the fact that the slips exhibit two distinct handwritings I conclude that there were two scribes employed in copying them. These, with the compiler of the Hebrew text, and the chemist who manipulated the slips, account for my remark that there were four or five persons engaged in the forgery."

Ginsburg's verdict was endorsed by other authorities in this field. "Let us hope, however," commented Adolf Neubauer of Oxford with acrimony, "that this will be the end of the publication of these forged texts and their useless commentaries, unless they are intended as exercises for beginners in Hebrew, for whom practice in the correction of bad grammar may be desirable."

"Without evidence more trustworthy than hitherto adduced we are naturally inclined to reject the Manuscript as spurious," agreed Dr. Michael Friedländer, principal of Jews' College. "The Scotland Yard officials may perhaps be in a better position to remove any doubt as to the origin of the manuscript than orientalists and archaeologists. It is surprising that the Trustees of the British Museum allowed the MS. to be exhibited contrary to Job XI:14, 'If iniquity be in thy hand, put it far away and let not unrighteousness dwell in thy tents'."

The London *Times,* in an editorial on August 27, 1883, commented severely and unsympathetically: "After Dr. Ginsburg's report the sale of the manuscript will hardly repay Mr. Shapira his expenses in coming over with it and his credit as an antiquary is certainly not raised. . . . He is so disappointed with the results of his bargain that he threatens to commit suicide. This venture we think he will not do. . . . He has survived the Moabite pottery fraud, and he will probably survive this new one." But the *Times* erred in its augury. Shapira was humiliated and heartbroken. "You have made a fool of me by publishing and exhibiting things you have believed to be false," he wrote to Ginsburg. "I do not think I will be able to survive this shame." On March 11, 1884, the unhappy book collector shot himself in a Rotterdam hotel.

In recent years certain scholars, impressed by the similarity between Shapira's story and the incidents relating to the discovery of the Dead Sea Scrolls at Qumran, have suggested that "the Shapira Manuscript was in fact a genuine ancient document; that Shapira was ruined and hounded unjustly and that his manuscript was never returned to him but was lost somewhere in the vaults of the British Museum." This is certainly a disquieting suggestion.[6]

In 1924 the Museum acquired for the sum of £10,000 the collection of Dr. Moses Gaster, *Chakham* of the Sephardi community and principal of the Lady Montifiore College. Its thousand manuscripts are rich in works relating to the Bible, Midrash, and Kabbalah. On May 9, 1924, the London *Jewish Chronicle* proudly announced: "We are grateful to learn that the invaluable collection of Hebrew manuscripts possessed by *Chakham* Gaster is to remain in this country and not to go to America as was at first, we gather, contemplated."

The British Museum has well over 3,000 Hebrew manuscripts. This estimate is indefinite because many of the volumes contain a number of items bound together for either convenience or economy. This vast and varied collection mirrors Jewish thought throughout the ages. A perusal of the catalogues published by the Reverend George Margoliouth and Jacob Leveen is in itself a rewarding experience. Among the Geniza fragments are two leaves of the Hebrew text of Ecclesiasticus, portions of the Zohar and a book of *selichot* (penitential prayers), written by Isaac ben Moses at Fostat in 1066. There is even a Hebrew Pentateuch, dating to the year 916, which is one of the oldest Hebrew Bibles in existence. The name of Ben Asher (Aaron ben Moses ben Asher), the Hebrew Masorite who lived in Tiberias during the tenth century, occurs in the text, indicating that he was still alive when this was written. *Responsa* often give revealing glimpses of social and religious customs of the times. For example, one Geonic *responsum* describes the burning of Haman: "Four or five days before Purim the young men take an effigy of Haman and hang it on the roof. On Purim itself they build a bonfire on which they light the effigy while they stand around joking and singing and at the same time holding a ring about the fire and waving it from side to side through the fire."

Autographed *responsa* of Maimonides deal with day-to-day problems. One letter concerns a dispute between merchant and customer. The second *responsum* refers to a teacher of Jewish girls who had vowed in anger not to teach them any more and then repented his rash oath. The hot-tempered teacher inquired whether he would be allowed to resume instruction. Maimonides gave an affirmative reply, but first required the questioner to declare his change of mind in the presence of three Jews.

Occasionally the manuscripts throw light on their copyists. Rabbi Moses ben Mordecai was the scribe who copied Rashi's commentary on the Five Megillot. It is with pathos that he describes his difficult working conditions, and many contemporary writers will read his plaint with sympathy. "I have strayed like a lost sheep," he laments. "I have no fixed place to write and I am obliged to move from my place a hundred times by day and by night." Into the preface of another manuscript a lady copyist injects a personal note: "I beseech the reader not to judge me very harshly when he finds that mistakes have crept into this work, for, when I was engaged in copying it God blessed me with a son and thus I could not attend to my business properly." [7]

Of specifically Anglo-Jewish interest is a receipt for £4 written on the back of a Latin charter. The recipient was Solomon of Paris, the donor Richard de Malebys, and the date 1183. Another manuscript records the Jewish verdict on Henry VIII's marriage to Catherine of Aragon. Rabbi Jacob Raphael Peglione of Modena replies to a question addressed to him by Messer Francisco Curtiso on how to reconcile the conflicting Biblical injunctions regarding levirate marriages.

The glory of the Museum is its "gallery" of seventy-five illuminated manuscripts. Art lovers and bibliophiles alike feast their eyes on exquisitely wrought Bibles, *machzorim,* and Haggadot. Of consummate craftsmanship are these pictorial records of Jewry's ecclesiastical artistry in the Middle Ages. Outstanding among them is a Hebrew Bible in vellum with 700 leaves and 40 miniature illustrations. Biblical scenes are portrayed: Abraham receiving the angels, the two angels leading Lot, Moses striking the rock, the High Priest Aaron pouring oil into the menorah, King David wearing a crown, and the judgment of Solomon.

Apparently the saintly illustrators found greatest scope in Haggadot.

An exemplar is a vellum volume consisting of forty-nine leaves, one of the finest of all illuminated Haggadot. The commentary is by Eleazar ben Judah of Worms (d. 1238) and the scribe was Joel ben Simon, called Feibusch Ashkenazi, from the city of Cologne. Some pages have a plain gold border, others are inscribed in different colors with scrollwork between the letters. Finely executed is the theme of the Four Sons and a vividly painted vignette represents Rabbi Akiba and his companions at Bnei Berak. "My heart has counselled me to reply to the questioners who may ask 'Who has ornamented this?' " reads the colophon: "It is I, Feibusch, known as Joel and I did it for Rabbi Jacob Mattithiah, may he live for ever." Outstanding from the standpoint of antiquity is another Haggadah of the thirteenth century, which contains fourteen pages of miniatures. Illustrations show Eve emerging from the rib of Adam, Adam naming the animals, Noah shepherding the animals out of the Ark (and prominent among the animals is a pig!).

Liturgy, too, allowed full latitude to the artist. A thirteenth-century *machzor* is noted for harvest scenes from the book of Ruth in which human figures were drawn with animal heads.

Many of the manuscripts in the Museum virtually await discovery. There are gems here which have not yet seen the light of day: authentic documents from the second century before the common era, Hebrew charters of pre-expulsion England, works on ethics, philosophy, poetry, mathematics, astrology, liturgy, and Kabbalah. This literary land has still to be charted.

HEBREW PRINTED BOOKS

On January 15, 1759 the Library of the British Museum was opened to the public. It contained 500,000 printed books; among them was one book in Hebrew. This was the first edition of the Babylonian Talmud, and had been owned by Henry VIII. To this solitaire of Hebraica Solomon da Costa Athias added 180 volumes originally intended for the shelves of Charles II. For some time after this phenomenal acquisition the Museum's collection of printed Hebraica expanded very slowly. During the first eighty-nine years of its existence it increased by only six hundred items, an average of barely seven books a year.

In 1848 the Museum acquired the 4,420 volumes collected by Heiman Joseph Michael (1792–1846) of Hamburg. Not since Oxford University's purchase of Rabbi David Oppenheimer's collection in 1829 had a library obtained with one single purchase so momentous an array of Hebrew books, embracing every department of Jewish literature and learning. The

Accounts and Papers of the British Museum [8] record the transaction with pride:

The most remarkable addition to the library is the collection of Hebrew works formed by the late H.J. Michael of Hamburg. The collection, well known and highly praised by critics—among others by Zunz—consisted according to the printed catalogue of 5,400 volumes of which, after the rejection of duplicates or of copies otherwise objectionable, 4,420 forming 3,970 distinct works were purchased by the Museum. Among them are about 400 Bibles and Commentaries, 2,020 theological works, 380 Liturgical works, 230 works on the Kabbalah, 860 on Science. The volumes are enriched by the manuscript notes of several distinguished Hebrew scholars. The MSS. notes of the collector himself, the learned Dr. Michael, deserve special mention. Up to the moment of his death (in 1846, at the age of 54) he was indefatigable in collating his printed books with manuscripts, marking the variations.

In 1867 there were "upwards of 10,000 printed books" enumerated in Zedner's 900-page *Catalogue of the Hebrew Books in the Library of the British Museum.* By 1894, when Samuel Van Straalen, assistant in the Department of Oriental Printed Books and Manuscripts, published his *Catalogue of Hebrew Books in the British Museum acquired during the years 1862–1892,* there were another 7,800 entries. It is difficult to ascertain with any degree of accuracy the number of Hebrew books in the Museum today. A rough estimate would be 30,000. But in addition to the Hebrew books in the Oriental Room there are many books of Judaica, including a number in Yiddish and Ladino, scattered through the huge general catalogue.

The library possesses most of the works printed in Italy by the preeminent printers of the sixteenth century. From Elizabethan England stems *Oratio de laudibus & utilitate triu linguar Arabice Chaldacae & Hebraice* by R. Wakefield (d. 1537), professor of Hebrew at Louvain. This book was printed in London in 1524, and contains one of the earliest specimens of Hebrew and Arabic type in England. Noteworthy, too, is the first all-Hebrew book printed in England, *Decision del Doctissimo,* by Zevi Hirsch ben Jacob Ashkenazi, the Chakham Zevi (1660–1718) which appeared in 1705. The Museum has nearly a hundred incunabula, 237 books printed between 1500 and 1540, and 38 books which are either unique or exceedingly rare.

The British Museum has always led the way in catalogue publication. Its library was the first in the world to publish (1881–1905) a complete catalogue of its books (except for Orientalia and manuscripts). George M. Margoliouth, who in 1891 succeeded Reinhardt Hoerning as assistant keeper in the Oriental Department, compiled the *Catalogue of the Hebrew and Samaritan Manuscripts of the British Museum.* This comprehensive work, issued in three volumes, describes 1,206 manuscripts. A fourth volume of the same catalogue by Jacob Leveen, at the time assistant keeper and later keeper in the Department of Oriental Printed Books and Manuscripts, was issued in 1935 and deals with eighty-nine manuscripts not treated of in the earlier parts. A handwritten list of the Geniza fragments is available on request. A list of the Gaster manuscripts is to be found in the Students' Room. Two Hebrew manuscripts are described in the supplement by Charles Rieu (1820–1902) to his great Catalogue of Persian Manuscripts (three volumes, 1879–1883). But with regard to its sizable collection of Hebrew books the Museum somehow lagged behind. No Hebrew catalogue has been published since 1894. The Oriental Room has a card index of Hebrew books acquired since 1953; but for the Hebrew books acquired between 1894 and 1953 there is not even a card index. A new printed catalogue, or at least an up-to-date index, of the acquisitions of the last half century is now some fifty years overdue.

Chapter II

The Bodleian Library, Oxford

Asleep beneath fair Oxford's dreaming spires are some of the most important Hebrew manuscripts in existence. Among the treasures of the far-famed Bodleian Library are more than three thousand priceless Hebrew manuscripts, over thirty thousand Hebrew books, sixty-seven incunabula, thousands of rare Judaica, and a noteworthy collection of Jewish periodicals. Altogether 2,000,000 volumes and 40,000 manuscripts are housed in Oxford's stately new Bodleian Library building, designed by Sir Giles Gilbert Scott.

Remarkable achievement though it is, surprisingly little use is made of this splendid collection. Relatively few scholars consult these historic works. One book in a hundred so much as leaves its well-earned resting place upon the shelves, and modern scholarship is the poorer for this negligence.

The Bodleian is the possessor of 146 handwritten Bibles, the oldest dating to 1140. It has accumulated many commentaries on the Talmud, works on liturgy, philosophy, ethics, Kabbalah, astronomy, medicine, and mathematics. Thus the library has become a microcosm of the Jewish contribution to culture. The writings of rabbis, philosophers, mystics, *mithnaggdim,* and *chassidim* have gradually gravitated from Spain and Poland, from Egypt and North Africa to this celebrated seat of learning.

Oxford owns the Elephantine Papyri, discovered by archaeologists in Egypt between 1898 and 1908. These papyri record that a century and a half before Nehemiah, Jews had hired themselves out as mercenaries to guard the southern frontier of Egypt against Ethiopian invasion. They consist of marriage settlements, legal briefs, transfers of property, and letters referring to the temple erected by the Jews at some time before 495 B.C. on an island of Elephantine in the Nile.

Long before the erection of the temple at Leontopolis by Onias IV (*ca.* 160 B.C.), the military colony at Elephantine and Syene in the south of Egypt had its own house of worship, built before the Persian conquest.

The temple contained an altar on which burnt offerings were offered to Yahu. The Jews lived on equal terms with the Egyptians. The documents outline for us a picture of a Jewish community, its life and manners in the fifth and sixth centuries B.C. In the year 410 their temple was destroyed and the Jews of Elephantine wrote a moving appeal to the Persian governor Bagoas imploring his aid "that the Temple be rebuilt in the fortress of Elephantine as it was built before, and let meal-offering, incense and burnt-offering be offered upon the altar of God Yahu in your name and we will pray for you continually, we, our wives and our children and all the Jews." [9]

With the exception of that at Cambridge University, the Bodleian possesses a larger number of Geniza fragments than any other library in England. Some of these parchment pieces were acquired a few years before Schechter made his eventful expedition to Egypt. The Bodleian also has a number of books from the presses of Spanish and Portuguese printers in Constantinople and Salonica which were preserved in the Cairo Geniza.

The Hebraic jewel of the library is the Kennicott Bible. Dr. Benjamin Kennicott (1718–1783), an English divine who became keeper of the Radcliffe Library in 1767, spent a lifetime in the collation of Biblical manuscripts. In 1771 this manuscript was acquired by the Radcliffe trustees at the suggestion of Dr. Kennicott. It was transferred to the Bodleian Library in 1872. Written at Corunna in northwest Spain by Moses ibn Zabara for Isaac de Braga and completed in the summer of 1476, this Bible consists of 900 pages (444 folios) with 77 full-page illustrations and 173 marginal decorations. A fourth of the entire book is made up of illustrations. The beautiful Hebrew text is accompanied by the grammatical compendium by Rabbi David Kimchi (1160–1225) entitled *Sepher Mikhlol.* Among the subjects depicted are Phineas, grandson of Aaron, armed with shield and lance; Jonah and the whale; the seven-branched candelabrum; Balaam holding an astrolabe; David enthroned; an army of cats storming a castle defended by mice; an army of dogs attacking a castle garrisoned by a solitary deer. There are half-naked human figures, dragons, beasts, and birds.

A glimpse of the items on Maimonides alone affords a good example of the Bodleian's wealth. Not only does it possess all the first printed editions of theRambam's work, together with subsequent reprints and innumerable super-commentaries, but also manuscripts and even autographs. Maimonides finished his commentary on the Mishnah at the age of twenty-three, in the year 1168. The Bodleian's copy is probably in the hand of the author himself. It shows many signs of revision; and David, grandson of Maimonides, testifies on the title page: "This original copy . . . is in the handwriting of our Master, Moses of blessed memory." Another priceless possession is a copy of *Mishneh Torah,* Maimonides' compendium of Mosaic and rabbinic law dated 1173, thirty-one years before the death of the author.

Of Anglo-Jewish relevance is *Sepher ha-Shoham* ("Onyx Book"), a Hebrew grammar and lexicon by Moses ben Isaac haNessiah (d. 1215) of London. It is regarded as one of the greatest literary relics of the Jews in mediaeval England. The author relates, "Already in the days of my youth, I opened my mouth, I Moses son of Isaac, known as the son of the Princess, who is from the land of *Engleterre*." The book was preserved in only two manuscript copies. Leopold Dukes described it fully over a hundred years ago, and on August 8, 1849, the London *Jewish Chronicle* appealed to English Jewry "to publish this newly found literary treasure." Yet it took ninety-eight years for the book to find a publisher. The postscript of a letter to Edward Montagu from the diarist Samuel Pepys (1633–1703), bearing the date December 3, 1659, describes Pepy's second visit to Creechurch Lane Synagogue to attend a memorial service to Antonio Fernandez Carvajal (c. 1590–1659), founder of the modern Anglo-Jewish community. Also on record is the plan of the Marrano adventurer Simon de Caceres (d. 1704) for the conquest of Chile. A merchant and ship owner born in Amsterdam, de Caceres settled in London, and in 1653 offered to raise an army of Jewish soldiers to co-operate with the English forces in the campaign. Unfortunately, Cromwell's reply is not recorded.

EARLY HISTORY

Historians trace the origin of the Oxford University library to the fourteenth century, when the Old House of Congregation was built by Thomas Cobham, Bishop of Worcester, who died in 1337. Another great benefactor was the Duke of Gloucester, known as the "good Duke Humphrey," who died in 1447. A library deriving partly from the good Duke's bequests was built over the Divinity School in the second half of the fifteenth century. However, it was Sir Thomas Bodley (1545–1613), "a worthy of Devon" and a Fellow of Merton College, whose name is inextricably and immortally linked with the Library at Oxford.

Bodley's father, a zealous Protestant and a victim of that bigoted era, had been forced to leave his native England for a more hospitable dwelling place. For a time he lived with his family in Germany and Switzerland. In Geneva the youthful Thomas Bodley attended the Hebrew lectures of the Hebraist Anthony Rodolph Chevallier (1523–1572). Later he was entrusted by Queen Elizabeth I with diplomatic work in the Netherlands, Denmark, and France. When his royal assignments were accomplished, the diplomat returned to England and "set up his staff at the Library door in Oxford."

Bodley was proud of his command of Hebrew. He is said to have "equalled or even surpassed most of his contemporaries in his knowledge of that language." To the present day there is a *shetar* (a Hebrew deed) in Merton College, Oxford, which Bodley translated into Latin in 1554. An ardent bibliophile, he spent vast sums collecting books from all over Europe, and on November 8, 1602, in the "bare room" above the Divinity School, the first public library in the British Isles was officially opened. Around this nucleus of 2,000 volumes and 299 manuscripts the library expanded rapidly in many directions.

Little is known about its early Hebrew section. It is recorded that a Hebrew lexicon was presented by John Savile in 1601 and that a number of manuscripts were added by Dr. John Lhuid a year later. Bodley insisted that no effort be spared with regard to accurate classification. "For albeit I could correct at first sight a great part where but a letter or two are amiss in a word," he emphasized, "yet there are in divers titles so many letters changed that I cannot conjecture what the words should be." He urged his assistant librarian, Thomas James (1573–1629) that he "forget not to procure an exact catalogue to be taken of all the Hebrew books in the library." In nineteen of the more than two hundred letters that Bodley wrote to James, he refers to Hebrew books and to the necessity of cataloguing them.[10]

By the time James retired Oxford owned 16,000 books and manuscripts, including 150 Hebrew books. In the catalogue of 1620 the Hebrew books are enumerated in Roman characters. Nine years later a forty-page special catalogue, *Bibliotheca Rabbinica,* was printed, listing 150 titles of Oxford's Hebraica. It is no longer extant.

By then the library was already famous, in Bodley's own estimation. "The general conceit," he writes to James, "as well as of other nations, as of our own at home, of the library-store, is so great that they imagine in a manner there is nothing wanting in it." [11] Needless to say, this was an optimistic exaggeration. Much was still wanting.

The collection expanded gradually. In 1630 a London bookseller, Henry Fetherstone, donated a number of Hebrew books; and a pair of gloves valued at 3*s.* 6*d.* was given to a Mr. Johnson "for transcribing the register of the Rabbins of Mr. Fetherstone's gift." [12] From William Laud (1573–1645), Archbishop of Canterbury, the library received forty-two Hebraic items in 1633. A year later, the Archbishop procured a royal letter to the Turkey Company requiring that each ship returning from the East bring back a Persian or Arabic manuscript.

Hebrew was an integral part of the university curriculum and there were many Hebrew teachers on the faculty. In 1633 Victorius Bythner (1605–1670) a native of Poland, arrived in Oxford, where he became a member of the University in 1635. Anthony Wood describes him as "one who was blessed with a most admirable genius for the obtaining of tongues . . . He became a useful person in instructing many scholars in this University." Between 1636 and 1650 Bythner published half a dozen books on Hebrew grammar and the Bible.

It was during this period that the Orientalist, jurist, and archaeologist John Selden (1584–1654), whose familiarity with rabbinical literature was such as has been acquired "by few non-Israelite scholars," bequeathed twenty-one Hebrew manuscripts to Oxford.

Next luminary in the life of the Bodleian Library was Dr. Edward Pococke (1604–1691). Chaplain at Aleppo from 1630 to 1636, he had many opportunities of collecting manuscripts. Pococke, a fine scholar who had studied under the German Arabist Matthias Pasor as well as with William Bedwell, father of Arabic studies in England, was himself the author of commentaries in Micah, Malachi, and Hosea. The Bodleian possesses Pococke's notebooks with annotated extracts from rabbinical works in Hebrew and Arabic.

Pococke's *Porta Mosis* (1655), consisting of extracts from the Arabic commentary of Maimonides on the Mishnah, was one of the first books printed in Oxford from Hebrew type, which the University had purchased. The accounts for 1651 record that "222 pounds weight of Hebrew letters with pricks at four shillings a pound, –45.8.0, were purchased from a London letter-founder." [13] Dr. Pococke's collection was bought in 1693 for £600. Among the seventy-four Hebrew items are the works of master poets: Judah Halevi (1085–1140), Solomon Ibn Gabirol (1021–1058), author of the *Royal Crown,* and the Spanish Jewish scholar Moses Ibn Ezra (1060–1138).

Apparently the chaplains at Aleppo had a tradition of benefactions to libraries. Through Robert Huntingdon (1637–1701), who became Bishop of Raphoe in Ireland after holding the Aleppo office from 1671 to 1681, the Bodleian obtained via purchase and gifts some two hundred manuscripts. Among noteworthy Hebrew items is a copy of the *Mishneh Torah* which contains the autograph of Maimonides. In 1685 Thomas Marshall (1621–1685), Rector of Lincoln College, Oxford, contributed fifty-one manuscripts acquired from Huntingdon. From 1650 to 1672, Marshall too had served as a chaplain to the merchants at Rotterdam and at Dort. One of his contemporaries was Isaac Abendana, brother of the *Chakham* of the Spanish and Portuguese community in London in 1681. Abendana (1650–1710), who translated the whole of the Mishnah into Latin, sold many manuscripts to the Bodleian. The *Annals of the Bodleian* record, for example, that in 1668 he received £37 from the Bodleian for some Hebrew books.[14]

Little progress was made during the eighteenth century. In 1787 Johannes

Uri (1726–1796), a Hungarian scholar who had studied oriental literature under H. Schulterns (1749–1793) at Leyden and who was for twenty years a member of the Oxford University faculty, completed a catalogue, *Bibliothecae Bodleianae Codicum Manuscriptorum Orientalium,* which was printed in Oxford in the same year. There were 2,708 entries with 500 Hebrew, 127 Syriac, and 6 Samaritan items.

The nineteenth century saw the rise of the Bodleian in size and significance. This was largely due to Bulkeley Bandinel (1781–1861), a man of considerable enterprise. As a librarian he was indefatigable, and as a connoisseur of books he had few equals. In 1813 he succeeded the Reverend John Price as librarian, and the "sums expended in purchases rose from 2,611 pounds to 7,251 pounds and the Catalogue of annual additions from two pages to seventeen." In 1817 he acquired 2,045 manuscripts from the collection of Matheo Luigi Canonici (1727–1806) for the sum of £5,444. There were 110 Hebrew manuscripts in this important collection.

THE OPPENHEIMER COLLECTION

"The ownership of a fine library is the surest and swiftest way to immortality", is an remark which can aptly be applied to Rabbi David Oppenheimer. It was with the purchase of the Oppenheimer library that Oxford really made bibliographic history. Never before and never since has a library bought so much for so little. With this one transaction the Bodleian became the foremost Hebrew library in the world.

David ben Abraham Oppenheimer (1664–1736), an Austrian, was a rabbi, mathematician, and liturgist. He was also one of the foremost Jewish bibliophiles of all time. From his father he inherited both a substantial fortune and a love of books. His father-in-law, Leffmann Behrends Cohen (1630–1714), was financial agent of the dukes and princes of the Court of Hanover and a trusted servant of King George I before his ascent to the throne of England. A distant cousin was Joseph Oppenheimer, known as "Jew Süss" (1692–1738), who served as finance minister to Prince Carl Alexander of Württemberg. Samuel Oppenheimer, a banker who was in charge of the Austrian commissariat during the wars of the Spanish Succession, was one of David's uncles. On one occasion when Prince Eugene of Savoy returned from the Turkish wars he brought with him a number of Hebrew books and manuscripts which he had found among the booty captured by his soldiers. Through the banker, Samuel, this literary loot passed into the hands of the nephew.

Legacies and high-ranking relatives in strategic places helped, of course, but basically Oppenheimer's library was the result of a half century of tireless and determined acquisition. No price was too high, no obstacle too great. In 1688, at the age of twenty-four, he made his first alphabetical catalogue, listing 480 titles. A number of books were printed expressly for him on vellum. In 1715, when a new edition of the Talmud was being published, Oppenheimer ordered a special set of twenty-four volumes to be struck off on parchment at a most extravagant cost. Four years earlier, in 1711, Oppenheimer had published a broadsheet with a list of desiderata. The Lutheran divine, Johann Christoph Wolf (1683–1739), used the Oppenheimer library for the compilation of his *Bibliotheca Hebrea,* which was published in Hamburg (1713–1723) in four massive volumes.

When Oppenheimer was appointed rabbi of Prague he was reluctant to take the collection with him, since the Holy Office made periodic visits to the Jewish quarter and was quite capable of confiscating the books. The library was consequently transferred to the care of his father-in-law in Hanover. After Oppenheimer's death on September 12, 1735, it passed first to his son Joseph (d. 1739), who was a rabbi in Hildesheim, then to his son-in-law, Hirschell, subsequently to his widow, and after that to Isaac Seligmann Cohen of Hamburg. In the course of the next ninety years it changed hands many times. When Seligmann Cohen died in 1761 his widow, Genendel, owed her servants wages from two to eight retrospective years. Finally, the Oppenheimer collection was pawned with a senator of Hamburg for 50,000 marks ($12,000) and stored away in twenty-eight cases. Special catalogues were printed in 1764 and 1824 to facilitate its sale. On March 22, 1807, the lawyer Hubner even approached Napoleon's Sanhedrin, but without success.

Would-be purchasers were notified in a third catalogue that "should the Library not be sold as a whole, a public auction would be held on *Sivan* 16, 1827." The philosopher Moses Mendelssohn valued the collection at £22,000. It was then that Alexander Nicoll of Balliol College, Regius Professor of Hebrew at Oxford since 1822, began negotiations for the purchase of the library. Writing from Hamburg on January 6, 1827, his agent, Dr. F.C. Pappe, reported on the situation: "I have been informed that besides my application another one had already been made to them about the price of the said library and that £1,850 had already been offered by some person in England, but that this offer had been rejected. In order to pay all his debts to cover the expenses which the library has incurred over many years, and beside the fees and the expenses of the catalogues printed, the sum of £2,000 sterling would be required and this would therefore be the cheapest price at which it could be sold in private by the heirs."

In a further communication, dated February 6, 1827, Dr. Pappe sent this warning to Dr. Nicoll: "I should advise you in the meantime, in case the proprietors should still insist upon the first demand of £2,200 sterling, not to be very precipitate in granting their request . . . I am fully convinced that the trustees will at last part with the Library for £2,000, this being a sum which they have indeed very little prospect of reaching in a public sale." [15] The prospect was, however, somewhat brighter than it appeared to Pappe. The Bodleian bought the collection for 9,000 thalers (about $6,435), and the statement of account for November 8, 1829, carries the following entry: "Cost £2,080.0.0; Brokerage £2.1.0; Insurance £23.8.6; Commission and packing £53.3.4; Freight and dues £31.0.0; Carriage from London £11.8.0; Total £2,201.1.4." This represents a considerable sum, particularly in view of the fact that the Bodleian's entire expenditure for the year totalled £3,338.16*s*.11*d*.

The Oppenheimer collection comprised 780 manuscripts and 5,421 printed books. Most bibliophiles are familiar with its contents, which have often been described. A writer in the London *Hebrew Review* [16] castigated Anglo-Jewry for allowing this collection to pass into non-Jewish hands: "To our national discredit it must be stated, none of our wealthy Jewish brethren could be found to buy them, either for themselves or for a Jewish college library. They prefer holding stock which yields good interest, but they forget that when they, their stock and the interest shall be eaten up, these works will live and yield interest, not only for those who read them but also for the public, as they may perhaps be republished to perpetuate their valuable contents for generations to come. Our great loan contractors and bondholders might have erected for themselves an everlasting monument by securing these great works for a Jewish institution."

The Oppenheimer purchase was not the only extraordinary transaction in the development of the Bodleian. In 1845, for the negligible sum of £176.14*s*.6*d*., it acquired 483 printed books which had belonged to the German Orientalist and professor of theology at Halle, Heinrich Friedrich Wilhelm Gesenius (1786–1842). Three years later the Bodleian paid £1,038 sterling for 860 manuscripts, bound together in 629 volumes, which had belonged to the bibliophile Heimann Joseph Michael. He had begun to collect books at the age of thirteen, and had subsequently corresponded with Leopold Dukes, Franz Delitzsch, and Leopold Zunz.

In 1853 the Bodleian acquired sixty-three manuscripts, at the cost of £108, from the library of the Austro-Italian scholar Isaac Samuel Reggio (1784–1855), who was regarded as the Moses Mendelssohn of Italy and who founded the Rabbinical College at Padua. A prolific writer, poet, and artist, he inscribed the whole Book of Esther on a parchment scroll one and a half hand-breadths long. Among his manuscripts are an alphabetical listing of proverbs occurring in the Talmud, Midrash, Tanchumah, and Zohar, completed in 1777, and an index to the Zohar compiled by Moses Galanti in 1575.

There were no spectacular purchases during the next half century, but the Bodleian continued to increase its collection year by year. On March 24, 1869, it acquired twelve Hebrew manuscripts from the Jewish scholar and writer Samuel David Luzzatto (1800–1865), through Asher & Company, for the sum of £124.12*s*.5*d*. In 1890 it bought several Samaritan manuscripts for £144. The well-known booksellers of the nineteenth century found a ready customer in the Bodleian. Entries such as "4 manuscripts from Nathan Coronel, October 23, 1871, for £20.15*s*.6*d*.", or "17 manuscripts from I. Fischel, May 14, 1873, for £65," occur with great frequency in the University accounts. The rate of progress slowed down to a trickle in the last decade of the nineteenth century and almost came to a standstill in the twentieth. A perusal of the *Oxford University Gazette* reveals that 1894 was a peak year in which twenty-two manuscripts were acquired. In the two decades between 1894 and 1914 only twenty-six manuscripts were added. On December 8, 1933, six hundred Hebrew and Yiddish books were purchased from a private collector.

THE CATALOGUE

One of the major factors contributing to the development of the Bodleian was the high caliber of a number of distinguished librarians. Bulkeley Bandinel was not slow to recognize talent in others. It was he who commissioned Moritz Steinschneider (1816–1907), now regarded as the father of Jewish bibliography, to compile a catalogue of the printed books. Steinschneider looms as a nineteenth-century colossus, a scholar's scholar, a giant in an age of giants. He had no peer for thoroughness and mastery of sources. Born in Prossnitz, Moravia, the young Steinschneider studied under Rabbi Nechemiah Treibitsch of Nikolsburg, as well as under Rabbi Lazar Horowitz, and was ordained by Rabbi Hirsch ben Fassel. He acquired secular knowledge from such outstanding teachers as Professor Joseph Karl of Prague and John August Wilhelm Neander (1789–1850) of Berlin. It was in Berlin that Steinschneider received his first assignment in bibliography. In 1847 he compiled an auction catalogue for the bookseller Abraham Asher (1800–1853). Impressed and appreciative, Asher referred the young cataloguer to Bandinel.

Steinschneider spent five summers in Oxford and was thirteen years at his task. He was paid £1,300. The printing alone lasted from 1853 to 1860, and cost the library £2,050. The resulting monumental *Catalogus Librorum Hebraeorum in Bibliotheca Bodleiana* comprises 3,104 columns. Each book in the Bodleian is minutely described, and each of the 20,488 entries is furnished with most exhausting biographical, historical, and critical information. A total of 7,622 authors, 1,704 Jewish printers, and 232 Christian printers are enumerated. It is easy to understand why Steinschneider said that he "put a fourth of his life" into this complex compilation. He began by composing a catalogue and ended by writing a bibliography of Hebrew literature, which has been described by Neubauer as the "Bibliotheca Judaica." He recorded not only the printed books that are to be found in the Bodleian, but almost all the Hebrew books printed up to 1732. "The purpose of every author is to be understood", wrote Steinschneider in a letter to Professor R. Payne Smith (1819–1895) dated June 29, 1860, "and in a matter so little known as Hebrew bibliography the necessary perspicuity is very much injured by the use of an old language." [17] Despite its clumsy, crabbed, and most difficult Latin, its uncommon abbreviations, and its lack of conciseness, the catalogue is, in the words of Schechter, the "Urim and Thumim" of every Jewish scholar.

The Reverend Henry Octavius Coxe (1811–1881), who had served twenty-two years in the British Museum, succeeded Bandinel in 1860. On February 18, 1861, he asked Steinschneider to "undertake the sole charge of the Catalogue [of the Hebrew manuscripts] and proceed with it with all the expedition you can." Presumably the assignment was not confirmed; at any rate, it was never carried out by Steinschneider, who continued with his other literary activities.

In 1886 a list of his books filled 35 octavo pages of print. There, in Berlin, in his house on Wallnertheater Strasse, this Nestor of Jewish science worked incessantly until his death in 1907.

Adolf Neubauer (1831–1907), who was a relative of Dr. Adolf Büchler, principal of Jews' College in London, devoted the years 1873 to 1900 to the Bodleian. Born in Bittse, Hungary, he had fought with Louis Kossuth's army at the storming of Budapest. At one time he served in the Austrian consulate at Jerusalem, and in 1864 he was summoned to the Asiatic Museum at St. Petersburg to examine the Karaite manuscripts collected by Firkowitch. In 1868 he published his *La Géographie du Talmud*. He spent eighteen years compiling his *Catalogue of Hebrew Manuscripts in the Bodleian,* listing 2,541 items. Appearing in 1886, it was so fine a piece of work that the compiler could afford to ignore the strictures of the Cambridge critic Schiller-Szinessy, who declared: "Mr. Neubauer has no mastery in the theological science. He knows no Hebrew, no Rabbinics, no Talmudics, no Theology, either Jewish or Christian. He has indeed a smattering of all these things but no real knowledge." [18]

Oxford reacted with appreciation and tangible tributes. On December 7, 1900, a decree was passed in Convocation which brought the veteran cataloguer a retirement pension of £250 a year (instead of the statutory £200) and granted him the freedom of the library.[19]

The work was continued by Sir Arthur Ernest Cowley (1861–1931). In 1892 Sir Arthur had accompanied John Frederick Stenning on an expedition to the library of St. Catherine's monastery on Mount Sinai. In 1896 he acted as an assistant to Neubauer, and three years later he succeeded him as sub-librarian. The second volume of the catalogue appeared in 1906, bringing the number of manuscripts listed to 2,918, including 316 volumes made up of 2,675 Geniza fragments. In 1916 Cowley began work on the compilation which finally appeared in 1929 under the title *A Concise Catalogue of the Hebrew Printed Books at the Bodleian Library*. For brevity and accuracy this has no equal in bibliographic literature. Apart from a typewritten catalogue of Geniza fragments, no furtrer listing has appeared.

On November 13, 1891 Dr. Solomon Schechter wrote: "We are by no means so unreasonable as to entertain the hope that the time will soon come when the attendants of the British Museum and Oxford will complain of the crowds of Jewish students inquiring there for Hebrew manuscripts." [20] Seventy years have made no change in the cultural scene. The Bodleian Library today is a treasure house which has taken three and a half centuries to build. Despite its lucid catalogues, it is still largely terra incognita to Jewish scholarship. Here, as in the British Museum, rich discoveries, "the spoils of time", await the erudite explorer.

Chapter III

Cambridge, the World of the Geniza

Cambridge is the home of the Taylor-Schechter Geniza. Only fifty-six miles northeast of London, by the banks of the Cam, are to be found the frail but famous fragments of historic writings that throw valuable light on the life of the Jews who lived on the banks of the Nile, and of the Tigris and the Euphrates from the ninth to the eleventh century.

Just as the discovery of the Dead Sea Scrolls in 1947 electrified mid-twentieth-century scholars, so the discovery of the Geniza thrilled the scholarly world during the last years of the nineteenth century. The story of the discovery has often been told. The word *Geniza* means hiding place or repository. Old copies of the Law and time-worn Hebrew books were either buried in the cemetery or stowed away in the store room which was called the Geniza. The Talmud states specifically: "If a scroll of the law has two mistakes per page it must be corrected; if three mistakes, it must be hidden away." [21]

For a century and a half the Geniza of the Ezra Synagogue in Cairo had attracted the attention of scholars. As early as 1752 it had been visited by Simon von Geldern (1720–1744), a great-uncle of Heine. A century later, a traveling rabbi, Jacob Saphir (1822–1886) spent two days in that doorless, windowless room, yet discovered nothing of importance. However, Saphir realized that he had not delved deeply enough. "Who knows what is to be found underneath," was his prophetic comment.

More successful was Abraham Firkowitch (1786–1874), whose collections at Leningrad contain innumerable fragments from the Cairo Geniza and include the text of a letter sent by *Kagan* Joseph, last of the Jewish Chazar kings, to Chasdai Ibn Shaprut (915–970) of Cordova, chief counselor to Caliph Abdel Rahman I.

In 1891 Cyrus Adler (later president of Dropsie College) picked up the trail and acquired a goodly number of fragments, which became the nucleus of the New World collections. In January 1896, the tireless traveler Elkan Adler journeyed to the Cairo Synagogue. "The authorities accompanied me to the Geniza," he related, "and permitted me to take away the first sackful of fragments from the famous hoard. Neubauer rated me soundly for not carrying the whole lot away. Schechter admired my continence but was not foolish enough to follow my example." Further fragments were acquired through dealers towards the end of the nineteenth century. Through the Reverend G. J. Chester, Solomon Aaron Wertheimer, and Professor S.H. Sayce, the Bodleian obtained 2,600 items. The British Museum, The Cambridge University Library, and the Bibliothèque de l'Alliance Israélite Universelle of Paris were also successful in accumulating some of these precious pieces of history.

Dr. Solomon Schechter is a vital part of the Geniza epic. He was not far wrong when he said to his wife: "As long as the Bible lives, my name shall not die." [22] Born in Forscani, Rumania, the son of a *shochet* and follower of the rabbi of Lubavitch, he had received a traditional Jewish education. At the age of ten the boy entered the *yeshiva* at Pistra, and at sixteen he began his studies under Rabbi Joseph Saul Nathanson (1808–1875) of Lemberg. With a sound training in rabbinics, young Schechter progressed to Vienna, and there he came under the influence of three outstanding scholars: Meir Friedmann (1831–1903), teacher of Bible and Mishnah at the Vienna *Bet Hamidrash,* Isaac Hirsch Weiss (1815–1903), author of *Dor Dor Vedorshov,* a history of the development of oral tradition, and Adolf Jellinek (1820–1893), rabbi of the Great Synagogue in Vienna. To supplement his scant income as a teacher, Schechter catalogued the library of Adolf Jellinek. From Vienna he proceeded to Berlin, where he studied at the Academy of Jewish Science and came into contact with Israel Lewy (1847–1917), authority on the Jerusalem Talmud, and with the bibliographer Moritz Steinschneider.

In 1882, on the recommendation of Dr. Pinkus Friedrich Frankl, Schechter became tutor to C.J.G. Montefiore (1858–1938), whose grandfather was a brother of Sir Moses Montefiore. In this capacity, Schechter accompanied Montefiore, a disciple of Benjamin Jowett, to England. "To Schechter," declared the pupil in his preface to the Hibbert Lectures, "I owe more than I can adequately express here. My whole conception of the law and its place in Jewish religion and life is largely the fruit of his teaching and inspiration."

Schechter showed little enthusiasm for his new milieu. After the stimulating circles of Berlin and Vienna he found the atmosphere in London alien and sterile. "There is no spiritual life here," he lamented, "and I feel myself dead. The manuscripts in the British Museum are my only consolation." However, in this "dead" setting he completed his critical edition of *Avot de Rabbi Nathan* and his essay on Chassidism. Talmudist and Hebraist, this "Jewish Carlyle" joined "The Wanderers," a coterie of intellectuals among whom was Israel Zangwill.

The death of Dr. Schiller-Szinessy in March 1892 left an academic post at Cambridge unoccupied, and Schechter was appointed reader of Rabbinics. In 1892 the degree of Master of Arts was conferred upon him, and in 1894 he went off to study Hebrew manuscripts in Italy on the Worth Studentship (worth in fact £100). Later Schechter became curator of the Oriental Section under chief librarian Francis Jenkinson. Dr. F. C. Burkitt of Trinity College, Dr. Rendel Harris, Professor Robertson Smith, and other such intellectual giants of Cambridge held him in high esteem. After his death Sir James G. Frazer (1854–1941) author of *The Golden Bough,* said in warmhearted eulogy: "In him we have lost one of our truest friends and one of the finest and most remarkable men we have ever known. It would be difficult to say whether he was admired for the brilliance of his intellect and the readiness of his wit, or for the warmth of his affection and the generosity and nobility of his character, but I think it was the latter qualities even more than his genius which endeared him to his friends."

THE GREAT DISCOVERY

On May 5, 1896 Mrs. Agnes Smith Lewis, widow of the librarian of Corpus Christi College, and her sister Mrs. Margaret Dunlop Gibson returned from southern Palestine with a bundle of fragments. Schechter identified one fragment as consisting of Chapter 39 verse 15 to Chapter 40 verse 7 of Ecclesiasticus, by Joshua Ben Sira (who lived in Jerusalem in the early part of the second century B.C.), a Hebrew text which had disappeared for more than a thousand years. "The last Christian who saw the original Hebrew text of Ben Sira was Jerome in the fourth century and the last Jew Gaon Saadia in the tenth century." Schechter was elated. "I think we have reason to congratulate ourselves", he wrote to Mrs. Lewis, "for this fragment I took with me represents a piece of the original Hebrew of Ecclesiasticus. It is the first time that such a thing was discovered. Please do not speak about the matter until tomorrow. I will come to you tomorrow about 11 p.m. [sic] to talk to you, how to make the matter known. In haste and great excitement, Solomon Schechter."

The secret was soon out. On May 13, 1896, Mrs. Lewis addressed a letter to the *Academy,* a weekly review of literature and science:

> All the students of the Bible and of the Apocrypha will be interested to learn that among some fragments of Hebrew manuscripts which my sister Mrs. Gibson and I have just acquired in Palestine, is a leaf of the Book of Ecclesiasticus, has been discovered today by Mr. S. Schechter, lecturer in Talmudics to the University of Cambridge. The Talmud contains many quotations from the Book of Ecclesiasticus which are not always accurate and Jewish writers of the 9th century have also preserved some fragments for us. But now for the first time we have a leaf, albeit a mutilated one, of the original. The leaf is paper

and measures 7½ inches by 7¾ . . . Mr. Schechter is now studying it and hopes soon to publish its text.

Supported by Professor Henry Sidgwick (1838–1900), Dr. Donald MacAlister (1854–1934), and Dr. Charles Taylor, editor of a critical edition of the *Mishnah Pirke Avot* ("Sayings of the Jewish Fathers"), Schechter sailed for Egypt in December 1896, armed with a University commission. Never has an explorer been more richly rewarded at such small financial cost. From the Synagogue of Ezra the Scribe he collected as many as 100,000 fragments. To Herbert Bentwich (1856–1932) Schechter reported: "The work was done thoroughly, as it is written 'And they despoiled the Egyptians.' It is not safe to keep the fragments here. There is such a thing as the Evil Eye. I have spent a fortune in *Backsheesh*. Part goes to the dealers. People steal fragments and sell them to the dealers, but by buying from them I get what is more valuable." [23] With the help of Lord Cromer, British agent in Egypt, these thirty bags containing the treasure were removed to Cambridge.

Schechter himself, in a letter to the London *Times* dated July 5, 1897, announced his momentous discovery: "It will be of interest to Biblical scholars to know that I have discovered more fragments of the original of Ecclesiasticus in the library, here among the Hebrew Collections lately brought home by me from the Eastern Genizot. As only a small portion of the vast collections has as yet been examined, and as they all come from one and the same place, there is every reason to hope that further examination may bring still more fragments to light of this lost Apocryphal book."

On June 8, 1898 the Library Syndicate informed the University:

Dr. Taylor, Master of St. John's College, and Dr. Schechter, the Reader in Talmudics, have offered to the University on certain conditions the valuable collection of MSS. which Dr. Schechter has brought back from the Geniza of Old Cairo with the consent of the heads of the Jewish Community.

Among the more noteworthy treasures which this Collection contains are fragments of the Book of Ecclesiasticus in Hebrew and certain Palimpsests of which the underwriting is Greek and which preserve to us unique fragments of the Hexapla and of Aquilas's version of the Old Testament.

There are, moreover, about twenty large boxes of fragments which contain matter of much interest to Semitic scholars; for example, Biblical fragments in an early Hebrew hand presenting in some instances the super-linear punctuation, liturgical fragments and portions of the Talmud and of commentaries thereon: Historical documents (wills etc.); fragments in Arabic mostly written in Hebrew letters; and a few fragments in Syriac.

The Conditions upon which the collection is offered to the University are the following:

1. That the MSS. be kept in the University Library as a separate collection,

to be called by some such name as the Taylor-Schechter collection from the Geniza of Old Cairo.

2. That the thanks of the University be given to the heads of the Jewish community at Cairo with whose consent the MSS. were brought to England.

3. That the collection be not used without the consent of the donors for three years from the date of acceptance by the University.

4. That Dr. Schechter have the right to borrow manuscripts of which Facsimiles are not accessible, from the collection, on giving a receipt to the Library for them.

5. That the University undertake to make such provision as is possible by binding, mounting or otherwise for the preservation of the MSS. and to have them sorted, and a list or Catalogue of them drawn up within ten years from the acceptance of the collection.

6. That the fragments of Ecclesiasticus and those with Greek writing remain in the possession of the donors until after they have brought out complete editions of them.[24]

On November 10, 1898 the University accepted the Geniza. A letter by the Public Orator, Sir John Edwin Sandys (1844–1922), Fellow and tutor of St. John's College, expressed official yet ardent appreciation to Dr. Schechter: "We congratulate you that you divined with singular sagacity that there was a treasure of Hebrew manuscripts hidden in Egypt . . . 'Search and examine, seek and find; and hold her fast, let her not go.' Whatever truth shall be found in future in so great a treasure, the name of the finder shall remain inscribed on the grateful tablets of our heart." [25] Tribute was paid to the Jewish communty of Cairo, "not only on account of the singular goodwill with which you received our Reader in Rabbinic, but also on account of the conspicuous liberality with which you permitted him to return to us laden with so many fragments of books from your treasury."

There, in the great basement room of the Cambridge Library, Schechter sat with his boxes of jumbled treasures, trying to put them into some kind of order. There, history was pieced together, if not actually made. "My most glorious Geniza day," he noted, "was last Friday when I discovered in one afternoon a piece of Greek, a Syriac Palimpsest and a most important portion of Ben Sira. *Hodoo Ladonai* (Praise ye the Lord)."

There are few departments of Jewish literature which are not enriched by the Geniza findings. "How a Weiss or a Friedmann would rejoice in his heart at the sight of these Talmudic fragments!" [26] declared the almost ecstatic finder.

In this book *The Cairo Geniza* Professor Paul E. Kahle classifies the materials, which are stored in 164 boxes, in the following categories: [27] Biblical texts, writings with supralinear punctuations; phylacteries; Apocrypha, and Pseudepigrapha; Hebrew, Aramaic, and Arabic versions of the Bible; Bible with Targums; Midrash; Masorah; Mishnah; Talmud, text commentaries; Talmud Yerushalmi; *responsa* in general and *responsa* of the Geonim; Liturgy; Documents and Letters; Bills and Lists; Historical Letters; Amulets; Calendars; Catalogues; Dictionaries; Illuminated fragments; Medicine; Magic and Charmes; Saadiana; Arabic fragments; Lexicography; Polemics against the Karaites.

The Geniza provided proof that Saadia Gaon was born in 882 and not in 892. A letter of Rabbi Chusiel ben Elchanan of Kairouan to the head of the Cairo community, written about 1000 C.E., shows that he went to North Africa from Italy and not from Babylon, a misconception current for hundreds of years. A remarkable *responsum* of Gaon Samuel Ibn Chofni concerns the Witch of Endor.[28] The Gaon surmised that the "familiar spirit" of the Biblical narrative employed a cunning ruse to foster in King Saul the illusion that he had seen and heard the Prophet Samuel risen from the dead.

Schechter unearthed and identified many lost or obscure annals, including extracts from a Zadokite work (probably by the Dositheans, a Jewish sect dating from the Greek period and now known to be identical with the Dead Sea Sect of Qumran), and nineteen fragments of *Sepher Hamizvot* ("Book of Commandments") by Anan, who flourished in 750 and was the founder of the Karaite sect.

"I would not change this for all Wall Street," wrote Schechter to Sulzberger with a scholar's ecstasy and a historian's sense of true values. "I am finding daily valuable treasures. A whole unknown Jewish world reveals itself to us."

Fifty years have elapsed, and despite the pioneer work of Schechter, Louis Ginzberg, Paul Kahle (b. 1875), Jacob Mann (1888–1940), Menachem Zulai (1889–1954), Shelomoh Dov Goitein (b. 1900), and others, the bulk of the documents have not as yet been utilized. The chronicler of 1962 recalls with a particular poignancy, as he gazes at the four handwritten lists compiled by Schechter and Hartwig Hirschfeld, the prophetic words of the Reader in Talmudics: "Looking over this enormous mass of fragments about me, in the sifting and examination of which I am now occupied, I cannot overcome a sad feeling stealing over me, that I shall hardly be worthy to see all the results which the Geniza will add to our knowledge of Jews and Judaism. The work is not for one man and not for one generation. It will occupy many a specialist and much longer than a lifetime. However, to use an old adage, 'It is not thy duty to complete the work, but neither art thou free to desist from it.' "

Chapter IV

The Development of the Cambridge University Library

The present library building, designed by Sir Giles Gilbert Scott, and formally opened by King George V on October 22, 1934, was largely made possible by a £250,000 contribution by John D. Rockefeller. Within this edifice are forty-three miles of shelves, housing 2,000,000 books and 4,227 incunabula. The Anderson Room contains over a thousand Hebrew manuscripts, while many thousands of Hebraica and Judaica are dispersed through the general catalogue of the library.

The most prized possession is the Nash Papyrus, one of the finest relics of antiquity and one of the oldest Biblical fragments in existence. It is named after its discoverer, L.W. Nash, secretary of the Society of Biblical Archaeology, who purchased it in 1902 from a native dealer in Egypt. The papyrus dates from the end of the first century of the current era, or the beginning of the second, and consists of four small fragments covered with Hebrew script. The four pieces when fitted together measure five inches in length and nearly three in width. In all, twenty-four lines of writing are preserved. They contain the Ten Commandments, followed by the beginning of the Shema (Deut. VI:4–5). The Decalogue has a number of remarkable divergencies from the traditional Masoretic version of the Pentateuch. It follows neither the text of Exodus (XIX:2–XX:17) nor that of Deuteronomy (V:6–21), but agrees in the main with the Hebrew which lies behind the Septuagint. The phrase "the house of bondage" is deleted, no doubt to safeguard against giving offense to Egypt, where the papyrus was written, and the prohibition against adultery precedes the prohibition against murder. "The Masoretic text," says Professor Burkitt, "appears to me the more archaic, and therefore the more genuine. In these passages the Masoretic text reads to me like the scholarly reproduction of a MS., which happens to contain no serious errors, while the Nash Papyrus is not the scholarly reproduction of a MS. but a monument of popular religion, giving the text of the Commandments with the grammatical difficulties smoothed down."

The thirteenth century is well represented in the manuscript collection. When the Talmud was burned in Paris in 1244 a few charred fragments of the tractate *Baba Batra* survived the flames, and those are today preserved in the library. Of deep intrinsic merit is *The Book of the Intelligent Soul,* copied out by Moses ben Shem Tov de Leon (*ca* 1250–1303), Spanish writer and Kabbalist.

Fourteenth-century items include a Haggadah of 1347 with illustrations of Job, his wife and the devil, and the four epic poems entitled, "Our Rabbi Moses," "The Paradise," "Patriarch Abraham," and "Pious Joseph", earliest Yiddish literary manuscript, dated November 1332. More numerous are manuscripts of the fifteenth century such as the unpublished *responsa* of Solomon ben Abraham Ibn Adret (1235–1310), and a formula for the "Calling up of the Bridegroom of the Law on Simchat Torah."

Among the rich assortment of eighteenth-century manuscripts is a Reader's *Kol Bo* ("All is therein"), a collection of prayers for an English congregation, in which the prayers for the royal family refer to Queen Anne (1702–1714).

Numbered among notable nineteenth-century manuscripts is a letter in ryhmed prose dated February 9, 1851, from the Chief Rabbi of Padua, Mordecai Samuel Ghirondi (1799–1852), to the author and rabbi, Zevi Hirsch Chajes (1805–1855). The letter concerns the pedigree of Saul Wahl, a legendary figure who according to folklore had been king of Poland for one day.

The library has a number of specialized technical manuscripts: a textbook with diagrams and colored drawings using the Hebrew names of plants, reptiles, insects; names of the seven planets in Hebrew, Greek, Latin, Persian, and Arabic; an Italian vocabulary for the Targum; and an Italian translation of Hebrew scientific terms.

THE BEGINNING

The history of the Cambridge University Library goes back to the thirteenth century. It is far older than that of its celebrated rival Oxford. As early as 1286 Hugh Balsham, Bishop of Ely and founder of Peterhouse, bequeathed "many books in divinity and other sciences" to his students. Two early catalogues are preserved; one, dated 1425, enumerates 52 volumes, while the second catalogue, compiled in 1473, lists 330 volumes.

In 1438 King Henry VI responded to the "prayers of the Chancellor, Masters and Scholars of the University" who appealed to him for his help on behalf of the "Common Library." On the Feast of St. Hugh, November 17, 1444, the new library was opened under royal patronage.

The library acquired Hebraica gradually. Among the eighty-seven volumes given by John Lord Lumley (1534–1609) in 1598, and brought to Cambridge by Hobson the carrier, at a charge of 16*s*.4*d*., was the Hebrew incunabulum *Sepher Ha-Sherashim* by David ben Joseph Kimchi.

In 1625 George Villiers, Duke of Buckingham and Chancellor of the University, purchased the library of Thomas van Erpen (Erpenius 1584–1624), a distinguished linguist of Leyden. Seven years later the Duke's widow Catherine presented Cambridge with several important items, eleven of them Hebraic. Five years later Thomas Waley, Vice-Master of Trinity College, presented a commentary on the Pentateuch by Moses ben Nachman of Gerona (1194–1270). Another scholar who fostered the interest in Hebraic studies was John Lightfoot (1600–1673), who according to Gibbon "by constant reading of the rabbis became almost a rabbi himself." When he was appointed to the rectory of Ashley, Staffordshire, in 1630, he built himself a garden-study and devoted all his time to the study of Hebrew.

Cambridge had no Thomas Bodley and its purchases were rarely spectacular. Lack of private initiative prompted Parliamentary intervention, notably in the instance of the Thomason collection. George Thomason (1600–1666) carried on business at the sign of "The Rose and the Crown" in St. Paul's Churchyard, London. He was a most unusual bibliophile. Throughout the period of the Civil War and the Commonwealth he made it a principle to obtain a copy of every book and every pamphlet published in England and abroad.

Thomas Carlyle describes this collection as "the most valuable set of documents connected with English history." On May 21, 1647, Thomason issued a catalogue listing 1,970 books and manuscripts: 1,302 in Latin, 294 in Italian, 36 in Spanish, 6 in Scandinavian languages, 300 in Hebrew, 32 in various languages including Arabic, Coptic, Syriac, and Turkish. The preface reads: "Courteous Reader. The following is a Catalogue of books brought over from Italy of the greatest use, if I am not mistaken, to all who are interested in theology, medicine, philosophy or belles lettres. I have spared no expense in my attempt to satisfy your needs and to gratify your curiosity. You will find here more rabbinical and oriental books and manuscripts than have ever before been collected together." [29]

On March 24, 1647 the Commons passed this resolution:

Ordered, by the Lords and Commons in Parliament assembled, that the sum of Five hundred pounds be charged upon, and forthwith paid out of the Receipts at *Goldsmiths Hall*, unto Mr. Mr. *George Thomason*, Stationer, for buying of the said *Thomason* a library or Collection of Books, in the Eastern languages of a very great value, late brought out of Italy, and having been the library of a learned Rabbi there, according to the printed Catalogue thereof: And that the said library or Collection of Books be bestowed upon the Public

Library in the University of Cambridge; And the Acquittance or Acquittances of the said *George Thomason* shall be a sufficient Discharge to the Treasurers at *Goldsmiths Hall* for Payment of the said Five hundred pounds accordingly; and it is especially recommended to the Committee at *Goldsmiths Hall* to take care that present due Payment may be made of this Sum accordingly, that the kingdom may not be deprived of so great a Treasure, nor Learning want so great an Encouragement.

Parliament further "ordered that Mr. Selden and Mr. Lightfoot do take care, that the University of Cambridge may have the said Books; and that they may be preserved for them according to the printed Catalogue." [30]

It is established that these books arrived safely in Cambridge, but it is not certain whether Thomason was ever paid. On November 16, 1647, he was granted interest at the rate of eight per cent on the still unsettled bill. Nevertheless, Cambridge was grateful for the new acquisitions. The Commemoration Service of 1667 reads: "Mr. Selden (out of his love for learning) procured for us the Library of Isaac Prage, being a great collection of rabbinical authors valued at £500."

These books had once belonged to Rabbi Isaac Prage (Pragi or Faragi) and consisted of the sixteenth- and seventeenth-century works, editions of Soncino and Bomberg, together with six incunabula.

So famous was the library during the time of Cromwell that when the Council of State were discussing the re-admission of the Jews, it was alleged that the Jews had made an offer of a half a million pounds for St. Paul's Cathedral and the Cambridge University Library. "About this time, as it is said, certain Jews of the Western parts of Asia, who came to England at a private audience with Cromwell, negotiated the purchase of the Library of this University. They obtained permission to repair to Cambridge and in the presence of the Librarian examined and took a Catalogue of the most valuable books." [31] At that time it was rumored that the Jews were also contemplating the purchase of the Bodleian Library. These rumors were unfounded.

During the second half of the seventeenth century the Hebrew collection remained virtually static. In December 1672 Isaac Abendana, translator of the Mishnah into Latin, received from Robert Mapletoft (1609–1677), dean of Ely and sizar of Queen's College, Cambridge, "the sum of £5. for a Hebrew manuscript." In 1686 the library was enriched by thirty-eight manuscripts, nineteen of them in Hebrew, thirteen in Arabic, and six in Ethiopian, at the bequest of Dr. Edmund Castell (1606–1685). A Semitic scholar of note, Castell had assisted Walton in his Biblical Polyglot and was himself the author of a lexicon. "Wise men have no bread," says King Solomon. Castell spent £1200 of his own money on this work and was even imprisoned for debt.

In 1715 King George I presented the library of John Moore, Bishop of Ely. Moore was associated with Kennicott in the arduous task of collating the Hebrew manuscripts of the Bible. The royal purchaser had paid £6,450 for the 30,755 volumes and 1,790 manuscripts. In 1726 the Reverend George Lewis, Archdeacon of Meath, presented several Oriental manuscripts. Yet despite these bequests and acquisitions the entire Hebrew collection occupied but a single small section of the five library rooms around the school quadrangle.

More progress was made during the nineteenth century. In 1796 Claudius Buchanan (1766–1815) was appointed to the chaplaincy in Bengal. On May 3, 1806, he traveled to the coast of Malabar, where he acquired a number of Oriental manuscripts. The manner of the acquisitions makes almost pictorial reading:

> I negotiated for them hastily, and wrapped them up in two cloths and gave them to the Jews to carry them to my house. I had observed some murmurings amongst the by-standers in the Synagogue, while I was examining the chest; and before we appeared in the street, the alarm had gone forth that the Christians were robbing the Synagogue of the Law . . . The affair ended, however. I was to select which was old and of little use to the Jews and to give back to them what was new.[32]

Among the hundred manuscripts presented by Buchanan to the library in 1804 was a collection of historical notes, chiefly on the history of the Dutch Jews, written by an Ashkenazi author from France, and a history of the Black and White Jews of Malabar. There were a number of manuscripts, mainly Biblical, written in the Hebrew, Syriac, and Ethiopian tongues; a copy of the Hebrew Pentateuch written on goatskin, which had been found in Cochin; and a version of the New Testament rendered into Hebrew by a "learned rabbi in Travancore", containing portions of the Acts and of Revelation.

In the course of the nineteenth century Cambridge acquired many manuscripts from booksellers, from salesrooms, and from such benefactors as the Reverend William Henry Black of London. Another donor was Samuel Sandars (1837–1894), whose frequent custom it was to send a check for £50 to Francis Jenkinson (1853–1923) to be "spent in adding to the University Library any book which in your judgment may be desirable." Through this benefactor the library obtained the commentary on the Pentateuch by Nachmanides, printed in 1489. "I am glad," wrote Sandars to Jenkinson, "you have got the Portuguese early printed book. I wrote for it, too. If you have purchased it for the Library I shall be very pleased to donate it."

In 1908 the widow of Dr. Charles Taylor added three hundred of her husband's Hebrew books, many of them rare editions and fine specimens of printing, as were a number of manuscripts. Other twentieth-century donors were A.G. Murray (d. 1919), the Reverend A. Bueno de Mesquita, who presented an assortment of medical recipes in Judeo-German, and the Friends of the National Libraries, who gave a group of *shetars* (deeds) in 1945.

CATALOGUES

In 1825 the Orientalist Dr. Daniel Guilford Wait (1789–1850) was commissioned to prepare a catalogue of the Hebrew collection, but nothing came of this project. However, with the appointment of Henry Bradshaw (1831–1886) as librarian, the library entered into a more active phase. His resources were limited but his ideals were lofty. He felt that he had to make up for decades of neglect. "I cannot buy many books of this kind as I have to buy them out of my own pocket," he noted on November 9, 1865, "for our library authorities very rarely consent to the purchase of anything except what they chose to call modern, useful, scientific books." [33]

In a letter dated June 18, 1865, he wrote, "I have just set a Hungarian Rabbi at work upon our Hebrew manuscripts, and with his knowledge and my method of cataloguing I hope it may be a creditable book. But what with this, young Palmer [Edward Henry Palmer, 1840–1882] for the Arabic and Miss Shields for the Vaudois manuscripts, all being paid out of my own pocket, it leaves me but little prospect of going abroad this summer." [34]

An extraordinary personality and a key figure in the life of the library was Solomon Mayer Schiller-Szinessy (1820–1890), known in Cambridge as "the rabbi." He was born in 1820 at Alt-Ofen, Hungary—as it were with bibliographic blood in his veins, since he was a descendant on his mother's side of the Beks, well-known printers in Venice. Schiller-Szinessy graduated from Jena University and became professor *publicus extraordinarius* at the Lutheran College at Eperies, Hungary. During the Hungarian upheaval of 1848 he blew up the bridge of Szegedin, an act which checked the advance of the Austrian army.

In England the revolutionary became rabbi at the Manchester Reform Synagogue. But the Reformist ritual was not to the liking of this traditional Jew. He left the pulpit in 1863, and in 1866 Cambridge appointed him teacher of Talmudic and rabbinical literature, at a salary of £300 a year. On June 15, 1868, the Library Syndicate entrusted him with the task of compiling a catalogue dealing with (1) Bible, (2) Commentaries, and (3) Talmud, Liturgy, Religion, Philosophy, Kabbalah, Greek, Arabic, and Miscellaneous. The Syndicate watched him at work and on March 26, 1873 it reported approvingly that the "Catalogue of Hebrew Manuscripts continues to make satisfactory progress through the press."

A resolution was passed on May 23, 1872, to the effect that "a stipend of £200 a year be paid to Dr. Schiller-Szinessy from the library fund during such time as he may be engaged in passing the Catalogue of Hebrew manuscripts through the press, its payment to commence from midsummer 1871 when the Catalogue was first put to the press; provided that the time does not exceed five years and the work be carried out to the satisfaction of the Syndicate."

In 1876 the first part of the catalogue was published; it dealt with only seventy-two of the 762 codices. Some twenty-five sheets listing the Talmudic manuscripts were printed, but they were never published. Schiller-Szinessy received an honorary Master's Degree for his services. On November 14, 1876, he wrote to Edward Atkinson (1819–1915), Master of Clare College, Cambridge, "It has been a pleasure for me to devote the best part of the last 12 years to the service of the University and I hope that, if my life be spared, it will be found that the conferment of this honor will in no way diminish my willingness to do my utmost in prosecuting the work which has been entrusted to me." [35]

The great catalogue was finally completed, and filled six folio volumes. It describes all 762 of the literary manuscripts. On April 26, 1886 Schiller-Szinessy sent it off with a covering letter which read: "My dear Librarian, I send you the Catalogue. I beg you kindly to ask your Syndicate whether they would buy the former. Both catalogues were compiled by me at the request of your late Librarian . . . Many years ago a 'compliment' of £50 for the Catalogue (of subjects) which did not cover for me a tenth part of the labor which the one I send you now has cost me. I believe therefore, that £50 is a modest sum for it. Should you or your Syndicate have a different opinion, kindly return the Catalogue to me and it will remain my private property." [36] It is not recorded whether or not the manuscript was returned to the unhappy writer. It is a fact, though, that the Catalogue remained unpublished.

Schechter had hoped to continue this work. It was recorded on May 20, 1896, that "already the preparation of the Catalogue of the Cambridge Hebrew MSS. has been more or less formally committed to his charge." [37] Apart, however, from a number of articles in the *Jewish Quarterly Review* under the heading, "Notes on the Hebrew Manuscripts in the University Library at Cambridge," [38] nothing further was done.

Israel Abrahams, Schechter's successor, spent twenty-five years in Cambridge. "By his contribution to learning and his far-reaching vision", said Sir Albert Charles Seward, Master of Downing College (1915–1936) in tribute, "he loyally served the Hebrew Community. Honored for his erudition, he was revered for his humanity, sympathy and kindliness." [39] Despite the interest of the bibliophiles, William Aldis Wright and S.A. Cook, little progress was made with the catalogue. In 1913 the Orientalist Herbert Loewe (1882–1940) began to prepare a handlist of the Hebrew manuscripts. This work took him fourteen years and was subsequently revised by his son Raphael Loewe (b. 1919), Fellow of Caius College, Cambridge. Today Jacob Leveen (b. 1891), late keeper of the Department of Oriental Printed Books and Manuscripts of the British Museum (1953-56), has taken up where Schiller-Szinessy left off. He is preparing a catalogue of the whole collection (excluding the Geniza). But ninety years have passed and no catalogue has been published either of the manuscripts or of the printed books. In this respect Cambridge has fallen far behind all other British libraries.

Trinity College possesses the finest Hebrew collection of all the nineteen Cambridge colleges. It is based on the library of William Aldis Wright, one of the revisers of the Authorized Version of the Bible, and the 159 volumes from the collection of the Biblical scholar David Christian Ginsburg, the baptized Polish Jew. Among the manuscripts are a Karaite scroll dating to 1330 and a commentary on a portion of Canticles by Isaac ben Judah Abravanel (1437–1508), a Biblical exegete, statesman, and treasurer to the King of Portugal. A controversial manuscript is *The Satan on the Day of Atonement,* a satiric attack on the *maskilim.* The author refers to his home town of Sadigura, to Rabbi Israel of Rizhyn (1798–1851), and to Sir Moses Montefiore. A catalogue of Trinity College Orientalia, published in 1868 by E.H. Palmer, included a section on the Hebraica by Schiller-Szinessy. In 1926 a catalogue of the Aldis Wright collection was published by Herbert M. Loewe.

The Hebraica in St. John's College were included in the catalogue of Western Manuscripts published by Montague Rhodes James (1862–1936) in 1913. Three Hebrew manuscripts were given by Richard Horne, Bishop of Winchester (1560–1579) in 1646. In addition to two mediaeval Bibles there is a copy of Rashi's commentary, with the colophon "I concluded this book on the day before the New Year, 1238."

These are some of the treasures that glitter at Cambridge, accumulated over the course of almost seven centuries.

Chapter V

Jews' College Library, London

"Despise no man, and consider nothing impossible, for there is no man who does not have his hour and there is not a thing that does not have its place." This Mishnaic adage[40] comes to mind when one considers the size and significance of the library of Jews' College, which recently celebrated its centenary. Admittedly the library lacks the wealth of printed books and manuscripts which the Bodleian possesses. It has none of the Geniza fragments that are the glory of the Cambridge collection. Nor has it any treasures to compare with those that adorn the British Museum. Yet Jews' College Library has other advantages. Although smaller than some of the other Hebrew collections in England, it is the one most widely used. It is no mere depository of books. It is a living and lively center of Jewish study and research. Each day there is considerable traffic in books borrowed, returned, read, and consulted. It is housed in a contemporary showpiece setting, in the new College building in Upper Montagu Place, London, and every item is carefully and accurately classified.

EARLY HISTORY

Jews' College opened its doors on November 11, 1855, with thirty-three pupils. In his inaugural address Chief Rabbi Nathan Marcus Adler said: "We have, thank God, a house to work in, teaching power to work with and minds to work upon." No mention was made of provision for even a skeleton library. In 1860 Lewis Mayer Rothschild (1809–1884) presented the College Council with books that had formerly belonged to the General Literary and Scientific Institution in Sussex Hall. This had been the first Anglo-Jewish venture in popular education. Named after the Duke of Sussex, a noble friend of Jewry, Sussex Hall was opened on January 20, 1845, through the efforts of the public-spirited president of the Sephardi community, Chananel de Castro (1796–1849). The poet and novelist

Grace Aguilar (1816–1847) was among those who presented books to the Institution.

The experiment was not a success, and when Sussex Hall closed its doors Rothschild purchased its library. However, before bestowing it upon Jews' College, he carefully removed "a number of worthless works of fiction, befitting a literary institution and intended for general circulation but which would not only have been out of place in a college for the study of divinity, but that might have tempted youthful scholars to waste their precious time in the reading of useless books to the detriment of their grave and sacred pursuits." [41]

The Sussex Hall collection, valued at £500, was the nucleus of the Jews' College Library. It was opened to the public on Sunday afternoons and Wednesday evenings, and literate Londoners were quick to take advantage of this opportunity. "In common with numerous individuals who will doubtless make use of the Library of Jews College," wrote an anonymous "lector" to the *Jewish Chronicle* on November 16, 1860, "I feel a debt of gratitude to the Council for their liberality and public spirit." Soon afterwards Walter Josephs (1804–1893) added 250 volumes inherited from his father Michael.

However, the library was still poorly stocked and many basic books were lacking. According to the Reverend Isidore Harris (1853–1925), one of the early students, "It proved so inadequate for our wants that we can remember the time when the addition of such works as Munk's translation of the 'Moreh' or Webster's Large *English Dictionary* was regarded as a major event in the history of the College."

Steadily the number of printed books increased. In 1873 the collection was enriched by the Orientalia of Emanuel Deutsch (1829–1873), who had been assistant keeper at the British Museum from beginning in 1853. Five years later the College received yet another gift from Lewis Mayer Rothschild, who presented the books of Abraham Benisch (1811–1878), editor of the *Jewish Chronicle* and founder of the Anglo-Jewish Association and of the Society of Biblical Archaeology.

The year 1883 was another landmark in the history of the library. The widow of the Reverend Aaron Levy Green, honorary secretary of the College from 1852, handed over some six thousand valumes originally belonging to her late husband. In a letter to the Chief Rabbi dated June 13, 1883, Mrs. Phoebe Green wrote: "If the books should find a resting place in the College, which will I trust be consolidated as an important center of Jewish learning, it would afford me peculiar gratification to know that the students could find invaluable source of information in the library." The A.E. Green Memorial Fund brought in £500. In the course of the next half century Jews' College received many bibliographic contributions from faculty and alumni. Among notable acquisitions were the books of Dr. Adolf Büchler (1867–1939), the music library of the Reverend Herman Mayerowitch (1882–1945), and some volumes which had belonged to the former Chief Rabbi, Dr. J.H. Hertz.

MANUSCRIPTS

Through the Spanish and Portuguese Synagogue the College received on loan in 1898 the main contents of the collection then in Ramsgate, so lovingly and laboriously amassed by Dr. Louis Loewe (1809–88) and the *Chakham* Moses Gaster, while a mere fifty or sixty manuscripts and several hundred volumes were retained in Ramsgate. The Montefiore Collection, as it was called, consisted of three celebrated and separate entities: manuscripts collected by Sir Moses Montefiore and by Loewe; twenty-seven manuscripts once the property of Leopold Zunz (1794–1886), founder of the modern Science of Judaism, and a total of 512 items previously owned by Solomon Zalman Chayyim Halberstamm (1832–1900).

For forty years Halberstamm had combined a successful mercantile career in Bielitz with book collecting. He himself edited several manuscripts, such as the *novellae* of the fourteenth-century Talmudical commentator, Rabbi Yom-Tov ben Abraham Ishbili, the Ritba of Seville, and Abraham Ibn Ezra's *Sepher ha-Ibbur,* a manual of calendar science. In 1890 he published in Vienna a catalogue of his manuscripts entitled *Kehilat Shlomoh.* His printed books were bought by the Vienna Jewish community, and by Mayer Sulzberger for the Jewish Theological Seminary of America, while his manuscripts were acquired by Montefiore College. These were catalogued by Hartwig Hirschfeld (1854–1934), tutor at Jews' College and translator of Judah Ha-Levi's *Kuzari.* His catalogue was published in 1904 and contains 586 entries.

A number of the Montefiore manuscripts are of great antiquity. A copy of the Book of Job with anonymous commentaries is dated 1394. Another manuscript consisting of glosses on the Halakhic compendium of Rabbi Mordecai ben Hillel Ashkenazi (d. 1298), is dated July 1312. As many as forty-one of the 586 manuscripts are actually dated. In 1952 the library acquired a manuscript which had been the property of Solomon Bennett (1761–1838). He was a prolific writer and had begun a complete new English translation of the Bible.

Many manuscripts bear witness to the impact of the life and works of Sir Moses Montefiore on his contemporaries. A Montefiore diary of a journey through England, Holland, and Germany describes the itinerary in lively detail, noting expenses incurred en route along with unusual incidents. There are letters and petitions received by Sir Moses and Lady

Montefiore in the Holy Land in 1839, and a diary of Lady Montefiore from November 11, 1827, to February 20, 1828.

In its second half century of existence the library of Jews' College continued to develop at a steady pace. It received nearly 10,000 volumes from the Committee on the Restoration of Continental Jewish Museums, Libraries and Archives, in addition to the valuable rabbinic library of Aaron Blumenthal and the Aria College collection.

The library now possesses 60,000 books and 20,000 pamphlets, nearly 700 manuscripts, and 8 incunabula, plus a collection of portraits of Jewish notables. Its original departments, devoted to history, Bible, and prayer books, have been extended beyond recognition. It has excellent sections on folklore, Talmud, and Geonica and a nearly complete set of *Festschriften* (jubilee and memorial volumes), and is slowly amassing new treasures. Its latest acquisition, for example, is the Mishnah with Maimonides' commentary printed by Joshua Soncino at Naples in 1492. Most important, the library has excellent reference facilities. The researcher can gain quick and easy access to all basic rabbinic works, to all current encyclopedias, and to a wide range of rare and contemporary periodicals.

Chapter VI

The Bet Hamidrash Library, London

"The sun also ariseth and the sun goeth down," says Ecclesiastes [42] and this verse well applies to Woburn House. On September 12, 1957, Jews' College was transferred to a newly built campus, and the college library left the shelves which it has occupied for a quarter of a century. But those shelves were soon refilled. On July 14, 1959, Woburn House became the new home of the *Bet Din* and of the *Bet Hamidrash* Library consisting of 148 manuscripts, 12 incunabula, and 4,500 volumes.

Where there is a Jewish community there is always a synagogue and an academy of learning. So it is not surprising to find reference to a *Bet Hamidrash* in records of Jewish life in pre-expulsion England. In the Common Pleas of the seventeenth year of the reign of Edward II (1284–1327) there is an allusion to a "dwelling place in the Parish of St. Mary Creechurch next to the house which was formerly the great school of the Jews." [43]

After the resettlement there is little information regarding the *Batei Midrashim* of the fledgling community. It is recorded that a *Bet Hamidrash* was established, probably in 1776, in Booker's Gardens under Rabbi Zalman Ansell (d. 1840). In 1783 Abraham ben Solomon Hamburger of Nancy (known as Abraham Nanzig) participated in a *siyyum* (the completion of a study course that embraces the entire Talmud). His discourse there was printed in his work *Ale Teruphah* (London, 1785), which consisted of a treatise on the legal permissibility of vaccination, notes on tractate *Berakhot,* and sermons. In the same year "Dr." Chayyim Samuel de Falk, the *Baal Shem* of London (1708–1782), a dabbler in magic and practical Kabbalah, left a ten-guinea annuity to the *Bet Hamidrash.*

In 1802 Solomon Hirschell (1761–1842) was appointed Chief Rabbi of the Great Synagogue of London. The *Gentleman's Magazine* viewed the appointment with approval: "The Congregation of German Jews in London have elected, after a vacancy of ten years, a High Priest of their Nation." As a descendant of Rabbi Meir ben Isaac Katzenellenbogen (*ça.*

1482–1565) of Padua, and as a rabbi for nine years at Prenzlau, Prussia, Hirschell now had an authority extending far beyond the confines of his own community. Even the B'nai Jeshurun (oldest Ashkenazi congregation in New York, established in 1825) submitted ritual questions to him and sent him Purim offerings for distribution among the poor of London.

Hirschell was an ardent educator. He supported the efforts of the Polish scholar Solomon Jacob (Shalom) Cohen to establish a model Hebrew school in England. In 1829 Solomon Arnold of the New Synagogue bequeathed one thousand pounds to the *Bet Hamidrash.* But it was not until 1841 that a site was acquired, for the sum of £370, at No. 1 Smith's Building, Leadenhall Street. The *Bet Hamidrash* was also to be a training college, "to train up youth for the various offices connected with the ministrations of our religion." [44] A report in the *Jewish Chronicle* [45] gives this revealing glimpse: "The Old *Bet Hamidrash,* miserable as was its locale, there was there an element of life and earnestness. Every evening without exception might be seen between Afternoon and Evening Prayers a crowd of scholars and during health and vigour Dr. Hirschell in their midst, pursuing the study of the Talmud."

After the death of Hirschell on October 31, 1842, an Anglo-Jewish periodical, *Voice of Jacob,* raised the problem of the Chief Rabbi's library: "With the exception of four *Siphrei Torah* which are bequeathed to his male descendants all his other property will have to be sold. It would be highly discreditable if his excellent library should be permitted to be distributed: it is hoped that it may be, in some wise, secured as a public library, for the use of Biblical and Rabbinical students; a great desideratum in this country." *Vox populi, vox dei.* The *Voice of Jacob* was heard and the library was acquired for the *Bet Hamidrash.*

"We are gratified to learn," commented the *Jewish Chronicle* on October 6, 1845, "that this excellent library consisting of upwards of 4000 Hebrew books, among which there are many very rare and valuable books and manuscripts collected by our late Chief Rabbi, his father and grandfather, has been bought by the Committee of the Hebrew College, for the establishment of a *Bet Hamidrash,* for the very low sum of £300. By now in possession of so excellent a library we hope the community will soon set up and furnish the *Bet Hamidrash* with students who are able to profit by it. At present the visits of students are very 'few and far between.' We hope that this valuable library will be soon arranged and catalogued, so that the students desirous of information may have no hindrance in gaining access of its treasures."

The erudition of the new Chief Rabbi, Nathan Marcus Adler (1803–1890), did little at first to raise the cultural standards of the community. His major contribution at the outset was to deliver a Talmudic discourse on the Sabbath before the Day of Atonement. Once more the *Jewish Chronicle,* organ of Anglo-Jewry, sounded a pertinent note: "One thing is certain, that they must have convinced the Chief Rabbi of the small number of Talmudists in London. . . . Unless the *Bet Hamidrash* be converted into a college for students, we consider Dr. Adler's Talmudic discourses a waste of time and argument." [46]

Two years later, in 1847, a *Chevrah Shass* was established. It met on Mondays and Thursdays for the study of rabbinics. It was no doubt due to Adler's encouragement that in 1848 Abraham Lyon Moses (1775–1854), who erected almshouses and supported the Jews' Orphan Asylum, donated £2000 of Government stock "in order that thereby increased facilities and advantages may be obtained in respect of the said library." [47] The first librarian was Aaron Levy (1794–1876), a native of Lissa and pupil of Rabbi Jacob Lissa. Levy, a lawyer, came to England in 1811 and became a protégé of Hirschell. In 1830 he was sent to Sydney, Australia, a journey that took seven months, in order to effect a bill of divorcement. He was away on this mission for eighteen months. Levy served as librarian until 1872.[48]

In a circular dated December 8, 1852, dealing with the founding of Jews' College, Adler referred to the present *Bet Hamidrash* "with its excellent library, revenue and the munificent gift recently bestowed by A.L. Moses Esq." The Library of the *Bet Hamidrash* was not incorporated into the new college. The *Bet Hamidrash* could not support itself. On January 12, 1872, its treasurer, Jacob Henry Moses (1805–1875), applied formally to the United Synagogue for assistance. The organization responded to the appeal and on January 8, 1875, the *Bet Hamidrash* was taken over by the United Synagogue.

In a letter to the Council of the United Synagogue dated March 10, 1876, the Chief Rabbi made this request: "As you are at present inviting applications for the post of Librarian at the new *Bet Hamidrash* I beg to suggest that the gentleman to be elected as *dayyan* be also called upon to take charge of the library and to hold classes for instruction in Bible, Talmud, Hebrew literature as provided in your scheme." On July 13, 1876, Bernard Spiers (1829–1901) was elected *dayyan* at a yearly salary of £150, with an extra £80 to cover his labors as librarian.[49]

The new premises at No. 1 and 2 Saint James Place, Aldgate, acquired for £2424.10*s*.5*d*., were consecrated on September 7, 1876. It was formally decreed that "a sum of at least £20 per annum be devoted to the maintenance of the library including the purchase of new books; the library to be open to readers at least four hours daily, except on Sabbaths and Festivals." [50]

Dayyan Spiers edited two manuscripts, which he embodied in his Passover Haggadah published in 1877. "Should it be received favorably," Spiers wrote hopefully in his introduction, "I may perhaps be encouraged to publish other works likely to exhibit in more marked degree the beauties of this valuable collection of the *Bet Hamidrash.*" [51]

A number of attempts have been made to catalogue the library. A handwritten catalogue was compiled by Menachem ben Samuel Mansfield in 1846. In 1880 Spiers tried his hand at this task. However, the work was eventually brought to a conclusion by the experienced Adolf Neubauer, whose catalogue was published in 1886, dedicated to Moritz Steinschneider on the occasion of the latter's seventieth birthday anniversary, on March 30 of the same year.

The *Bet Hamidrash* also acquired the library of Dr. Asher Asher (1837–1889), first secretary of the United Synagogue in London. With the influx of East European Jews during the first two decades of the twentieth century, the Anglo-Jewish scene underwent many drastic changes. The East End of London became the center of activities and a new locale was essential for the *Bet Hamidrash.* It was generally agreed that "as regard the *Dayyanim,* one should be Librarian of the *Bet Hamidrash,* one specially conversant with Yiddish and one connected with the educational side of the East End Scheme." [52]

Rabbi Moses Hyamson (1862–1942), who was one of the first Jewish ministers to gain a Bachelor of Law degree and was later professor of codes at the Jewish Theological Seminary of America, succeeded Spiers as librarian. The new *Bet Hamidrash,* at the juncture of Mulberry and Holloway streets on Commercial Road, in the heart of the East End, was consecrated by the Chief Rabbi on December 12, 1905, in the presence of the first Lord Rothschild, Nathaniel Mayer (1840–1915). This was its home for half a century, up until it was damaged during the Nazi "blitz" in September 1940.

Manuscripts in the library consist of Biblical and Talmudic commentaries and works on liturgy, philosophy, ethics, Kabbalah, mathematics, astronomy, and medicine. Among notable items are a casuistic work by Abraham Rothenburg, brother of the famous scholar Meir ben Baruch of Rothenburg; a *responsum* of Zevi Hirsch ben Aryeh Leb Norden of London, and Haggadic notes on the Pentateuch by *Dayyan* Naphtali ben Abraham of Prague, son-in-law of Nathan Nata of Opatow, rabbi of the Hambro Synagogue in London. There are a number of items on "Dr." Falk, the *Baal Shem* of London, such as his permutations of the letters contained in the Name of God, his belief on angels and his formulae for amulets.

This is a wandering library, which has moved from place to place and yet remained static. In the course of more than 120 years it has in fact depreciated, and is actually poorer today than when it was acquired from the executors of Chief Rabbi Hirschell in 1845.

PART II

The Jewish Literary Treasures of America

Chapter VII

The Library of the Jewish Theological Seminary of America

The greatest Jewish library in the world belongs to the Jewish Theological Seminary of America. It contains 10,000 manuscripts, 145 Hebrew incunabula, and 200,000 printed books. This library of libraries is housed in the Jacob H. Schiff Memorial building, an impressive landmark on upper Broadway, between 122nd and 123rd streets. The six-story structure, Colonial in style, is dominated by a tower 165 feet high. The emblem of the Burning Bush, with the inscription, in Hebrew and in English, "And the Bush was not consumed" (Exodus III:2), appears above the entrance.

Two specially constructed rooms, fitted with steel cases and protected by locked doors and bronze wire guards, occupy an area 41 feet long by 22 feet wide and enshrine the accumulated wisdom of many climes and centuries. Crowded on the shelves are the writings of Samaritans, Rabbinites, Ashkenazim, Sephardim. Jewels of the library illumine every corridor of Jewish learning, every phase of Jewish history through two thousand troubled years. If only the inanimate were articulate! Scattered throughout the world, Jewery made its multiform contribution to civilization in a multiplicity of languages. Side by side with Hebrew texts are works in Aramaic, Arabic, Persian, Tataric, Provençal, Maharrati, Ladino, Turkish, and, inevitably, Yiddish.

The Jewish Theological Seminary was born in 1886, at a conference of Conservative clergymen in the Nineteenth Street Synagogue in New York. The ministers resolved unanimously "that it is indispensable for the welfare of Progressive Judaism in the country that there be founded a Seminary for the training of the teachers of the future generations in sympathy with the spirit of Conservative Judaism." The resolution might have remained a verbal gesture but for the zeal of Dr. Sabato Morais (1823–1897), rabbi of Mikveh Israel Synagogue in Philadelphia, second oldest congregation in the New World. On January 3, 1887, the Seminary opened with a *minyan* of exactly ten students at the Shearit Israel Synagogue in New York, and Dr. Joseph Herman Hertz (1872–1946), later to become Chief Rabbi of the British Empire, was its first graduate.

As early as 1890, at the second Biennial Convention of the Association of the Jewish Theological Seminary, the Honorable Joseph Blumenthal, president of the Board of Trustees (1886–1901) asserted, "There is an urgent and immediate necessity for the formation of a well equipped library. It is out of the question for us to attempt to obtain the best results without the essential supply of the scholar's tools. Many of our pupils have already reached the stage in their studies when original research must supplement the teachings of the class room. The fund necessary for purchasing the needful volumes of Hebraica and Judaica is not so large but that it ought to be readily forthcoming. Rightfully, however, we ought to have accessible to our pupils everything of value in literature relating to their sphere of study." [53]

The library at that time consisted of a mere 1,000 books, but in 1893 it was quadrupled by the addition of the 3,000-volume collection of Dr. David Cassel (1818–1893), historian and theologian and one of the founders of the *Jüdische Wissenchaft.* In the same year, to mark the seventieth birthday of Dr. Morais, large literary additions were made and the whole collection was designated as the Morais Library. The benefactors hoped that "the Morais Library of the Seminary might become so valuable and important a collection of works in Hebrew literature as to constitute it the Center of Hebrew Learning and Research in America." Dr. Morais himself bequeathed seven hundred volumes to the Seminary.

THE SULZBERGER COLLECTION

The great expectations of these scholarly pioneers were fulfilled. Under Dr. Solomon Schechter, second president of the Seminary, the institution gained in academic status. As lecturer in rabbinics at Cambridge, Schechter had fired the imagination of the world by his work on the Cairo Geniza. In July 1894 he had written to Richard Gottheil, professor of Semitic languages at Columbia University: "I believe that the future of Judaism is in America, and with God's help I am sure we could do much good there, not only for science but for the purpose of forming a school of young men who will unite enthusiasm with Jewish learning . . . I have come to London for *Kaddish* [the mourners' prayer]. In Cambridge there is no community and no synagogue. That is one of the principal reasons which drives me from Cambridge. I want to be a Jew and to bring up my children as Jews. Do not think I over-rate America. But with Jews I can get understanding. I lose my life among Christians." [54]

For thirteen years (1902–1915) Schechter was the patriarch of American Jewry. Shades of the academies of Breslau and Vienna and the *yeshivot* of Piatra and Lemberg hovered over the Seminary in New York. Under the new president it developed from a rabbinical school into a college of higher learning.

In his inaugural address on November 20, 1902, Schechter expounded his theories on the preparation of candidates for the ministry. "Now, we all agree that the office of a Jewish minister is to teach Judaism; he should accordingly receive such a training as to enable him to say: '*Judaeici nihil a me alienum puto* (I regard nothing Jewish as foreign to me).' He should know everything Jewish—Bible, Talmud, Midrash, liturgy, Jewish ethics, and Jewish philosophy; Jewish history and Jewish mysticism; and even Jewish folklore. None of these subjects, with its various ramifications, should be entirely strange to him." [55]

Schechter attracted to the Seminary men of exceptional talent. Louis Ginzberg (1873–1953), author of the monumental seven-volume *Legends of the Jews,* occupied the chair of Talmud. Israel Friedlaender (1876–1920), Orientalist and translator of Dubnow's *History of the Jews in Russia and Poland,* joined the faculty at the age of twenty-seven. He died while ministering to pogrom-stricken Jews in the Ukraine. Israel Davidson (1870–1939), author of the *Thesaurus of Mediaeval Hebrew Poetry,* a listing of 35,000 poetical compositions, was another star in this galaxy of scholars.

Alexander Marx (1878–1953), a devoted disciple of Steinschneider, became both professor of history and librarian, and this proved a most apposite appointment. While the master had spent a lifetime cataloguing libraries, the disciple dedicated himself to the formation of one great library, the Seminary collection. Marx was barely twenty-five when he entered upon this task, and he devoted fifty years to its fulfilment. The library became his preoccupation by day and his dream by night.

In this *annus mirabilis* of the library, Judge Mayer Sulzberger of Philadelphia presented his momentous collection. Sulzberger (1843–1923), a jurist and civic worker, and one of the early American Jewish bibliophiles, had begun to acquire books in 1890. Author of works such as *Am Ha-aretz, The Ancient Hebrew Parliament,* and *The Status of Labor in Ancient Israel,* he was a scholar who fostered scholarship. After the death of the bibliophile Solomon Zalman Chayyim Halberstamm, some 5,500 books and 200 manuscripts were secured by Sulzberger for the Seminary.

In a letter dated January 20, 1904 he wrote: "I hereby give to the Seminary a collection of about seventy-five hundred Hebrew and Jewish printed books and about seven hundred and fifty Hebrew manuscripts, all of which I have lately caused to be placed in your building . . . My hope is that the Seminary may become the center for original work in the science of Judaism, to which end the acquisition of a great library is indispensable.

We and our successors must labor many years to build up such a library, but I believe that a good foundation for it has now been laid." [56]

Judge Sulzberger's enthusiasm did not flag. At the dedication of the new building on April 26, 1903 he gave almost lyrical expression to hopes for the future: "The Bodleian Library at Oxford and the British Museum at London are, and perhaps will always remain, the most magnificent and complete Hebrew book museums in the world. But it is our business on this side of the Atlantic to hope and to work, undaunted by the magnitude of others' achievements; we should hold in view the purpose to make our collection as nearly complete as the resources of the world may render possible, and in so doing we should spare neither thought nor labor nor money." [57]

The Sulzberger collection included a large number of incunabula as well as sixteenth-century editions and an assortment of fine Judeo-Arabic manuscripts brought together by the bookseller Ephraim Deinard. Many items were unique. There was, for example, a fourteenth-century manuscript of a commentary on Genesis and Exodus by the Italian Jewish poet and exegete, Immanuel ben Solomon of Rome (1270–1328), in which the text is followed by Targum with vowels. There was a copy of the *Former Prophets,* written in 1580 in the house of Donna Peyna, widow of the Turkish-Jewish statesman Joseph Nasi (d. 1579). There was a commentary by Abraham Ibn Ezra (1093–1167), famous Hebrew poet and Biblical scholar. This manuscript was copied by Judah ben Namer in Magnesia in 1374, with many marginal notes by the scholar known as Moses "Twenty-Four" (*Esrim V'Arba*) because he was said to know the twenty-four books of the Bible by heart, who bought the text in 1478. This same Moses was involved in the controversy between the Italian rabbi Joseph Colon (1420–1480) and Moses ben Elijah Capsali (1420–1493), Chief Rabbi of Turkey. Also in the collection is a Hebrew Pentateuch, dated 1491, with the Targum Onkelos in which the Aramaic translation is not only fully vocalized but also provided with notes for cantillation in the same manner as the scripture text itself. Evidence of high standards of education in fifteenth-century Italy is found in the fact that the manuscript *Livnat Hasapir,* a grammatical treatise by Judah ben Jechiel Rofe Messer Leon (*ca.* 1470), was copied out by a boy of fourteen.

It was Judge Sulzberger who in 1907 acquired the four hundred and seventeen Haggadot lovingly amassed by Adolph Oster of Xanten. These became the nucleus of the Seminary's Haggadah collection, which now numbers 1,332 items.

In 1907 the books of Moritz Steinschneider, father of Jewish bibliography, reached the Seminary. This library consisted of 3,000 Judaica and 1,500 Hebraica as well as 30 manuscripts. It was acquired in 1897 by Jacob

Henry Schiff, financier and philanthropist, who with characteristic magnanimity permitted Steinschneider to keep the library until his death. Twenty-six years later, Miss Adeline Goldberg contributed the vast correspondence between Steinschneider and scholars both Jewish and non-Jewish. The twenty-six large packages of which it is composed are packed with material of sociological and scientific interest. Much of it is autobiographical, revealing many phases of Steinschneider's early life and career until he retired after twenty-one years of service as rector of the *Mädchenschule* of the Jewish community in Berlin.

Others followed Sulzberger's example. In 1909 New York's Temple Emanu-El, which had acquired the Almanzi-Lewenstein-Emden collection in 1871, divided it between the Seminary and Columbia University. A total of 620 Latin dissertations on Biblical and Jewish subjects were received by the Seminary. Two years later Jacob H. Schiff, who had been appointed a life Director of the Seminary, presented the Kautzsch collection of 4,600 books and pamphlets, rich in Semitic philology.

World War I (1914–1918) did not stunt the library's growth. The mantle of Jacob H. Schiff fell upon Mortimer L. Schiff (1877–1931), who rarely missed an opportunity of enriching the Seminary. At the death of Dr. Schechter on November 20, 1915, his family presented 1,475 books and 13 manuscripts, as well as some rare Geniza fragments. The Schechter acquisitions included a famous fund-raising letter, an appeal bearing the signature of Maimonides, in Arabic but using Hebrew characters, for support in the work of redeeming captives. Twenty years later Mrs. Frank I. Schechter presented a valuable supplement, her husband's notebooks and correspondence.

THE ISRAEL SOLOMONS COLLECTION

By the end of World War I the library prided itself on its 54,000 books and 1,800 manuscripts. The next decade, however, was the one most decisive in its development. Attention was focused on England, and the purchase of two great Anglo-Jewish collections placed the Seminary among the world's foremost Jewish libraries.

One day the attention of Israel Solomons (1860–1923) was caught by a print of the Great Synagogue, which he saw by chance in a bookseller's collection. He spent the rest of his life zealously accumulating books and pamphlets relevant to Anglo-Jewry, and contributed fifty items to the Anglo-Jewish Historical Exhibition of 1887. Moreover, Solomons was a bibliophile with a fine aesthetic taste. His books were finely bound by J. Zaehnsdorf (1816–1886), R. Riviere (1808–1882), and other skilled bookbinders. The Solomons collection of 1,800 books and pamphlets and 1,100 prints was bought by Mortimer L. Schiff for the Seminary.

Apart from British Museum holdings, no other collection throws so much light on Anglo-Jewish history from the resettlement to the mid-nineteenth century. Of paramount importance are the works of Manasseh ben Israel (1604–1657), which are mostly represented in the original first editions as well as in translation. There is a rare print of greetings in Portuguese to the Prince of Orange when he visited the Amsterdam Synagogue with Queen Henrietta Maria of England (1609–1669), wife of Charles I. Rabbi Manasseh's *Spes Israelis* ("Hope of Israel"), identifying the American Indians with the Ten Lost Tribes, is found in two Spanish editions of 1650 as well as in Latin, English, and Hebrew translations. Manasseh's role as statesman is documented by two copies of the original edition of a pamphlet entitled *To His Highnesse the Lord Protector of the Common-wealth of England, Scotland and Ireland. The humble addresses of Menasseh Ben Israel, a divine, and doctor of physick, in behalfe of the Jewishe nation,* and his *Vindiciae Judaeorum* (1656), a refutation of allegations against the Jews.

The results of Manasseh's interventions are reflected in a number of contemporary records. The Whitehall Conference, summoned by Oliver Cromwell, is described by Henry Jessey's *Narrative of the late proceeds at White-Hall, concerning the Jews; who had desired by R. Manasses an agent for them, that they might return into England, and worship the God of their fathers here in their synagogues* (London, 1656). Of great importance is the copy of a treatise by William Prynne, *Short demurrer to the Jewes long discontinued barred remitter into England,* citing texts that deal with Jewish life in pre-expulsion England.

There is much valuable eighteenth-century data. Solomons has no less than forty of the eighty-five tracts which discuss the ill-fated Jew-Bill, as the Jewish Naturalization Bill of 1753 was called. Also available is the sermon by *Chakham David Nieto* (1654–1728) on divine Providence (*De la divina providencia*), preached on November 20, 1703, which caused him to be charged with the heresy of transmitting Spinoza's pantheistic doctrines. Nieto's philosophical works are here in various editions, along with his denunciations of the Inquisition and his bitter attacks against Nechemiah Chayyun, a supporter of the pseudo-Messiah Shabbethai Zevi (1621–1676).

Among other little-known items are the tracts *Fair Hebrew; or A True But Secret History of Two Jewish Ladies, Who Lately Resided in London* (London, 1729), and *Narrative of the remarkable affair between Mr. Simonds, the Polish Jew merchant, and Mr. James Ashley, merchant of Bread Street, London. Wherein the robbery at Cranford-Bridge, the several trials at the Old-Bailey, King's-Bench, and Chelmsford, are particularly set forth* (London, 1752).

The nineteenth century, too, is well represented. In this category there is the satire on Catholic emancipation entitled *Epistle From a High Priest Of The Jews, to the chief priest at Canterbury, on the extension of Catholic emancipation to the Jews* (London, 1821). There is also evidence of the famous feud between the printer Levy Alexander (1754–1853), one of the earliest Anglo-Jewish typographers, and the first Ashkenazi Chief Rabbi in England Solomon Hirschell, who favored the work of a rival printer, E. Justin. Not satisfied with the abusive pamphlet *The Axe Laid to the root; or ignorance and superstition evident in the character of the Rev. S. Hirschell, High Priest of the Jews in England, in several letters to him on the occasion of his having ordered the trees to be felled in the burial-ground at Mile End Road* (1808), Alexander issued a prayer book in two parts, each with a special paper cover. These covers were used partly for advertisement and partly for bitter personal vituperation against the Chief Rabbi. In a similarly scandalous vein is Alexander's *Memoirs of the life, and commercial connections . . . of the late Benj. Goldsmid, Esq., of Roehampton; containing a cursory view of the Jewish society and manners, etc.* (London, 1808).

Less controversial, but equally illuminating with regard to contemporary mores, is such an item as *Funeral sermon delivered at the Spanish and Portuguese Synagogue . . . on the day of burial of H.R.H. Princess Charlotte Augusta, daughter of . . . the Prince Regent, etc. with a Hebrew elegy by David Meldola* (London, 1817). A significant pamphlet contains *Rules and Regulations of the Meshebat Nephesh established for the purpose of distributing Bread, Meat and Coal amongst the poor of the Jewish Nation* (London, 1825). Of these rules No. 25 states: "At the death of a member, two Hackney Coaches shall follow the funeral and if on Sunday, three coaches at the expense of the Society."

Of particular interest to America is the rare book of Thomas Thorowgood, lengthily entitled *Jewes in America, or probabilities that the Americans are of that race. With the removal of some contrary reasonings, and earnest desires for effectuall endeavours to make them Christians* (London, 1650). On a kindred theme, Hamon L'Estrange, the Elder, wrote *Americans no Jewes or improbabilities that the Americans are of that race* (London, 1652) discussing the origins of the American Indians.

The collection includes likenesses of prominent chief rabbis of England, as well as of such other notables as Montefiore, Rothschild, and Disraeli, and of various famous singers, actors, actresses, and pugilists. There is one of Lord George Gordon, hero of the "No Popery" riots of 1770, who was called up for the Reading of the Law in the Humbro Synagogue and made an offering of £100. Another is of the opera singer and composer Michael Leoni (born Myer Lyon), chorister at the Great Synagogue of London *circa* 1770, and teacher of the English tenor John Braham (1774–1856). Leoni appeared at the Covent Garden Opera, managed an opera house in Dublin, and was eventually appointed *chazan* at Kingston, Jamaica.

The collection is not confined to Anglo-Jewry. There are prints depicting the Paris Sanhedrin convened by Napoleon on February 9, 1807, and portraits of such leading personalities as Baruch Spinoza, the pseudo-Messiah Shabbethai Zevi, the Shabbethaian prophet Nathan Benjamin Halevi Ghazzati (1644–1680), the Kabbalist Naphtali Cohen (1649–1718), and Moses Mendelssohn (1729–1786), pioneer of the Judeo-German Enlightenment. There are eighty prints showing synagogues in different countries, and 270 caricatures of leading Anglo-Jewish personalities.

Chapter VIII

The Jewish Theological Seminary Library: the Adler Collection

Of great significance was the purchase for $100,000 (£20,000) of the Elkan Adler collection of 3,500 books and 4,000 manuscripts. Of this sum half was provided by Mortimer L. Schiff and Felix M. Warburg (1871–1937), while Louis Marshall and several other friends contributed $10,000 each. Abraham Simon Wolf Rosenbach (1876–1932), American bookseller and "Napoleon of the Auction Room," who in the words of the London *Times* (April 18, 1923) "spent £210,000 in public and private purchases of rare books and manuscripts since he came to England in February," concluded the transaction on March 16, 1923. On April 17, the month of Judge Sulzberger's death, sixty-four cases of material from the Adler collection reached the Seminary; two more cases arrived later. In an interview with the London *Jewish Chronicle* on May 4, 1923, Adler said, "I do not quite know how the news got abroad, that I was willing, for private reasons, to dispose of my collection. But I was approached from more than one quarter including a big University and two or three Seminaries. Negotiations were also set on foot to acquire the Library for Jerusalem, a distinction which would have been very agreeable to me, but they fell through and then cabled communications were instituted by New York, which were followed by a visit of Dr. Rosenbach for the sale to the New York Seminary. For sentimental reasons I should have preferred the collection to have gone to Jerusalem, but next to that there is nothing better than the Jewish Theological Seminary in New York."

On April 6, 1923 the *Jewish Chronicle* commented editorially: "The splendid Library of Mr. Elkan Adler became for sale and we suppose, that with the experience of the failure regarding the Brann Library led him to conclude that it would be hopeless to offer it in this country."

Not since the Bodleian's purchase of the Oppenheimer collection had a library acquired overnight so magnificent a treasure house. Understandably, Alexander Marx was elated. "I hope that it will be a cause of gratification to you," wrote the rejoicing librarian to Elkan Adler, "that your library will remain in Jewish hands and together with ours will constitute the greatest Jewish Library. Whilst most of the Jewish collections have finally landed in the great non-Jewish Libraries, yours will remain Jewish and will be situated in the largest Jewish center in the world where it will give great impetus to Jewish learning." [58]

Elkan Adler was born in London on July 24, 1861, the third and youngest son of Chief Rabbi Nathan Marcus Adler and half-brother of Chief Rabbi Hermann Adler (1839–1911). Little Elkan grew up, it might almost be said, between covers, surrounded by both books and bibliophiles. Joseph Zedner, Adolf Neubauer, Leopold Dukes, and Michael Friedlander (1833–1910), principal of Jews' College from 1865 and translator of Maimonides' *Guide of the Perplexed* were frequent and familiar visitors to his parents' home. Adler became a solicitor and founded the law firm of Adler and Perowne—humorously referred to in the City of London as "The Old Testament and the New Testament", since Edward Perowne was the son of the Master of Corpus Christi College, Cambridge.

Professional practice did not lessen Adler's passion for book collecting. He inherited several manuscripts from his uncle, Benjamin Adler. He bought items from the noted booksellers Jacob Lipschitz, Fischel Hirsch, David Frankel, and Ephraim Deinard. However, it was not Elkan Adler's custom to wait for manuscripts to come to the door. He preferred to seek them out.

In 1881 the young lawyer was sent to Jerusalem by the Montefiore Testimonial Trustees to deal with a case of trespass on the Montefiore estate. Like Saul who went to look for asses but found a crown, Adler set out on a legal errand and returned with a bibliophile's spoils. In 1895 he anticipated the exploits of Schechter by securing many Geniza fragments. During the next three decades there were few places in the world which he did not visit. His purposeful wanderlust took him to Spain, Portugal, North Africa, South Africa, Russia (which he visited six times), Turkey, and Central Asia. To the east, west, north, and south, Adler's "journeys were not holiday jaunts to satisfy a restless craving for excitement. They were part of a well ordered scheme of education that was ever growing. If, like the bee, he moved from flower to flower extracting the honey, it was always to the hive to which he returned with his store of books and manuscripts which continued to increase year by year." [59]

The Adler collection was described in a careful catalogue (consisting of 278 pages, with 104 illustrations) published by Cambridge University Press in 1921. It added seventeen new items to the Seminary's incunabula. There were also fragments of ten known and twenty hitherto unknown incunabula, including the only known copy of the two-volume commentary on the Pentateuch (1484) by Bachya ben Asher ben Chalawa (1255–1304), the Spanish Biblical exegete.

A Hebrew Bible manuscript on parchment, finished in Toledo in the spring of 1492, adds a new chapter to the tangle of Jewish history. The copying had been interrupted by the expulsion of the Jews from Spain. Vocalization and Masoretic notes were meticulously added in 1497 by a scribe in Constantinople. The colophon explains: "This volume, which contains the Twenty-Four Sacred books was written by the learned Rabbi Abraham Calif in the city of Toledo, which is in Spain. It was finished in the month of *Nisan* 5252 *Anno Mundi* [spring 1492], for the very learned R. Jacob Aboab, the son of the esteemed gentleman R. Samuel. May the Almighty find him and his descendants worthy of meditating in it for ever. And on the seventh day of the month of *Av,* in the self-same year, the exiles of Jerusalem, who were in Spain, went forth dismayed and banished by the royal edict. May they come back with joy bearing their sheaves. And I Chayyim Ibn Chayyim have copied therein part of the *Masorah* and the variants in the year 5257 [1497] in the city of Constantinople. May salvation be at hand."

For the student of Jewish history the Adler collection is richly rewarding. In a letter in Spanish, written from Amsterdam and dated January 21, 1648, Manasseh ben Israel speaks of employing "my Portuguese mother tongue for I am a Lisbonian by patrimony . . . I have lost my estate in the varying fortunes of America."

Eighteenth-century documents include the thirty-nine-page diary (1747–1758) of the valet of "Dr." Chayyim Samuel Jacob Falk, the *Baal Shem* of London, which gives an odd insight into this extraordinary character. Interspersed with Kabbalistic and mystical notes are bills and accounts of excursions to what appears to have been Epping Forest in a four-horse coach. "On Friday, 28th *Nisan* 5532 [1772] R. Abele, who is well known as a heretic, came to bid farewell. I did not see him and sent him by Gedaliah [his stepson] three shillings for the third time." There are several references to Prince Czatorysky: "On Monday 23 *Tevet,* Norden received a letter from the Prince. R. Jacob was with the Prince and said that he had handed to Salli Norden, the day before a letter of credit from R. Simeon Boaz." Mention is made of pills for the relief of gout, recipes for cakes and spiced liquor, lists of bottles of wine, accounts of garments that were his "suits of honor", and payments to tradesmen.

Adler collected a number of nineteenth-century items closely associated with his own illustrious ancestry. A minute book of the *Bet Din* at Frankfurt-on-Main from 1768 to 1792 has many references to famous Frankfurt families. Similar data are found in the records of the rabbinate at Hanover from 1785 to 1814.

Spotlighting the religious and social life of the Jews of England during the early part of the Victorian era is a minute book of the London *Bet Din* (1833–1845) as guided by rabbis Hirschell, Azriel, Aaron, and Samuel

Marcus Gollancz. Carefully recorded are divorces, *chalizot,* and proselytizations. It was not then permitted to circumcise a would-be proselyte in England, and such aspirants to Judaism had to travel to Amsterdam in order "to enter the Covenant of Abraham." The amount of work which engaged the *Bet Din* during those leisurely years was negligible; there are only eighteen entries for the whole year of 1841, seventeen for 1842, and a mere eleven for 1844.

Under *Kislev,* 1843, there is an entry involving a certain Mayer Phineas, a former resident of New York, who while living there had divorced his wife. The lady had remarried and Phineas had come to England. He now wished also to be remarried, to a young woman from Liverpool, and asked the London *Bet Din* to recognize his American divorce. His request was granted with great reluctance. The minutes state, "We never validate divorces that emanate from America for we are not cognizant whether they are reliable or not"—indicating a lack of confidence hardly calculated to strengthen Anglo-American ties.

Another pointed comment on the transatlantic scene is *Megillat America,* a parody on American Jewry written in 1830 by T. Ree of Copenhagen, with a German preface by Julius Fürst (1805–1873).

Printed books include rarities highly prized by bibliophiles, such as the first edition of *Mikhlol* (Constantinople, 1532), a comprehensive exposition of Hebrew by Rabbi David ben Joseph Kimchi (of whom it was said, "Without *kemach* [flour] no Torah" (*Abot* III:21).

Among the famous "firsts" are the homiletical commentary by Moses ben Chayyim Alshech (1508–1600), the first book printed in Palestine (Safed, 1563); *Nibchar,* a volume of sermons, the first book printed in Damascus (1605); *Abudraham,* an exhaustive work on Jewish liturgy by David ben Joseph ben David, the first book printed in Africa, with types which were brought over by Portuguese exiles.

The "ingathering of the manuscripts" by the Jewish Theological Seminary Library "reunited" volumes and fragments which fate had severed for centuries. A commentary on the Talmudical tractate *Yebamot* contains a very rare *Tosaphot* of Gurnay. On the same tractate is part of the *Shita Mekubezet,* including the commentary *Menorat Zechariah* by Mendel ben Aryeh Lob Zechariah (d. 1791) on ten tractates of *Moed,* which breaks off in the middle of the tractate *Sabbath.* The second half of the same manuscript was found in the Sulzberger collection. Now these two manuscripts have been brought together.

In the 1930's purchases, gifts, and legacies filled many lacunae. The library was fortunate in its benefactors. Dr. Hyman Gerson Enelow (1877–1934), a rabbi and scholar who was the editor of *Menorat Ha-Maor* by R. Israel Ibn al-Nakawa, enlisted the help of Mrs. Nathan J. Miller, who presented the library with nearly 1,100 manuscripts. These were brought to America in 1932 by Jacob Halpern from North Africa, Antolio, Syria, Palestine, and Yemen. Among the rabbinic texts and Midrashim is a manuscript whose moving prelude tells of the suffering of an aged scholar, Shem-tov ben Jamil, who managed to flee the Spanish Inquisition but whose child was captured and baptized. At the age of eighty ben Jamil wrote *Keter Shem Tov,* an elegy of which only four leaves survived.

While European libraries were being ravaged by the Nazis, the Seminary consistently added to its treasures. In 1940 the library of the Graduate School for Jewish Social Work was transferred to the Seminary. It consisted of 5,000 books, a number of rare pamphlets, and 144 bound typewritten theses carefully accumulated by Dr. Maurice J. Karpf (b. 1889), an American sociologist and director of the School. The focus here is on sociology, education, psychology, and cognate subjects.

An important step was the establishment in 1953 of the Louis Ginzberg Microfilm Memorial Library. This served the dual purpose of expanding immeasurably the scope of the library and of honoring the memory of Dr. Louis Ginzberg, professor of Talmud and Bible from 1902 until his death in 1953. Already this relatively new division has more than 750 microfilm reels, each containing several thousand manuscripts. Here are the microfilms of all the Hebrew manuscripts (2,700 items) in the British Museum, of the 1,500 manuscript items in the Bibliothèque Nationale in Paris, of the 550 in the Bibliothèque D'Alliance Israélite in Paris, of the Taylor-Schechter Geniza in the Cambridge University Library, and of the Hebrew manuscripts in the Biblioteca Escorial in Madrid. Eventually microfilms of the Hebrew collection at the Bodleian and in the libraries of the Vatican, Leningrad, Munich, Amsterdam, Vienna, and Jerusalem will find a second home at the Jewish Theological Seminary in New York.

Chapter IX

The Jewish Theological Seminary Library: Unique Aspects

For six decades devoted bibliophiles labored, and their work brought dividends. The library is in many ways unique. It possesses over 15,000 Geniza fragments, including leaves from the original Hebrew text of Ecclesiasticus by Ben Sira. There are 145 incunabula, among them such rarities as the Book of Esther from the Gutenberg Bible; a Scriptural commentary by the Franciscan monk Nicholas de Lyra, who wrote under the influence of the works of Rashi; and Petrus Niger's work *Against the Perfidious Jews* (Esslingen, 1475), the first book containing Hebrew characters to be printed in Germany. The library owns forty of the one hundred non-Hebrew books published by Gershon ben Moses Soncino, as well as the only illustrated incunabulum in the Hebrew tongue, a book of fables, *Meshal ha-Kadmoni* ("Easterner's Parable") by the Spanish Hebrew author Isaac ben Solomon Ibn Sahulah, printed by Soncino in 1480.

Other valuable acquisitions are leaves of the first Hebrew book printed in Spain, consisting of Rashi's commentary on the Pentateuch (Guadalajara, 1476). The one complete copy of this edition in existence is now in the library of the Jewish community of Verona. Another prize is the first Hebrew jubilee volume, published (Venice, 1624) in honor of Joseph Chamitz when he was simultaneouly awarded the degrees of Doctor of Philosophy and of Medicine. It was edited by the famous scholar Leon of Modena, and only two other copies are extant.

Important Biblical manuscripts have been assembled from various countries including Persia, Yemen, Spain, and Italy. There are leaves from tenth-century Egypt, and there are thirty-five Babylonian fragments dating back to the ninth century. Particularly famous is the Pentateuch with marginal Masoretic annotations, written at Toledo in 1241 by the scribe Israel ben Israel, who based the text upon the Codex Hilleli, the most reliable manuscript of the Hebrew Bible in Spain, written by Rabbi Hillel ben Moses ben Hillel in the year 600 as a model for Torah scribes.

Printing pecularities include the "Bug Bible" of 1551, in which Psalm

XCI:5 contains the phrase "afraid of bugs by night," instead of the traditional rendering, "terror by night." Sometimes books were burned, sometimes their owners perished in furnaces fiercer than the testing ground for Shadrach, Meshach, and Abednego. In Nazi Germany in 1933, six de luxe copies of a Pentateuch were printed on parchment. One copy was brought to London, where it remained until it was reclaimed by a nephew of the former owner, a survivor of the concentration camp, who brought it to the Seminary Library.

The library has accumulated 195 super-commentaries on the master commentator, Rabbi Solomon Yizchaki (1040–1105), sixteen of which writings have never appeared in print. Unique is a Rashi manuscript on Exodus, written in thirteenth-century Spain: every verse has Targum Onkelos and Arabic translation as well as Rashi's commentary. The Rashi collection ranges from a leaf belonging to the first printed Hebrew book, the commentary of Rashi on the Pentateuch published in Reggio di Calabria on February 5, 1475, to a manuscript of Rashi's commentary on the Pentateuch copied out by hand in Yemen as late as 1845.

The Seminary Library has the first book printed in the Balkans, *Arbaah Turim,* a code of Jewish law in four parts by Rabbi Jacob ben Asher (1269–1343), printed in Constantinople in 1493. The Library also possesses a copy of this Code which was one of the first Hebrew books to come off a printing press in Piove di Sacco; it is dated July 3, 1475.

In addition to standard editions of the Midrashim, 3,330 copies of Hebrew Codes, and 1,729 volumes of rabbinic responsa, the library owns *Sepher Russiano,* a Midrashic commentary on the Pentateuch written on parchment and paper by Rabbi Samuel, a Russian scholar of the twelfth century. It was copied in Brusa, Turkey, in 1377, by Solomon ben Jesse ha-Nasi, who claimed descent from King David. For centuries this manuscript was literally lost and no one knew its whereabouts. Then in the enghteenth century it reappeared. It is known that in 1727 *Sepher Russiano* belonged to a Jesuit college in Paris. A century later it became the property of Augustus Frederick, Duke of Sussex (1773–1843), the eccentric son of George III, who kept it in Kensington Palace, London; and so this much traveled opus made the transition from priestly precincts to royal palace and after various other adventures finally reached the haven of the Seminary.

The Library is rich in liturgical works. Among them is a fragment of *Seder Rav Amram,* the first great liturgical collection. It was compiled by Amram ben Sheshna (late ninth century), head of the Talmudic Academy in Sura. The library has liturgies of many lands: rites of Aleppo, Ancona, Padua, Persia, North Africa, Corfu, Algiers, Carpentras, Avignon, Rovigo. A Spanish prayer book for the Day of Atonement was printed in an unusual oblong form, perhaps to permit the unfortunate Marranos to slide it hastily into their pockets.

A not untypical travel tale is told by a festival prayer book copied in Germany in 1296. Around 1300 this *machzor* was taken by its owner to Spain, where it remained until 1492. From Spain it was carried to Egypt. In 1928 it was acquired by a German-Jewish bookdealer who took it back to Germany. It finally reached the Seminary after having spent the war years in England.

Many of these prayer books are very rare. A valuable first edition is a prayer book of the Italian rite, called *Sidorello* (Soncino, 1486); only one other copy of this edition is known to exist. Another rarity is the first German translation of part of the Hebrew prayer book composed in 1523 by the apostate Johann Boeschenstein. An Italian translation was copied in 1714 by Eli, daughter of Menachem Halevi Meshullam. The title page bears a picture of a lady sitting at a table and writing a manuscript with a quill—evidently a self-portrait of the copyist. Next to it are depicted the ewer and basin which constitute an emblem of the Levites.

The Passover Haggadah has always been popular. The library has no less than 1,332 different editions, including many illuminated copies. A Haggadah with a rather remarkable interracial background was written by the Italian scholar and geographer Abraham ben Mordecai Farissol, and illustrated by the Venetian engraver Agostino Veneziano, a Christian. The library has the second printed edition of the Haggadah, produced by Soncino in 1486, and the first Haggadah to be published in London, dated 1770 and "containing the Ceremonies and prayers, which are used and read by all families in all houses of the Israelites, the two first Nights of Passover; faithfully translated from the original Hebrew by A. Alexander, and Assistants." It has a Haggadah with an Arabic translation, lithographed in Alexandria in the nineteenth century, and still another with Arabic rubrics and a Persian translation.

The library is well equipped for the Jewish historian. Obscure epochs and remote events are often illumined by the time-worn witnesses on the shelves. There are, for instance, a fragment of the Biblical history by Saadia Gaon and a document written by Nathan Gaon in 1041 dealing with the appointment of Bostanai ben Chaninai as the first Babylonian Exilarch after the Arab conquest in the mid-seventh century.

Particularly moving is the material on the Marranos. The researcher can study original documents from the court of Ferdinand V of Aragon (1452–1516) and Isabella of Castile which contain grants of property confiscated from the Jews. A missive to Ferdinand and Isabella from Ferdinand Gonzale de Cordobis, Viceroy of Naples, reported among other things that the latter was hesitant to execute the royal decree that expelled the

Jews from Naples because of their small number. "For when Charles II of the House of Anjou came to this kingdom, all of them became Christians under compulsion and called themselves baptized Jews and they live as they used to only nominally Christians. So that they cannot be expelled as Jews." In six folios, which were found in a monastery in Portugal are the meticulously recorded proceedings of the Portuguese Inquisition. In 113 printed and 475 hand-written lists are the names of the victims of all the autos-da-fé held in Lisbon, Coimbra, and Evora between 1553 and 1784.

The student of Italian Jewry of the sixteenth century will find a wealth of documentation in such items as autographed *responsa* and the widely assorted letters of scholars and laymen. In one letter, dated 1592, a Jew of Mantua complained to the leading Italian rabbis that he could not get justice from the head of the community, Zalman Hurwitz, who terrorized everyone.

A Hebrew broadsheet published in Mantua in 1564 by David Provenzale appealed to notables of northern Italy to create a Jewish college which should teach Jewish and secular subjects simultaneously: "At special hours, the student will learn Latin which is almost indispensable now in our community, for no day passes by that we do not require this knowledge in our relations with officials. We have a precedent for this since even the members of the household of Judah the Prince were allowed to trim their hair like the pagans because they had frequent contact with the Roman Government."

The question, "May a woman serve as a ritual slaughterer?" was discussed at great length by the rabbis. Some Italian rabbis permitted women to act in this capacity. Rabbi Isaac ben Immanuel de Lattes (1495–1570), tutor to Don Isaac Abravanel's sons, authorized two women as ritual slaughterers in Mantua. Isota, daughter of Elchanan Da Fano, was licensed as a *shochet* in Mantua in 1614. Nine years later, after her marriage to Menachem Maziach Foa, she was also allowed to porge meat. There is a little *Mohel* book dated 1666 with the heading, "The first year of the arrival of our Messiah," a revealing reference to the momentous if delusional news of Shabbethai Zevi.

A manuscript entitled *Chizzuk Emunah* ("The Strengthening of Faith") —classic refutation of Christian attacks on Judaism by the Karaite Isaac ben Abraham Troki (1533–1594) copied in Metz in 1681 by Feibusch Joel ben Samuel—contains historical notes which end with the year 1681. It refers to the conquest of Strasbourg, the "metropolis of Alsace", by Louis XIV of France in 1681, and to the flight of the persecuted Calvinists and Lutherans.

The library possesses hundreds of documents dating to the French Revolution and the Napoleonic period. A petition drawn up by the merchants of Paris protests against the decree allowing Jews to live and trade in the city. An anti-Napoleonic pamphlet printed in Russia in Church Slavonic and Greek in December 1806, relates how to the disgrace of the Christian Church "he [Napoleon] convoked the Jewish Synagogue, ordered that their rabbis be openly honored and established a new great Hebrew Sanhedrin, the same ungodly council which had once dared to condemn to crucifixion our Lord."

Moving from scene to scene, from century to century, the historian finds perennial problems, perennial parallels. In a document published in Warsaw in 1838, Solomon Zalman Posner and the Chassidic Rabbi Isaac of Warka (d. 1848) appealed to Polish communities to be particularly careful in their religious observances and to appoint supervisors to enforce this rule. The rabbis cover every phase of life under some twenty headings. They point out, among other things, that "at weddings, males should not, God forbid, dance with females and that every man should watch that the members of his family should not frequent coffee houses on the Sabbaths and holidays."

Among items of Anglo-Jewish interest is a little book, *Haec sunt verbi Dei,* printed in Cambridge in 1597 by the Polish convert Philip Ferdinand (1555–1598). Ferdinand, who made a reputation for himself as a teacher at Oxford and Cambridge, stayed for a time at the London *Domus Conversorum* (home for converted Jews), which gave him a stipend.

Of special significance to Anglo-Americans are the *Prayers for the service arranged by order of King George III of England (December 13, 1776) beseeching Divine assistance for the British armies in restoring peace and prosperity to the kingdom.* One prayer reads: "We, Thy servants, pray before Thee, for our master, the king, against the American provinces, which rebelled against their king, and refused to acknowledge his rule according to the law and custom of the kingdom."

The library now houses nearly ninety per cent of all Yiddish books and manuscripts dating from the sixteenth to the eighteenth century. Treasures include the first edition of the Pentateuch to be printed in *weiber deutsch* (Cremona, 1560), and a Pentateuch and Megillah translated and printed in Constantinople in 1544. Only four other copies of the latter are known to exist, and this is the only copy in the United States. Other rarities are leaves of several sixteenth-century fables in rhymed Yiddish, written in Germany and found in Mosul, where they were probably brought by a European traveler. The library has the only known copy of *Meneket Rivkah* (Cracow, 1618), written by the sixteenth-century Austrian writer, Rebecca bat Meir Titkiner. There are also two numbers of one of the earliest Yiddish newspapers, the *Dyhernfurther Privilegirte Zeitung,* carrying the coat of arms of the city of Dyhernfurth, *Germany,* and dated 1771.

The Arabic works contain the Epistle to Yemen, a reply by Maimonides to an inquiry by Jacob ben Nethanel Al Fayyum, head of the Jewish community of Yemen. In it Maimonides condemns belief in astrology, pointing out that its predictions have always been wrong. He urges hope and patience, illustrating by examples from Jewish history the tragic results of blind belief in claims of a pretender.

The translator and Talmudist Moses Arragel, a Spanish rabbi who flourished in the first half of the fifteenth century, translated the Bible into Castilian at the request of Don Luis de Guzman, Grand Master of the military Order of Calatrava. The work was begun in 1422 and completed in 1430. Rabbi Moses often deviates from the Latin of Jerome. "This is the opinion of the Christians", writes the traditionalist, "but the Jews hold the opposite view." This Bible of the House of Alba is a striking example of mutual understanding, unhappily so infrequent, between Jews and Christians in the Middle Ages.

The well-stocked "medicine chest" holds Maimonides' *Treatise on Hygiene,* written for Caliph Alfadal, and the *Treasure of the Poor* of Petrus Hispanus (later Pope John XXI) in a Hebrew translation. There is also a small book in which thirteen hundred prescriptions are written in almost microscopic characters. Many of these are magical incantations. A sleep-inducing spell advises the physician to take a tooth from a black dog and place it beneath the pillow of the insomniac. Another spell is warranted to make a wife confess her thefts.

The library has a treasured assortment of miniature books. The smallest is a Hebrew Bible measuring three quarters by one-half inches, with letters so tiny that the silver case which houses the Bible necessarily contains a magnifying glass. The same miniature script is found in illuminated Jewish marriage contracts where extra clauses and subclauses were added to the legal texts. The intricate geometric and floral designs of one such *ketubah* contain the texts of the Book of Ruth, the Book of Esther, and the Song of Songs in microscopic script. There are pocket-sized editions of prayer books, Mishnayot and tractates of the Talmud designed to be carried on the owner's person and studied during every free moment.

Many books are, so to speak, of royal descent. Here are volumes that once belonged to the royal families of England, Spain, and Germany, and to Czars Alexander III and Nicholas II. There are others from the libraries of such famous book collectors as A.G.S. Graciano, the Russian poet and grammarian; the German exegete Wolf Benjamin Heidenheim (1757–1832) ; and the Jewish scholar and writer Samuel David Luzzatto (1800–1865) .

Dedications and inscriptions are often very revealing. The Italian exegete, philosopher, and physician Obadiah ben Jacob Sphorno (1475–1550) wrote a book, *Or Ammim* ("The Light of the Peoples,") , in which he countered Aristotelian theories with Biblical arguments. He himself translated it into Latin and sent it to Henry II of France. An Antwerp Bible was once the property of Bishop Berkeley, who in 1750 inscribed it *Non tibi sed toti*; later it passed to the poet Robert Browning (1812–1889), who on April 17, 1883 wrote in it, "My wife's book and mine."

Many volumes could be written about these books, but a different type of bookkeeping engages the attention of the library executive. The budget of the library has risen by about fifty per cent during the last decade, yet it is far from adequate. Fifty thousand books need rebinding or repairing. Seventy-five per cent of the rare books require rebinding. There is no catalogue of the manuscripts—not even a card index—available to the general public. Recently Maurice F. Tauber, professor of library service at Columbia University, made a detailed study of all aspects of the library and formulated a number of thoroughgoing recommendations: the erection of a modern library building, the recataloguing of the manuscript collection, and the air-conditioning of the manuscript and reading rooms. Implementation is long overdue. So this library with a historic and somewhat hectic past has an ambitious and expansive program of development ahead, ever mindful of the words uttered by Solomon Schechter on November 20, 1902: "We dare not neglect any part of this great intellectual bequest but at a serious risk and peril to ourselves. And the risk is the greater in Jewish literature—a literature pregnant with 'thoughts that breathe and words that burn' whose very pseudography became the sacred books of other nations, whose most homely metaphors were converted from literature to dogma."

Chapter X

YIVO Institute for Jewish Research

On upper Fifth Avenue overlooking Central Park a stately six-story mansion, once a Vanderbilt residence, houses the YIVO Institute for Jewish Research, the Jewish Record Office.

Although it is one of the youngest such repositories in the United States, it already numbers 250,000 volumes, and tens of thousands of documents, all valuable sources of information on many facets of the political, economic, and social history of the Jews. The library has cast its net wide to include items on clothing and entertainment, on migrations and mores. But one of its chief concerns is the documentation of Jewish life in Eastern Europe and the detailing of Nazi crimes against the Jews. The twenty-five rooms of the Institute serve as workshops in which thousands upon thousands of photographs, letters, diaries, theater posters, and pamphlets are pieced together into moving and meaningful pictures of Jewish life.

At a five-day conference in Berlin in August 1925, a group of Jewish scholars and scientists from various countries decided, under the direction of the Yiddish critic and philologist Nachum Shtif (1879–1933), to establish in Vilna the Yiddish Scientific Institute (Known as YIVO from the initials of *Yiddischer Vissenshaftlicher Institut*). Dr. Simon Dubnow (1860–1941), historian of East European Jewry, greeted the idea with enthusiasm. "It is possibly no coincidence, but a profound symbol," he pointed out, "that in Jerusalem of Palestine and in 'Jerusalem of the Diaspora' two similar institutions were established in the same year."

The objects of YIVO were three fold: (1) to collect and prepare material mirroring Jewish life; (2) to study scientifically Jewish problems, material and spiritual, of the past and the present; and (3) to train new research workers in various domains of Jewish scholarship. YIVO's Vilna headquarters were dedicated in 1928. By 1939 the Institute had surpassed the expectations of its founders. It possessed a library of more than 100,000 books; a press archive of some 10,000 volumes; a manuscript collection of 100,000 units; a gallery of several thousand photographs; a museum of pedagogy and ethnography; and bibliography and records of Yiddish book production. The three-story building held 3,500 periodicals in Yiddish, Hebrew, and other languages.

In the course of two decades YIVO published a total of sixty thousand pages of scholarly research. Among the publications were *Studies in Economics and Statistics, YIVO Annual of Bibliography,* and *Studies in History.* A significant sociological study by Professor Libman Hersch (1882–1955), *Delinquency among Jews,* appeared in Yiddish, English, Polish, and French.

For the training of archivists, YIVO in 1935 established the Aspirantur, a graduate school for research techniques. Three years later the undergraduate school was founded. In 1941, during the Hitler occupation of Vilna, the authorities of the Vilna Ghetto decided to merge the famous Strashun Library of the *kehilah* (community) with the YIVO collection. Matthias Strashun (1817–1885) had studied under Manasseh of Ilye and Isaac of Volozhin, and had corresponded with eminent Jews like Zunz, Rappoport, and Professor Wuensche. His Library consisted originally of 7,000 volumes, which he bequeathed to the community. It was housed in the *schulhof* (synagogue courtyard) in Vilna. Later it was augmented by several other collections. In 1940 the Strashun library consisted of 35,000 volumes, a number of incunabula, and about 200 manuscripts, and was housed under the same roof as the YIVO collection.

THE STONE WHICH THE BUILDERS REJECTED

When YIVO was founded in October 1925 branches for fund-raising were established in Warsaw, Berlin, Paris, London, and New York City. A decade later, in the fall of 1935, a group of Jewish leaders, among them the Yiddish literary critic Samuel Niger (pseudonym of Samuel Tscharny), Mendel Elkin (b. 1874), and Jacob Levin (1884–1958), conceived the idea of establishing in New York a library dedicated to American-Jewish writings. They resolved that "it was essential to gather in one place in America the fruits of our creative efforts and the records of our accomplishments", and the resolution was strongly supported by the Y.L. Peretz Writers' Association, the Workmen's Circle, and the Sholem Aleichem Folk Institute.

At 1133 Broadway, in a small room rented by the American branch of YIVO, the Central Jewish Library and Archives began its activities. Shlomo Mendelson and Morris Odoner searched diligently for material. They were instrumental in obtaining for YIVO the collection of Morris Vinchefsky (1870–1920), known as the grandfather of Jewish socialism, who had amassed a considerable library on the history of the Jewish labor movement. It included nineteen letters from Aaron Samuel Liebermann (1844–

1880), founder of the first Jewish socialist organization, *Agudat Ha-Sozialism ha-Ivrim* (1876), and the first Hebrew socialist periodical *Ha-Emet.*

Within three years the Central Jewish Library needed *Lebensraum.* It moved to the HIAS (*Hebrew Sheltering and Immigrant Aid Society*) building at 425 Lafayette Street on October 22, 1938. The outbreak of the European War and the destruction of the European archives brought home to American Jews the importance of developing their own collections. In October 1939 the Central Jewish Library and Archives were incorporated in the American branch of YIVO.

In September 1940 Elias Tcherikover (1881–1943), secretary of YIVO's history division for fourteen years, escaped from the Nazis in Paris and brought 2,600 volumes and many historical records to YIVO in New York. Similarly, the sociologist and economist Jacob Letschinsky (b. 1876) brought the division of economics and statistics to New York. This move was an impetus to further expansion. Among notable acquisitions at that point were the Ceshinsky collection from Chicago, consisting of several thousand volumes of rare Yiddish periodicals; the A. Litwin (1862–1943) collection of folklore, and the letters of the Yiddish playwright and novelist David Pinski (b. 1872).

In 1942 YIVO transferred to its third home, in the former building of the Jewish Theological Seminary of America.

A BRAND PLUCKED OUT OF THE BURNING

On September 19, 1939, Vilna was occupied by the Soviet armies. At the end of October the city was handed over to the Lithuanians. In the summer of 1940 it was re-occupied by Russia. On July 24, 1941, the German army entered Vilna and on September 7, 1941, the Jews were confined to the Ghetto. Between July and December of that year, 48,000 of the 60,000 Jews were taken to Ponary and executed. Early in 1943 Jewish Vilna was completely liquidated. The Nazi occupation of Vilna spelt doom for YIVO. An eyewitness gave this account: "The archives, book collections and other materials were cast like dung into the basement of the building. . . . Hitler's experts came hurriedly to the Institute . . . opened the safe and seizing the manuscripts of Sholem Aleichem and Peretz, hurled them to the ground and trampled on them."

In January 1942 the Nazis moved most of the books of YIVO and the Strashun library to the Institut zur Erforschung der Judenfrage in Frankfurt-on-Main. Devoted YIVO workers were forced to participate in this work. In January 1944 Dr. Emanuel Ringelblum, historian of the Warsaw Ghetto, sent a coded message containing this bleak, and cryptic obituary: "Chayyim Vivulsky recently died and his possessions are scattered."

Events moved fast. On July 15, 1944, Vilna was again occupied by Soviet forces. Intensive Allied bombing forced the Germans to hide the Hebrew repositories in the village of Hungen. In 1945 Corporal Abraham Aaroni informed YIVO headquarters in New York that the YIVO Vilna collection had been found in caves at Offenbach near Frankfurt-on-Main. This report was confirmed on July 23, 1945, by the State Department. Concerning the discovery, Captain I. Bencovitz of the U.S. Army wrote: "I would pick up a badly worn Talmud with hundreds of names of many generations of scholars. Where were they now? Or rather, where were their ashes? In what incinerator were they destroyed? I would find myself straightening out the books and arranging them in their boxes with a personal sense of tenderness, as if they had belonged to someone dear to me. Someone recently deceased."

YIVO in New York claimed the Vilna collection and on May 7, 1947, was recognized by the Secretary of State as the rightful owner. On July 17, 1947, three freight cars carried 420 cartons to Bremen, and a few days later the steamer *Pioneer Cove* sailed with the material for New York. Upon their arrival the 79,204 documents and 54,000 volumes were stored by B. Manischewitz and Company until they found a home in the new YIVO building.

This was not the only rescue operation. The sequel came in 1957. The Germans had stored many books in an old castle in the Austrian province of Carinthia, and some of these found their way to the Museum für Völkerkunde in Vienna. Attorney Dr. Friedrich Weissenstein took legal steps to reclaim them. Eventually these books were handed over to YIVO, together with the library of the linguist Dr. Alfred Landau (1850–1935) of Vienna, which contained many published doctoral dissertations. The Institute also received 11,681 volumes from Jewish Cultural Reconstruction, Inc.

Among the treasures rescued from Europe were a number of early sixteenth-century books that bear the signs of severe censorship, many with entire passages obliterated in ink. In a popular homiletical exposition of a Pentateuch commentary by Rabbi Bachya ben Asher ben Chalawa (1350–1440), the censor deleted the word *prophet* and all references to the coming of the Messiah. Jewish nationalistic aspirations similarly received harsh treatment. For example, the Talmudic dictum, "He who resides outside Palestine is like one who has no God" (quoted by Israel's Premier David ben Gurion at the twenty-fifth Zionist Congress in 1960) was blotted out by the reviewer.

Among other rarities is *Asaph Ha-Mazkir* (Venice, 1675), containing a list of all the explanations found in the Haggadic *Ein Yaacov* by the seventeenth-century Italian scholar Rabbi Zechariah ben Ephraim Ponto of Urbino. The Rabbi's will appears on the title page and includes several communal bequests. "Some fifty thousand piasters to charity, four thousand florentine piasters for the great *Mitzvah* of *the Redemption of Captives* and 18,000 piasters for the 'dowering of virtuous maidens.' "

Emphasis is naturally upon the Yiddish language and the theater. Books and manuscripts from the sixteenth century are well represented. There are many of the works of Elijah Levita (1468–1549), known as Elijah Bachur, tutor of Aegidius of Viterbo. Another important possession is *Mirkevet Ha-Mishnah* ("The Second Chariot"), printed in Cracow in 1534—a Judeo-German Biblical concordance by Rabbi Asher Anschel ben Joseph of Cracow, who flourished in the first half of the sixteenth century, and one of the oldest Yiddish books published in Poland. YIVO also has *Undzer Shprach,* a Yiddish textbook printed in Jassy, Rumania, in 1941, by Nachum Hertzberg, but carrying the inscription "Warsaw, 1932," to mislead the Nazis.

The collection made by Abraham Liessin (1872–1938) provides a panorama of the Jewish literary world in the first half of this century. Liessin, the editor for three decades of the Yiddish monthly *Zukunft,* had brought together a wide assortment of literary, artistic, and scholarly publications by numerous authors. There are letters from the historian of Polish Jewry, Meyer Samuel Balaban (1877–1943), from Simon Dubnow, and from the Yiddish playwright Jacob Gordin (1853–1909), as well as 892 manuscripts from 626 authors.

Among the Hebrew and Yiddish writers represented in YIVO's two hundred boxes of manuscripts are Meir Dick (1814–1893), Sholem Asch, Nachum Sokolow, Samuel Niger. There are also letters from Sholem Aleichem, Yitchak Ben-Zevi, David Pinski, Theodor Herzl and Chaim Weitzmann to prominent Jewish and non-Jewish personalities dating from 1893 to the 1950's.

Particularly illuminating are the fifty letters by Simon Dubnow, who perished in the Hitlerian holocaust. That he was a stylist as well as a historian, is suggested by the remark in one of his letters, "I am a great admirer of succinctness and I maintain that every unnecessary word detracts." He suggested that John Stuart Mill's *On Liberty* could well serve as a model of style. Writing from Kovno to Maxim Vinaver (1862–1926) on May 11, 1922, the historian told of rejecting a professorship in Jewish history at the newly founded Lithuanian University, for the reason that he could allow nothing to delay the completion of his magnum opus, the *World History of the Jewish People.* From Danzig he wrote on July 30, 1922, of his unrest in the midst of the menaced Jewish microcosm: "After all, my dear friend, we are both emigrés. It is true that we are citizens of a World Diaspora, and members of a historical international, which was founded even earlier than the age of Alexander the Great. And yet, we cannot but feel the ache of one whose nest has been destroyed. Moreover, I myself cannot share the faith that still keeps you going, the faith in the resurrection of the Jewish center in Russia."

These premonitions of disaster increased and crystallized. On April 25, 1924, he voiced grim apprehensions: "This cruel and cold Berlin makes us foreigners feel our alienation even more strongly. . . . We are now living in Grueneberg, near a park, a beautiful section, except that it is a nest of Prussian Black Hundreds, of German Nationalists, and of the other scum, whom fate—this may well happen—can bring to victory in the next elections".

Theater archives containing 3,000 programs and numerous posters present a vivid panorama of the Yiddish theater. The curtain goes up in Kielce on January 1885; act follows act in rapidly changing settings; and the finale is played by Maurice Schwartz (1895–1960) of the Yiddish Art Theater in New York in the 1950's. A hundred programs were rescued from the Jewish *Kultur Bund* Theater in Berlin under the Nazis (1935–1939).

A special focus is on East European Jewry. Much of the vast mass of material has not yet been catalogued. Some of it was on display at the Vilna Exhibition held in New York in 1960 under the title "A Jewish Community in Times of Glory and in Time of Destruction." One hundred and twenty-two items trace the history of the Jews of Vilna, "the Jerusalem of Lithuania," from the end of the fifteenth century to modern times. A document with the heading "Regesti i Nadpisi" concerns a house that had belonged to a Jew, Janeszowski, and which the Lithuanian archduke Alexander Jagiello donated on July 28, 1495, to the municipality of Vilna. In *Megillat Sepher,* the autobiography of the Talmudist Jacob Emden (1697–1776), printed in Warsaw in 1896, the author asserts that "Vilna surpassed all other communities in wisdom and in fame." The title page of *Dos bilbl iz oyf di dray kdoyshim bekak vilne,* a poem on the blood accusation in Vilna in 1690, has been preserved. Numerous eighteenth-century documents include a facsimile of the proclamation of the Vilna *kehilah* against the Chassidim, dated the second of *Av* 5541 (1781), as well as books of Vilna's greatest son, Elijah ben Solomon, known as the Gaon of Vilna (1720–1797).

The last two centuries are well represented: a poem of the Vilna *kehilah* in honor of the coronation of Alexander I in 1802; an announcement by the Vilna police forbidding Jews to live on the five main streets and prohibiting Christian landlords from renting dwellings or stores to Jews, dated September 10, 1823; a letter from Sir Moses Montefiore to Isaiah Cramer in Vilna, written in 1885.

A fascinating miscellany reveals facts on living conditions, *kashrut,* Sabbath observance, funerals, houses, loan associations, people's banks, *kehilah* soup kitchens, educational systems, and trade unionism. World War II is documented by material on the Jewish administration of the Ghetto under the Nazis, including the order of July 21, 1942, decreeing the wearing of the Star of David, and an announcement made on December 3, 1942, to the effect that "all Jews are obliged to salute the representatives of the German authorities."

"Despite the danger of death, deportation, deprivation, famine, and misery, the Jews in Vilna felt it to be their mission . . . to continue the old, beautiful Jewish cultural traditions of Vilna." [60] Testimony to this effect is found in the lists of the literary evenings of the Amalgamated Writers and Artists Association; a motion for the purchase of a painting by Rachel Sutskever and a sculpture by Yudel Mut, which were displayed at an exhibition in Vilna on March 29, 1943; a program of twenty-five lectures and other activities at the Workmen's Forum on Rudnika Street; and an announcement of a "Sabbath festival for children and young people" to take place in the auditorium of the Kosher Kitchen, on December 26, 1942. There is also a sketch of the decorations for a performance in Hebrew of "Kindle the Lights," presented in the Ghetto Theater by the inmates of *Yeladim,* the children's home, on December 6, 1942. There are reports of the only open conflict between the Germans and Jews; it took place at the barricades on Strashun Street on September 1, 1943. "Let us not be led like sheep to the slaughter," ran the proclamation of the Vilna Ghetto fighters. Of great importance is the Vilna Ghetto diary kept by Z. Kalmanovitch, one of the YIVO leaders, covering the period from June 22, 1941 to August 31, 1943.

Another exhibition, "The Shtetl 1900–1939",[61] held in New York between February and August 1959, gave a graphic picture of Jewish life in a typical village in Eastern Europe. A total of 781 objects from YIVO archives were used to illustrate every aspect of life—typography, demography, homes, synagogues, stores, schools, libraries, cultural activities, persecutions and pogroms.

The whole Jewish world is the province of YIVO. An exhibition on Jewish life in Shanghai was held at YIVO from September 1948 to January 1949. Two hundred and seventy-nine items were used to present an exotic Far Eastern panorama, from the oldest Sephardi congregation of 1870 to the Ghetto established by the Japanese on February 18, 1943. Among the exhibits were: a map of Shanghai showing the boundaries of the Ghetto; badges with the inscription "Passage permitted"; documents on the Jewish Kitchen Fund established in August 1942, and the files of the Jewish Chamber of Commerce founded on November 11, 1946. Other historical documents include a brochure issued by the Shanghai community commemorating the death of Herzl, copies of the oldest Jewish publication in China, *Mevasser Yisrael* (1904–1941), and forty-four post-war publications, including such Chassidic works as *Tanya, Noam Elimelech, Or Torah,* and *Sephat Emet.*

Apart from its role as chronicler of contemporary Jewry, YIVO (like the Wiener Library in London and the *Yad V'Shem* in Jerusalem) is becoming a major repository of holocaust history. In 1945 Max Weinreich, research director of YIVO, issued a booklet, *Desiderata of Nazi Literature on the Jews,* appealing for material on this dark period. The response was overwhelming. YIVO now owns the collection, consisting of 179,339 items arranged into 2008 folders, made by UGIF (*Archives Union Général des Israélites de France*), which was responsible for the administration of French Jews in the free and occupied zones. It has the Displaced Persons Collection, comprising a million pages and including some highly significant Nazi papers which were used as exhibits at the Nuremberg Trial.

Fourteen files of Nazi documents deal with the policies and pronouncements of Himmler, Goebbels, and Rosenberg. Tragic tokens include Jewish money issued in the Ghetto, a piece of a prayer shawl found in a crematorium, a photograph of the ruined YIVO building in Vilna, and a copy of a sketch showing scenes of brutality, made by a child prisoner at Theresienstadt. Writing with fingers dipped in his own blood, a Jew had inscribed the words *Yiden Nekomoh* ("Jews take revenge") upon the wall of his cell. This inscription is recorded for posterity in a photograph at YIVO. Another such picture records a parent's cry of anguish, sharp enough to pierce a stone wall but not the stone of an inhuman heart: "I leave in peace. But how will my children live? What will happen to them?"

These contemporary records are of the utmost value. The Nachman Zonabend collection tells the story of the Lodz Ghetto, which became the second largest Ghetto in Nazi Europe, from its inception in March 1940 to its final transfer to Treblinka. Four hundred photographs taken by the donor and by local photographers M. Grossman and H. Ross convey a pictorial record of life and death in this doomed city. We see Jews carrying packs on their backs, pushing carts; men harnessed to wagons, doing the work of horses, even dragging refuse; scenes depicting resignation as Jews dragged themselves despairingly to the railroad cars bound for Treblinka; an old Talmudist bending over his *Gemara* (Talmud) and Jewish street singers drawing audiences around them.

The files of Rabbi Shneur Zalman Schneerson, a scion of Lubavitch, gives inside information regarding the dangerous underground rescue work carried out by religious Jews in Nazi-occupied France between 1943 and 1945. In 1936 Rabbi Schneerson established the Association des Israélites pratiquants, which carried out varied activities throughout France with headquarters first in Paris, then at Marseilles, Demu, and St. Etienne de Crossey.

The Jewish children of Nazi Europe left their mark, and many childish sketches and scribblings provide touching testimony to the inhumanities of that tragic period. The little victims drew the scenes they witnessed, including executions and bombings. One such drawing bears the matter-of-fact caption: "The Germans have killed the mother and now fire at the child." There are one hundred and sixty accounts—found written in school exercise books, diaries, and on scraps of paper—by the ill-fated children of Eastern Europe.

Many files bear witness to the rescue work that was carried out to help the youngsters in Nazi occupied France. Among the 160 folders containing 2,000 pages are the dossiers of children concealed in Christian homes through the efforts of this organization. Carefully recorded are the particulars concerning the child, the fate of his parents, his foster home. A total of four thousand documents deal with the problems of these children after the war, including attempts at "reclamation."

Close co-operation was established between YIVO and *Yad V'Shem* in 1954. Material was categorized under three independent but interrelated divisions: (1) Bibliography, (2) Archives, and (3) *Pinkas Hakehilot* (Annals of Destroyed Jewish Communities). Headquarters of the first two divisions are at YIVO in New York; the third is housed at *Yad V'Shem* in Jerusalem.

YIVO is assiduous in amassing material on the inter-war years. Of particular interest is the collection of the agronomist Dr. Joseph Rosen (1876–1949), of the Joint Distribution Committee, which gives a full account of activities in the Soviet Union during that period. Among the papers included is a draft of the agreement between the Soviet Government and the American Joint Distribution Committee, dated September 21, 1922, which guaranteed full liberty and protection to "Joint" personnel in Russia.

Chapter XI

YIVO: The Jewish Record Office

During the last decade YIVO has amassed material relating to Jewish communities scattered throughout the world, highly significant data for historians of the future.

Revealing commentaries on Palestinian affairs during the eventful octave 1940–1948 were obtained in 1951. Most were in the form of pamphlets published "illegally" by the *Irgun Zvai Leumi* (National Military Organization) and *Lochmai Cherut Yisrael* (Fighters for the Freedom of Israel), known by its opponents as the Stern Gang. Among them are a declaration of the principles of *Irgun,* a report of a meeting between an *Irgun* commander and United Nations officials, and day-to-day reports of fighting and "terrorist" activities marked "secret—to be destroyed".

YIVO has been fortunate in its English acquisitions. Through its London branch it received documents collected by Dr. Moses Gaster, honorary president of YIVO for many years; the Sussman collection concerning the London Yiddish Theater, and many letters by Anglo-Yiddish writers. It also acquired the Kalman Marmor collection dealing with the history of the Jewish socialist movement in England and America. Marmor (d. 1953) was one of the founders of the World Union of Poale Zion in 1907 and his documents reveal many aspects of party policy and planning. Equally important are the archives of Thomas Barnes Herwald (1872–1951) on the Jewish Territorial Organization (ITO), which campaigned for Jewish settlements in areas outside Palestine. It was founded after the seventh Zionist Congress (1905) by Israel Zangwill, and Herwald was an ardent ITO supporter. YIVO's material covers nearly half a century of ITO activities, dealing with proposals for Jewish colonization in Mesopotamia, Cyrenaica, Angola, and South America.

Among the documents is an undated letter, probably written in the fall of 1916, signed by Rabbi Abraham Isaac Kook (1865–1935), who resided in England during World War I. It was addressed to the Right Honorable Herbert Samuel, His Majesty's Home Secretary, and is an impassioned plea for the afflicted Jews of Russia and for the Russian Jews living in England who feared the new conscription laws [Conventions with Allies Act, 1917] which were being discussed in Parliament: "We, the Jewish Rabbis of London who consist mainly of unnaturalised Russian Jews, are emboldened by the high standards of justice and rights of the British people to submit this appeal. We are desirous of explaining the terrible plight of our brethren and to ask in the name of the Holy Light of the Almighty which illumines the just and righteous laws of Gt.Britain, that the matter upon which we are now approaching should be dealt with by the Government in accordance with the ideals of Justice and of law which have always glorified the annals of England."

World War II is vividly recorded in a Yiddish account of the Battle of Britain. The translation was prepared, at the formal request of the British Government, by Dr. Solomon Birnbaum (b. 1891), lecturer in East European Jewish studies at the University of London. Copies were dropped on the Warsaw Ghetto by the Royal Air Force.

The most important single Anglo-Jewish archive is the Mowshowitch collection. Dr. David Mowshowitch (1887–1957), a native of Minsk, came to England in 1915 to act as liaison officer for Russian Jews in England. At the outbreak of World War II he joined the staff of the Board of Deputies of British Jews. In the inter-war years he became a close associate of Lucien Wolf (1857–1930), civic worker, political journalist, historian, critic, and—above all—"Foreign Minister" of the Jewish people.

Wolf was born in London in 1857. After receiving an education at private schools, at the Athénée Royale in Brussels, and in Paris, at the age of seventeen he joined the staff of the *Jewish World* as sub-editor and editorial writer. For the next thirty years he was an active journalist, holding at various times the posts of assistant editor of the *Public Leader,* foreign sub-editor of the *Daily Graphic,* and editor of the *Jewish World.* From 1886 a member of the Council of the Anglo-Jewish Association, Wolf became the foreign secretary of the Conjoint (Joint) Foreign Committee of the Board of Deputies and the Anglo-Jewish Association. He took a leading part in securing the adoption of the Minority Treaties, which he devised at the time of the 1919 Peace Conference in Paris. He represented the largest Jewish organizations in Europe and was regarded by Jews in the East and in the West as their "Minister Plenipotentiary."

Throughout his life Mowshowitch collected documents, and after his death Mrs. Mowshowitch dispatched the entire collection to YIVO. It consisted of 1,000 highly specialized volumes, in addition to Parliamentary reports, rare pamphlets, and some 12,000 items of published and unpublished material illuminating the first three decades of the twentieth century, particularly in relation to the manifold roles played by Lucien Wolf. A typewritten copy of Wolf's diary for 1919 is augmented by his vast personal correspondence. There are also many letters exchanged by Jewish scholars and by such leaders as Israel Abrahams and Cyrus Adler and such statesmen as Arthur James Balfour (1848–1930), Foreign Secretary under Lloyd George, and James Ramsay MacDonald.

A founder, and seven times president, of the Jewish Historical Society of England, Lucien Wolf was a pioneer in Anglo-Jewish historical research and a contributor to nine of the eleven volumes which make up the *Transactions of the Jewish Historical Society*. In a letter of February 5, 1896, Robert Arthur Talbot Gascoyne Cecil, third Marquess of Salisbury (1830–1903), gives Wolf permission to examine Foreign Office files for historical purposes. Five years later, on October 31, 1901, a similar request was granted him by the Foreign Secretary, Lord Lansdowne. This zeal of Wolf's for historical research remained with him to the very end. There is a letter dated April 30, 1930, from the assistant clerk of the Governors of St. Bartholomew's Hospital, London, in reply to the researcher's query regarding Rodrigo Ruy Lopez (1525–1594), the Marrano physician who settled in London in 1559, became physician to the Earl of Leicester and Queen Elizabeth I, and was finally executed for high treason at Tyburn on June 7, 1594.

Lucien Wolf's philosophy is reflected in a number of letters. On January 21, 1907 he wrote to the novelist and poet George Meredith (1828–1909), "I am, too, for assimilation but I wanted mechanical and not chemical. I want the race preserved but the spirit merged." In another letter, written on September 28, 1913, he is even more specific if less consistent: "I like Yiddishkeit more than Judaism."

In 1903, after the Kishinev pogrom in which forty-five Jews were murdered and the Jewish quarter almost entirely destroyed, Wolf visited Russia and met Vyacheslav von Plehve, Russian Minister of the Interior and "Chief Executioner" of the "City of Slaughter." Wolf's deep distrust of the Russian policy towards the Jews was expressed in many of his writings, which appeared in various periodicals prior to World War I. Desperately he sought reassurance and remedies but was unable to find either. There is a letter dated January 13, 1904, in which David Lindo Alexander, K.C. (1842–1922), president of the Board of Deputies of British Jews, attempts to assuage Wolf's anxiety: "I have confidential information that His Majesty's Ambassador at St. Petersburg had received an official and confidential assurance that there is no foundation to the reports in question and the local authorities have taken every precaution to prevent any renewal of the late disturbances." The feebleness of these precautions was displayed only too disastrously in the pogroms that took place between October 18 and 29, 1905. In 725 different localities nine hundred persons were killed, and more than 200,000 persons suffered injury and loss as a direct result of these excesses.

The letters between Lucien Wolf and Dr. Moses Gaster were published in the *Jewish Chronicle* on December 4, 1908, under the heading "Extremely Curious Correspondence." "Mr. Lucien Wolf had the audacity," Dr. Gaster castigatingly wrote, "the cruel wickedness, to place a whip in the hands of the Rumanian Government, which no anti-Semite would have stooped to take up and to say that because the Jews were Zionists, they did not desire the emancipation or the freedom to which they were entitled under the Treaty of Berlin."

There are documents describing the attempt of Lucien Wolf and Claude G. Montefiore to persuade the British Foreign Office to intercede with the Russian Government for Jews expelled from Kiev. In March 1911 a thirteen-year-old boy, Andrei Jushtschinski, was found murdered near a brickyard belonging to a Jew. Menachem Mendel Beilis, one of the watchmen at the brickyard, was accused of a ritual murder and the infamous Beilis Blood Libel was born. On October 1, 1913, Lucien Wolf sent a draft petition to Lord Rothschild for submission to the Vatican.

Haunted by the knowledge that millions of Jews were being systematically destroyed, Wolf campaigned prolifically and passionately on their behalf. He wrote *The Persecution of the Jews in Russia.* He also revived the periodical *Darkest Russia,* originally edited by Sir Isodore Spielmann (London, 1891), which under the subtitle *Weekly Record of the Struggle for Freedom* was published from January 3, 1912 to August 4, 1914.

As foreign editor of the *Daily Graphic* Wolf took the stand of the Liberal Party and opposed the entry of Great Britain into World War I. For this he was bitterly attacked by L. J. Maxse, editor of the *National Review,* in September 1914: "All the gutter squirts of the Ghetto were turned upon Russia. Even good-natured, easy-going Englishmen accustomed to be trampled on by the least desirable aliens, are growing restive, under the odium of the Hebrew domination which is being operated exclusively in the interest of Germany. Mr. Wolf is a Russophobe Jew to whom Russia is always in the wrong." [62]

When World War I broke out Wolf suspended *Darkest Russia* in order to contribute "by his silence to the hushing up of differences among the allies." He then devoted himself exclusively to the work of the *Conjoint Foreign Committee.* A letter from the Foreign Office, dated March 3, 1916, assured Wolf that "Sir George Buchanan [1857–1924], British Ambassador in Russia, never came across any cases of ill-treatment of Jews in the Russian Army, during his repeated visits to the varied sections of the Russian front."

Wolf opposed the "Zionist peril." On January 7, 1915 he wrote: "While talking about Zionists, I explained to Mr. F. D. Acland [Parliamentary Under-Secretary of State for Foreign Affairs] that the question of Palestine was for us a subordinate one. I said that we were primarily interested in the safety of the Jews in Poland." In a memorandum dated October 16, 1916, his tone is milder: "The Jewish population in Palestine shall be secured in the enjoyment of civil and religious liberty, equal political rights with the rest of the population, reasonable facilities for immigration and colonisation, and such municipal privileges in the towns and colonies inhabited by them as may be shown to be necessary." [63]

Apparently there was little sympathy between British Jews and their transatlantic cousins. On April 5, 1916, Wolf wrote: "I went to the Foreign Office on Monday and saw Mr. Hubert Montgomery, who is in charge of the Publicity Section and who wishes to talk over with me the question of our propaganda in the United States. Sir Cecil Spring-Rice [1859–1918], the British Ambassador in Washington, says that the great bulk of the Jews of America are against the Allies, and many of them, especially writers in the newspapers, are specifically against Great Britain, as well as against Russia. He seems to be disposed, like Lord Robert Cecil, to hold all the Jews responsible for this attitude of their American co-religionists, and I was surprised to find Mr. Montgomery hinting at the same thing." [64]

Wolf's comments were always sharply pointed. On December 21, 1916, he wrote to Claude G. Montefiore, great-nephew of Sir Moses Montefiore: "Zangwill is of course angling for the leadership of the Zionists. The throne of poor Herzl is really vacant and Zangwill is not wrong, I think, in calculating that if he returns to the Zionist fold he is almost certain to become leader."

A perusal of the YIVO archives proves that Lucien Wolf was truly "a veteran soldier in the cause of righting injustice to the Jews for a half a century," as Dr. Stephen S. Wise termed him in an appreciative epitaph.

A special campaign has been launched for the collection of archives on the history of the Jews in the New World during the last eighty years. The backbone of this department is the archives of the Educational Alliance, together with the files of HIAS (the Jewish Colonization Association), which are a treasure trove of material on Jewish communities in Eastern and Central Europe.

Strenuous efforts are being made to catalogue this vast material, for "the care which a nation devotes to the preservation of the monuments of its past may serve as a true measure of the degree of civilisation to which it has attained." The achievements of YIVO are receiving recognition. The Librarian of Congress in Washington, D.C., recently declared, "The archival resources of YIVO for research in Jewish social life and culture are unequaled. In fact, one cannot visualize any serious research in modern Jewish history without access to and utilization of the YIVO Library and Archives. Its value cannot be overestimated."

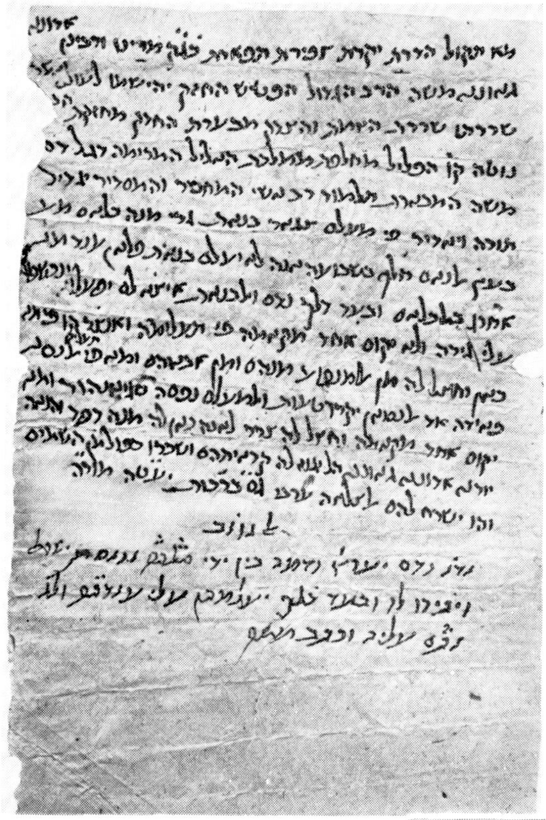

1. *Autograph* responsum *of Moses Maimonides found in the Cairo Geniza (British Museum, Or. 5519), twelfth century.*

2. *Haggadah (British Museum, Or. 2884). The family is shown at table reciting the Haggadah.*

3. *Pentateuch, Megilot and Haphtorot. A teacher and pupil are shown,* A.C.E. *1395. (British Museum, Add. 19776.)*

4. *Scene in a synagogue—a rabbi expounding the laws of Passover. (British Museum.)*

5. *Liturgical poetry with Palestinian vowels. (Bodleian Library, Oxford.)*

6. *Heading to the Book of Kings: David on his throne. The Kennicott Bible. (Bodleian Library, Oxford.)*

7. *Heading to the Book of Jonah: Jonah and the Whale. The Kennicott Bible. (Bodleian Library, Oxford.)*

8. Solomon Schechter, 1847–1915.

9. Psalm scroll with Palestinian punctuation. (University Library, Cambridge.)

10. *The Nash Papyrus. (University Library, Cambridge.)*

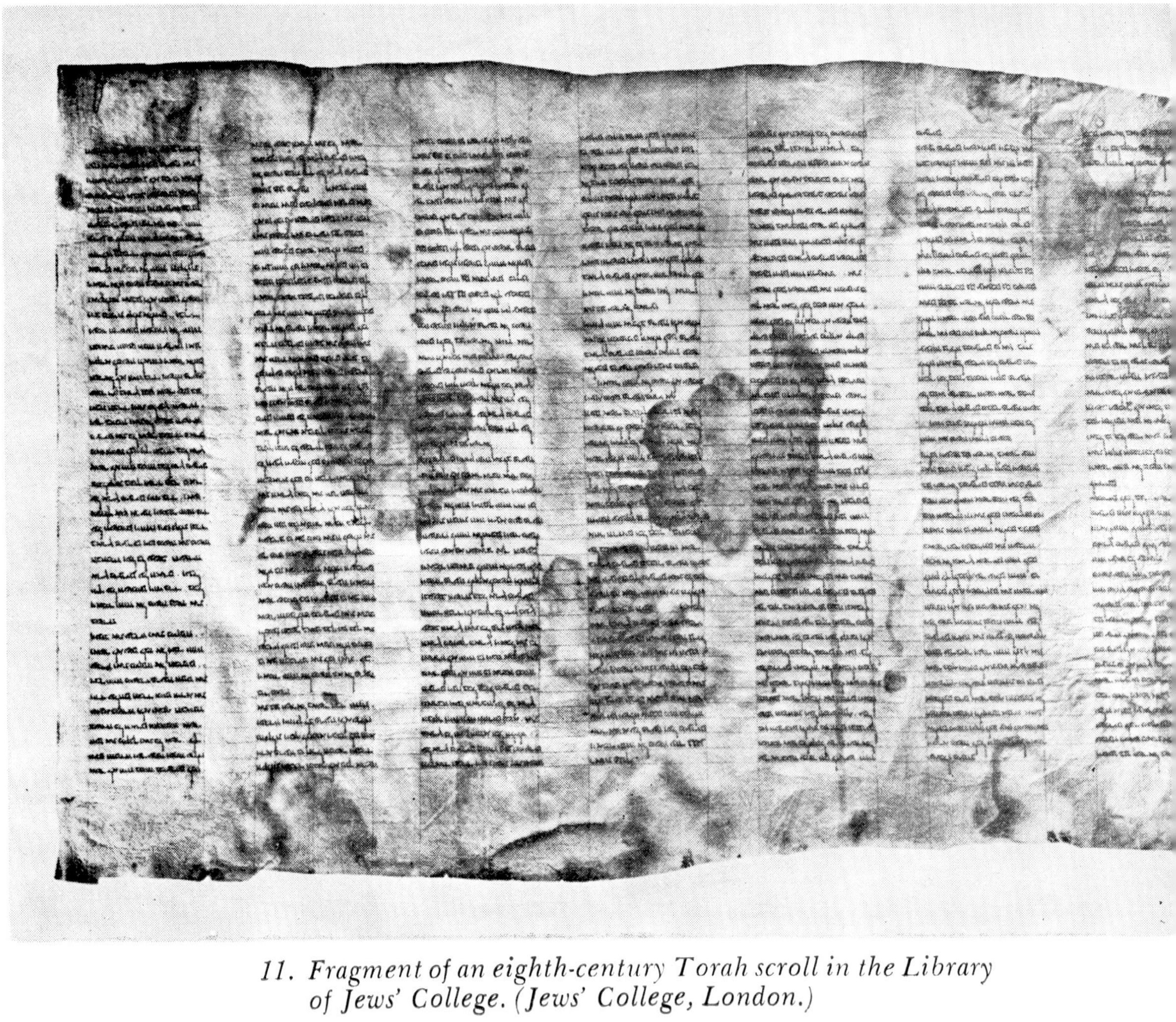

11. *Fragment of an eighth-century Torah scroll in the Library of Jews' College. (Jews' College, London.)*

תמונת אד״מו החכם הכולל הגאון הגדול מהור שלמה ·
בן אד״מו הגאון הגדול מהור צבי זצ״ל ·
א״בד דקק אשכנזים בלונדון והמדינה יע״א :
שלשלת היחוסי הגאונים מהו״ה העשיל והחכם צבי זצ״ל יחיה :
THE REV. SOLOMON HIRSCHELL;
Chief Rabbi of the German and Polish Jews in England.

12. *Solomon Hirschell, Rabbi of the Great Synagogue and Chief Rabbi, 1802–1842. (From an engraving.)*

13. *Memorandum by the Exilarch David ben Zaccai on the calendar controversy. (Jewish Theological Seminary of America.)*

14. *David Nieto, 1654–1728. (Jewish Theological Seminary of America.)*

15. *Sixteenth-century copy of the Adeshir Book, written by the Judeo-Persian poet Shahin in the fourteenth century. (Jewish Theological Seminary of America.)*

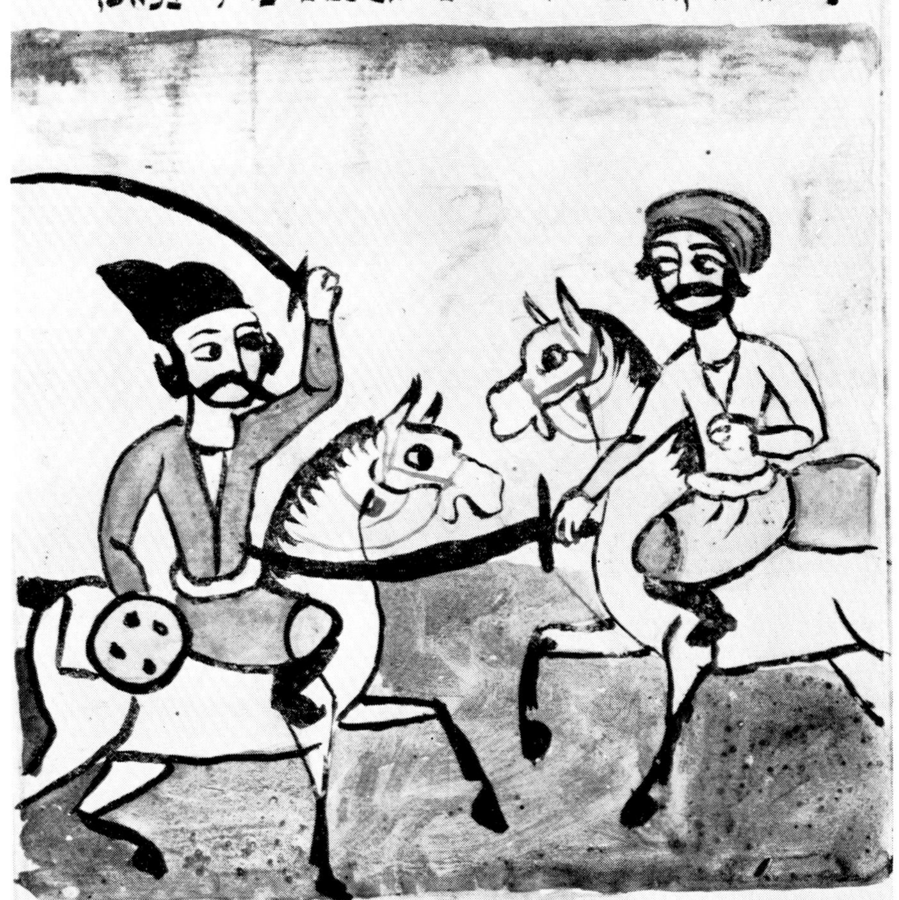

16. *A Jewish Persian manuscript containing a poetical paraphrase of the narrative portions of the Pentateuch. Illuminated in Persian style* ca. *1660. (Jewish Theological Seminary of America.)*

17. Prayer book, Austria, 1300. (Jewish Theological Seminary of America.)

18. Library of the YIVO Institute for Jewish Research. (YIVO Library.)

19. *The title-page of a Bible printed in Mantua, Italy, in 1742, containing eight biblical scenes, such as the exodus from Egypt, the judgment of Solomon, the giving of the Decalogue, Daniel in the lion's den, David and his harp, the vision of the dry bones, Esther before King Ahasuerus, and Joshua's stopping of the sun. (YIVO Library.)*

צוואת אמת אביכם

אמת תדברו ותכירו ותודו. ולא תאמינו לדמיוניכם
המעוור עיני השכל המפתיכם לשקר כי השקר אין
לו רגלים. ולא יעמוד. ושפת אמת תכון לעד והתחזקו
עד מאד בזה. אף כי השקר הוא המושל כעת בארץ
הזאת הנשמה. אל תיראו. כי במעט אמת תתגברו
ותדחו שקר הרבה כמו במעט אור אשר אחוז בנר
ידחה החשך מכל הבית ובזה יהי לכם קיום בזה ובבא
ותתדבקו נפשתיכם באחד האמות מוצא שפתיכם
תשמרו לקיים כי היא מצות עשה דאורייתא כדעת
הרמבם ומי שאין מקיים במאמרו חס ושלום עובר
על מצות עשה וכמה לאוין על התחזקו בכל
מאמצי כחכם נגד היצר. ותקיימו מצות עשה זו

20. *The writer of this will, who passed away in 1850, was rabbi in Olkusz, Poland. He penned this will, two pages of which are given here, for the benefit of his children, exhorting them to the good life. He called his will a "Testament of Truth," for above all other virtues he put truth. (Gift of Rabbi Hugo B. Schiff to the YIVO Archives.)*

Соломонъ Наумовичъ Рабиновичъ.
Кіевъ. Большая Васильковская, 5.

8.XII. 1901.

21. A letter dated 1901 from Shalom Aleichem, the Yiddish humorist. (YIVO Institute for Jewish Research.)

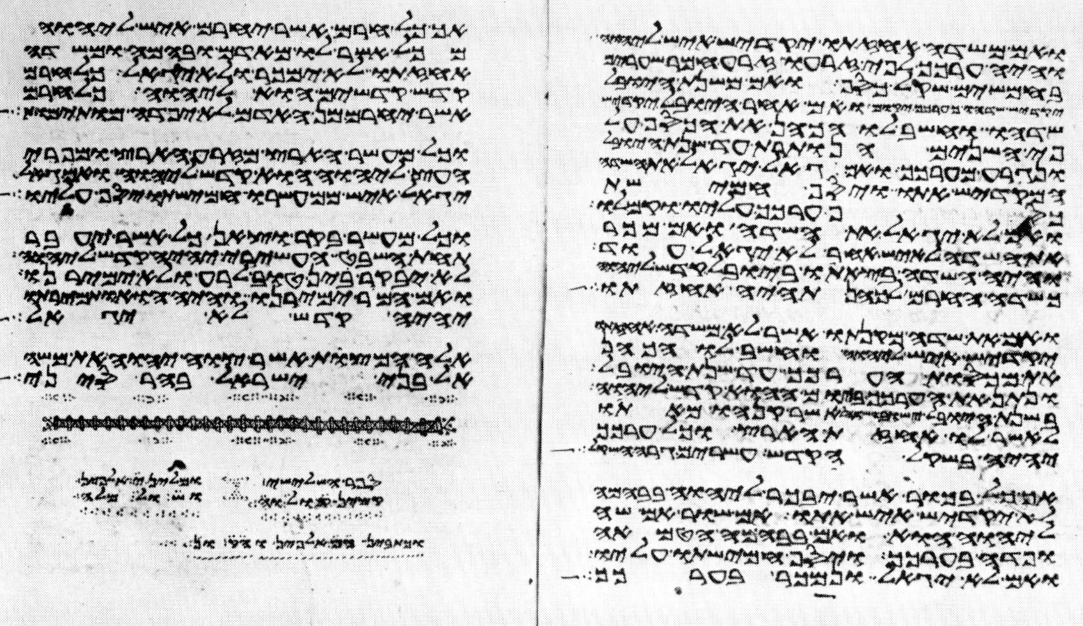

22. Samaritan Pentateuch written approx. 1231. (New York Public Library.)

23. *First word of* Kol Nidre, *in a fourteenth-century illuminated machzor. (New York Public Library.)*

24. Selichot *from a fourteenth-century illuminated* machzor. *(New York Public Library.)*

25. *First word of a* piyyut *from a fourteenth-century illuminated* machzor. *(New York Public Library.)*

מלך מלכי המלכים הקב״ה וגאלם שנאמר ויאפו את הבצק אשר
הוציאו ממצרים עגות מצות כי לא חמץ כי גורשו ממצרים ולא
יכלו להתמהמה וגם צידה לא עשו להם

מרור זה שאנו
אוכלים
על שום

מה על שום שמררו המצרים
את חיי אבותינו במצרים שנאמר
וימררו את חייהם בעבודה קשה
בחומר ובלבנים ובכל עבודה בשדה את
כל עבודתם אשר עבדו בהם בפרך

בכל דור ודור חייב אדם לראות את עצמו כאילו הוא
יצא ממצרים שנאמר והגדת לבנך ביום ההוא לאמר
בעבור זה עשה יי לי בצאתי ממצרים ולא את אבותינו גאל
הקב״ה בלבד אלא את אותנו גאל עמהם שנאמר ואותנו הוציא
משם למען הביא אותנו לתת לנו את הארץ אשר נשבע לאבותינו

לפיכך אנחנו חייבים להודות להלל לשבח
לפאר לרומם להדר לברך לעלה
ולקלס למי שעשה נסים לאבותינו
ולנו את כל האותות והמופתים והנסים האלו הוציאנו ממיצ
ממצרים מעבדות לחירות ומיגון לשמחה ומאבל ליום טוב
ומאפלה לאור גדול
ונאמר לפניו
הללו יה

26. Machzor, *Italian rite, fifteenth-century Seder service with illustration of bitter herb. (New York Public Library.)*

נדרים ואסרים והקדשות וחרמים ושבועות
וקיומים שנדרנו ושאסרנו ושהקדשנו
ושהחרמנו ושנשבענו ושקימנו ושקבלנו
על נפשותינו בשבועה מיום צום הכפורים
שעבר עד יום צום הכפורים הזה הבא
עלינו בכולם חזרנו ובאנו לפני אבינו
שבשמים אם נדר נדרנו אין כאן נדר אם
אסר אסרנו אין כאן אסור אם הקדש
הקדשנו אין כאן הקדש אם חרם החרמנו
אין כאן חרם אם שבועה נשבענו אין כאן
שבועה אם קיום קימנו אין כאן קיום
בטל הנדר מעקרו בטל האסר מעקרו

27. Kol Nidre *in a fifteenth-century manuscript. (New York Public Library.)*

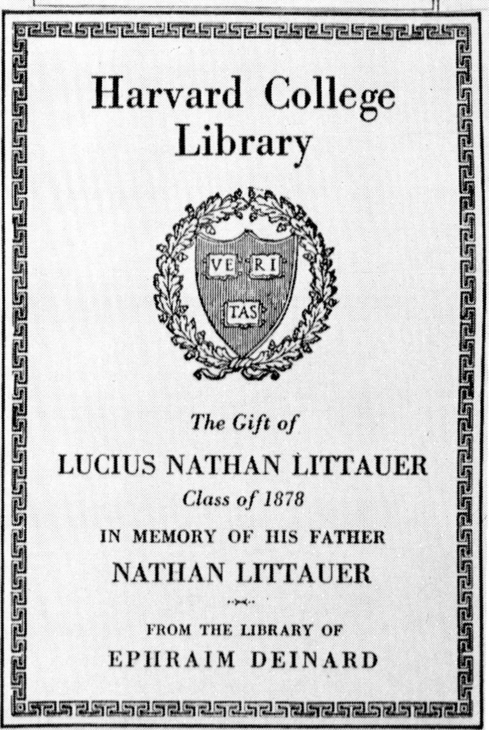

28. Bookplates used by various American colleges and universities.

HARVARD COLLEGE
LIBRARY

FROM THE LIBRARY OF HEBRAICA AND JUDAICA FORMED BY FELIX FRIEDMANN OF AMSTERDAM AND PURCHASED THROUGH THE GIFTS OF A COMMITTEE OF DONORS

YALE UNIVERSITY LIBRARY

YALE UNIVERSITY
LIBRARY

THE
SHALOM ASCH COLLECTION
OF JUDAICA

The Gift of
Louis M. Rabinowitz

29. Dr. Samuel Belkin, President of Yeshiva University. (Yeshiva University.)

30. Yeshiva University, main building. (Yeshiva University.)

עזר אלהי קדם שוכ
מעונה: אחל לפרש
תפלות כל השנה

INCUNABULA

1489 -- LISBON

No. 1

ABUDRAHAM

אבודרהם

Commentary on the Book of Prayers

Encyclopedia on matters of Jewish rituals and customs

נגמר ספר חמישי
והוא ספר קדושה

ספר ששי
והוא ספר הפלאה

פרק ראשון

INCUNABULA

1490 -- SONCINO

No. 2

The Repetition of the Law

משנה תורה

By Moses Maimonides (1135-1204), famous philosopher, astronomer, physician and outstanding scholar, the greatest mediaeval Jewish thinker (known as the second Moses).

31. *Incunabula. (The New York University Jewish Culture Foundation.)*

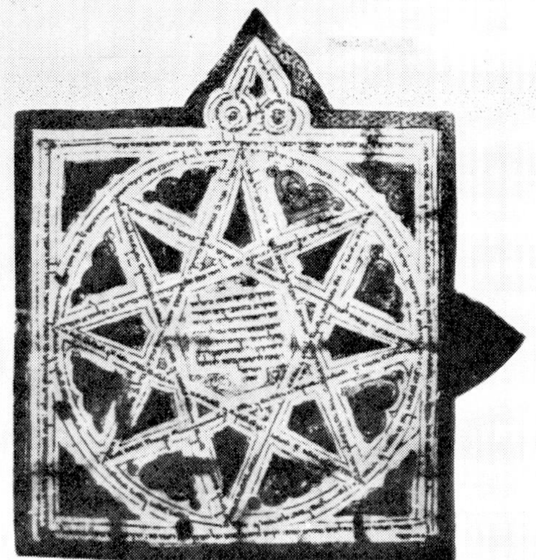

32. Geniza manuscripts in the Soviet Union. (The New York University Jewish Culture Foundation.)

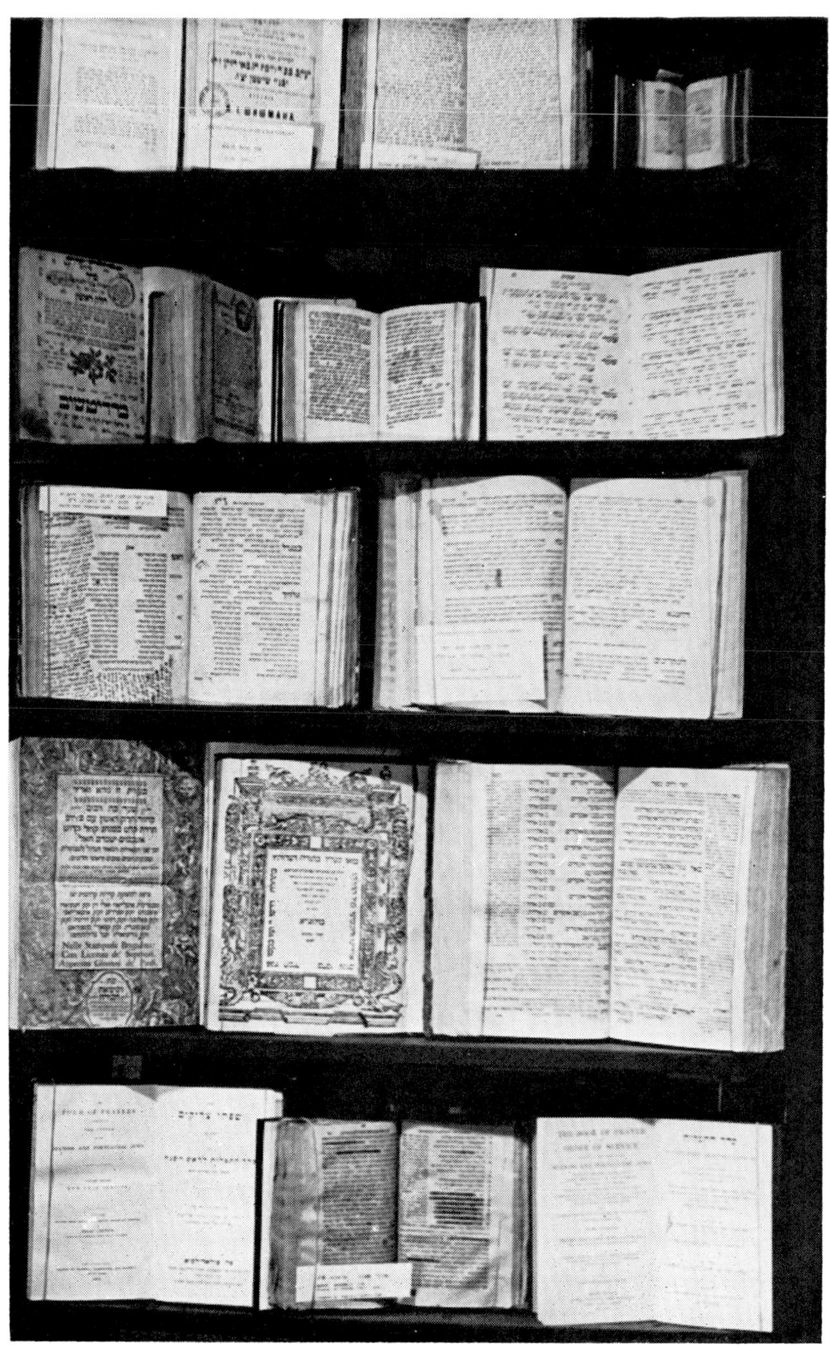

33. Rare prayer books. (Jewish Institute of Religion Library.)

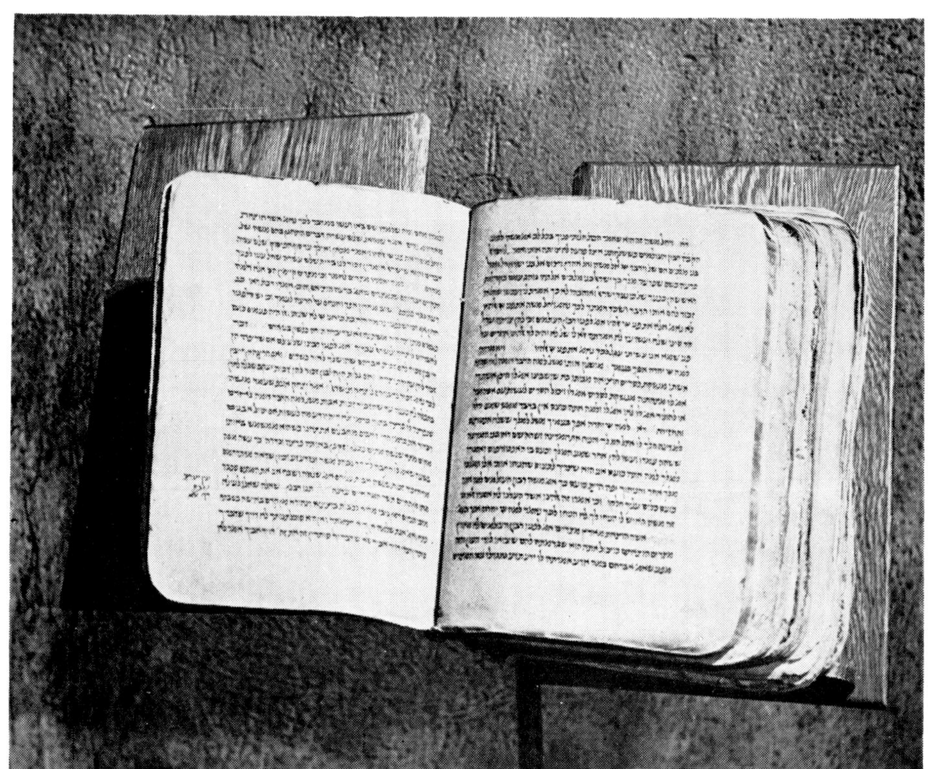

34. *Midrash Hagadol on Shemot. (Jewish Institute of Religion Library.)*

35. *Air-view of the Hebrew Union College campus and buildings. Inset, from old engraving, shows old Sixth Street building which the College formerly occupied. 1. Administration Building. 2. Dormitory. 3. Gymnasium. 4. Bernheim Library and Museum. 5. New Library. (Hebrew Union College Library, Cincinnati.)*

36. *Jacob journeys to Egypt,* top left, *Cincinnati Haggadah, 13a. Building the storage cities,* top right, *Cincinnati Haggadah, 17b. Colophon of the copyist,* bottom, *Cincinnati Haggadah, 68b, 69a. (Hebrew Union College Library, Cincinnati.)*

37. *The mnemotechnic "Jaknhas" (Hare Chase),* top, *Cincinnati Haggadah, 4a. Seder meal,* bottom left, *Darmstadt Haggadah, 37b. Seder meal in small family,* bottom right, *Cincinnati Haggadah, 2b. (Hebrew Union College Library, Cincinnati.)*

38. Chinese Jewish manuscript from Kai-Fung-Foo. (Hebrew Union College Library, Cincinnati.)

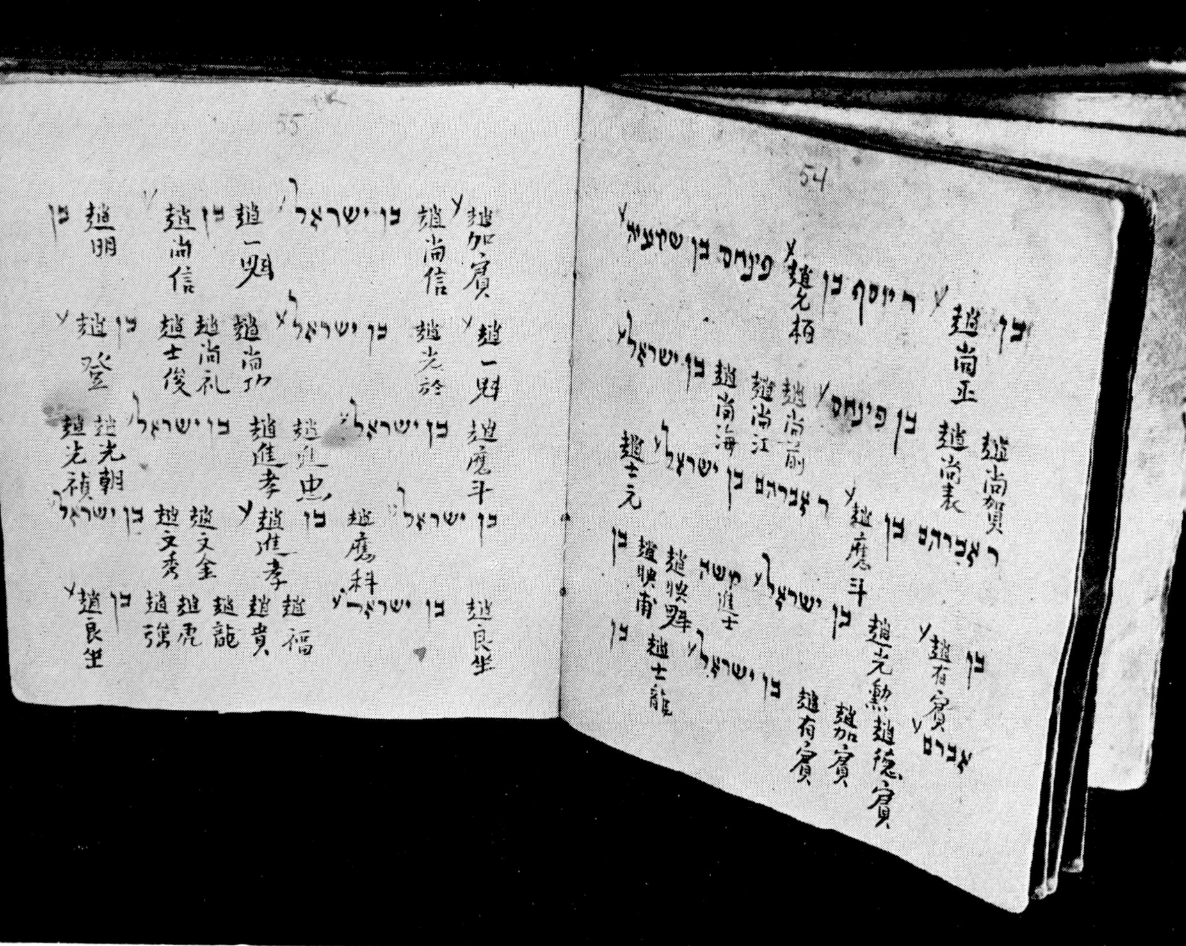

39. A genealogical register in Hebrew and Chinese. (Hebrew Union College Library, Cincinnati.)

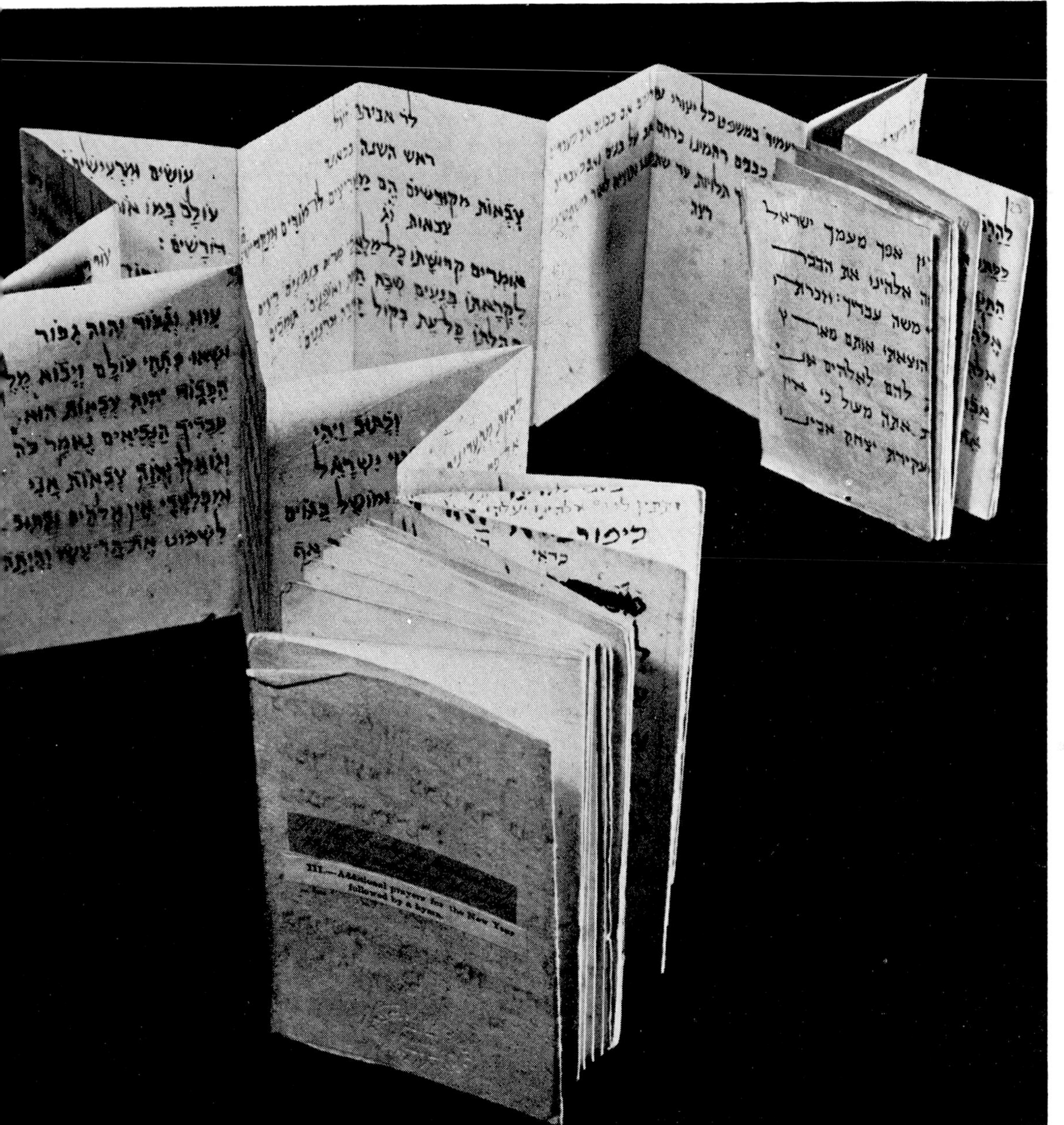

40. Manuscript from the Chinese community of Kai-Fung-Foo. (Hebrew Union College Library, Cincinnati.)

41. Dropsie College.

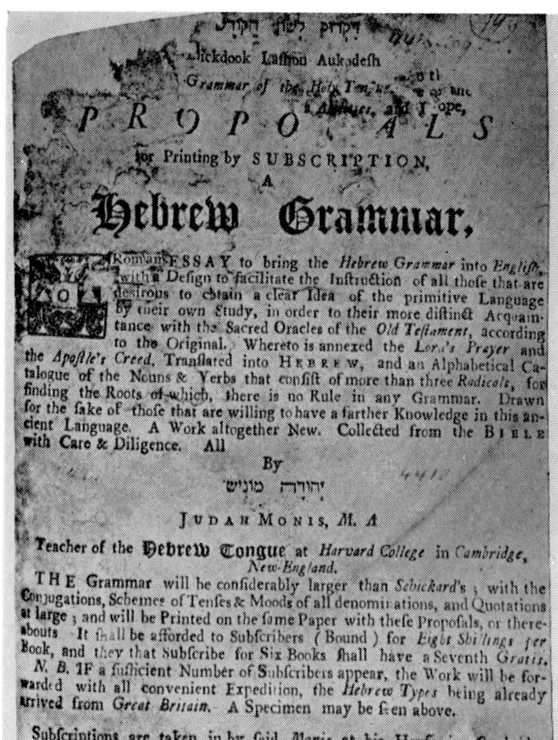

דקדוק לשון הקדש

Dickdook Leshon Aukodesh

Grammar of the Holy Tongue

P R O P O S A L S

for Printing by SUBSCRIPTION,

A

Hebrew Grammar,

Roman ESSAY to bring the *Hebrew Grammar* into *English*, with a Design to facilitate the Instruction of all those that are desirous to obtain a clear Idea of the primitive Language by their own Study, in order to their more distinct Acquaintance with the Sacred Oracles of the *Old Testament*, according to the Original. Whereto is annexed the *Lord's Prayer* and the *Apostle's Creed*, Translated into HEBREW, and an Alphabetical Catalogue of the Nouns & Verbs that consist of more than three *Radicals*, for finding the Roots of which, there is no Rule in any Grammar. Drawn for the sake of those that are willing to have a farther Knowledge in this ancient Language. A Work altogether New. Collected from the BIBLE with Care & Diligence. All

By

יהודה מוניש

JUDAH MONIS, *M. A*

Teacher of the **Hebrew Tongue** at *Harvard College* in *Cambridge*, *New-England.*

THE Grammar will be considerably larger than *Schickard's*; with the Conjugations, Schemes of Tenses & Moods of all denominations, and Quotations at large; and will be Printed on the same Paper with these Proposals, or thereabouts. It shall be afforded to Subscribers (Bound) for *Eight Shillings per* Book, and they that Subscribe for Six Books shall have a Seventh *Gratis*.

N. B. IF a sufficient Number of Subscribers appear, the Work will be forwarded with all convenient Expedition, the *Hebrew Types* being already arrived from *Great Britain*. A Specimen may be seen above.

Subscriptions are taken in by said *Monis* at his House in *Cambridge*, and *Daniel Henchman* Bookseller in *Boston*.

42. Broadside advertisement of Judah Monis' Hebrew grammar. (Harvard University Library.)

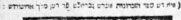

43. *A page from the* Tze'enah u-Re'enah *(ed. Amsterdam, 1792).* Upper scene: *Haman building the gallows for Mordecai.* Lower scene: *The book of records being read to Ahasuerus. (Yale University Library.)*

44. *Sepher Ziyyoni, Cremona, 1559. (Yale University Library.)*

אחרי מות

ספר ויקרא

45. The main reading room of the Library of Congress, as seen from the visitors' gallery. Collections of reference books are located in the alcoves which surround the room. (Library of Congress.)

Chapter XII

The New York Public Library

Eight thousand people a day and three million people a year pass through the portals of the New York Public Library, the second largest library in the United States. Located in the heart of Manhattan, at the bustling junction of 42nd Street and Fifth Avenue, the library somehow reflects this stupendous metropolis. Quiet though intense activity takes place within its stately walls. With a staff of 850, the library is open almost every day of the year, from 9 A.M. to 10 P.M. on weekdays, with an abbreviated eight-hour day on Sundays. It houses four million books on its eighty miles of shelves—enough books to make an unbroken line from New York City to Pittsburgh, 320 miles away.

Among its many specialized divisions is the Jewish Section in Room 217, with approximately 110,000 books on Judaica, Hebraica, Biblical literature, theater and belles-lettres, as well as an unsurpassed collection of Jewish newspapers and periodicals. Considerable material deals with Samaritans, Karaites, *Chassidim,* modern Yiddish literature, and Jewish apologetics. Moreover, even pietists for whom the libraries of the Jewish Theological Seminary and the Jewish Institute of Religion are "forbidden territory," feel at home in the paradoxically non-sectarian atmosphere of Room 217. It is not unusual to observe a bearded rabbi, immersed in a difficult passage of the Talmud, sitting alongside a journalist investigating suicide statistics among Jews. Scholars and laymen, Jews from every walk of life, gather around the long tables, united by a common quest for knowledge.

The New York Public Library owes its existence to three benefactors, Astor, Lenox, and Tilden. When John Jacob Astor died in 1848 he left $400,000 for the establishment of a library. Under the presidency of the writer Washington Irving (1783–1859), this fledgling library opened its doors to the public on January 5, 1854, with a stock of between 80,000 and 90,000 books. Thirty-six years later, in 1870, the Lenox Library was established by the New York merchant and philanthropist, James Lenox

(1800–1880). From the estate of the American politician Samuel Jones Tilden (1814–1886), candidate for the Presidency in 1876, the City of New York received in 1892 a sizable collection of books together with two million dollars for its development. In 1895 these three collections were consolidated. There were among them no more than 5,000 books of Hebraica, in addition to several Samaritan manuscripts and scrolls of the Book of Esther.

In 1897 the Jewish Division was established, and Abraham Solomon Freidus (1867–1923) was appointed its head. He was described by the editor of the *Jewish Encyclopedia,* Joseph Jacobs (1954–1916), as a "pocket Steinschneider." The preface to this magnum opus, to which there had been 400 contributors and whose index consisted of more than 25,000 entries, acknowledges handsomely that it could not have been produced without the help of the New York Public Library, and Freidus is thanked for "special privileges accorded and assistance rendered."

In 1897 the chief librarian, John S. Billings (1838–1913), wrote: "In their examination of the resources of the combined Libraries, the Trustees, becoming aware of the lack of a collection of Jewish literature, turned to Mr. Jacob H. Schiff, the foremost Jewish citizen of New York, among whose vast and varied interests, Jewish learning and education were by no means the least. He responded generously for the end that Jewish literature may take its honorable place in the library among the literature of the world."

Schiff, born in Frankfurt in 1847, of the family of David Tevele Schiff, rabbi of the Great Synagogue in London (1765–1792), became the library's Maecenas. In November 1897 he donated $10,000 for the purchase of Semitic literature. This was the first of many contributions, which totalled $100,000 during his lifetime in addition to a final bequest of $25,000 and the donation on March 17, 1909, of 317 original water-colors on Biblical subjects by the French painter Jacques Tissot (1836–1902) valued at $100,000.

To this Hebraic nucleus was added the valuable library of Leon Mandelstamm (1809–1889) of St. Petersburg. A Hebraist, poet, and educator, Mandelstamm had been secretary to the Rabbinical Commission convened at St. Petersburg in 1834 to draw up an educational program for Russian Jewry. His collection contained 2,135 volumes of Hebraica, including 237 Bibles with and without commentaries, and 184 volumes of Talmudical tractates, as well as volumes in Yiddish, German, and Russian.

Through J. L. Joachimsthal of Amsterdam the Jewish Division in 1899 acquired a few hundred volumes from the library of Meijer Lehren. Another notable acquisition was the collection of 530 books, periodicals, and pamphlets in Hebrew and Yiddish by Rabbi Benzion Eisenstadt (1873–

1951), editor of the *Aspeklariah,* a Hebrew monthly published in New York beginning in 1907.

"Persistent drippings will bore through a rock" must have been the motto of the Jewish Division. Purchases were never dramatic, bequests never spectacular; yet year by year the library enlarged its collection. Among its innumerable benefactors were Isaac Meyer (100 volumes on mysticism), Dr. Henry M. Leipziger (100 books and pamphlets), David Blaustein (588 books and 3,000 pamphlets), Dr. S. Brainin (Russian and Hebrew books), and Dr. Alfred L. Shapiro (1,350 books and 120 pamphlets).

There are only a handful of manuscripts, and these are confined to Samaritan, Biblical, and liturgical texts. A Samaritan Pentateuch consisting of 549 leaves and written in 1231–1232 is one of the finest in existence. The colophon gives this information: "I, Abraham son of Israel, son of Abraham, son of Joseph, the prince, king of Israel, have written this copy of the Holy Law for myself in the name of my son in the year 629 of the Ishmaelites [Mohammedans] which is 3200 years after the Children of Israel settled in the land of Canaan and 4993 years after the Creation of the World."

Similarly, an illustrated manuscript Bible in two volumes, dated January 1294, carries the colophon: "I, Joseph of Xanten, son of Kalonymus from Neuss (Rhine) have written and illustrated these twenty-four books for my friend Moses, son of Jacob, and finished it on Monday, the 21st of the month of *Sivan* in the year 5054 [1294], of the creation of the world. May the Creator keep him alive to study these books until the end of days. Amen, Selah."

Among the library's forty incunabula is *Arbaah Turim* by Jacob ben Asher (*ca.* 1269–*ca.* 1340), produced at Piove de Sacco in 1475—the first Hebrew printed book. The colophon reads: "Wisdom am I, and crown of all science, hidden am I, a mystery to all. Without pen-stroke, my imprint stands patent, without scribe, lo! a volume appears. One instant, and ink o'er me flowing, without guide lines, straight stands every word. Do you wonder at Deborah, the mighty, who ruled with the pen of the scribes? Had she seen me displaying my power, she had taken me, a crown for her head." The commentary on the Pentateuch by Rabbi Solomon ben Isaac, known as Rashi, printed in Zamora by Samuel ben Musa and Immanuel in 1487, is to our knowledge the only Hebrew book published in Zamora that has survived to this day.

The library has many books printed before 1600. Of particular interest are the works of a Christian printer of Hebrew books, Daniel Bomberg, son of a wealthy Antwerpian burgher, Cornelius van Bamberghen. From 1517 to 1549 he published many editions of rabbinic works. Pope Leo X officially endorsed Bomberg's project of publishing the first complete edition of the Babylonian Talmud (with the commentaries of Rashi, *Tosaphot,* and R. Asher ben Jechiel) —a work "involving greatest labor and expense."

The printers of Venice, the "city of books", produced two thousand eight hundred volumes before 1500, yet of these not one single Hebrew incunabulum has survived. However, the New York Public Library holds copies of virtually all the Hebrew books printed in Venice during the sixteenth century. It also has many works originating at Naples, also a center of Hebrew printing, and second in importance only to Soncino, the town in the Duchy of Milan from which a noted Italian family of printers took its name. Unlike Ferdinand V (1452–1516) of Spain, Ferdinand I of Naples (1423–1494) gave royal encouragement in practical terms to the reborn printing trade: "For printed books," ran the edict, "no custom duty need be paid."

E.N. Adler in *A Gazetteer of Hebrew Printing* (1917) enumerated 549 localities of Hebrew printing. Alexander Marx brought the number up to 626,[65] and in 1946 Aron Freimann (1871–1946) listed 939 localities.[66] Of these works 253 are represented by books at the New York Public Library.

One such collector's piece is the first printed text of the *machzor* according to the Roman rite, in two volumes the first printed at Soncino by Joshua Solomon in September 1485 and the second at Casal Maggiore in 1486. This latter also has the first printed illustration of a *matzah* (unleavened bread).

The library is the proud possessor of *Maasseh Tuvyah* ("Work of Tobias") by the Polish physician Tobiah ben Moses Cohen (1652–1729), published at Venice in 1707–8. The author lived in Adrianople, where he was physician to five successive sultans. He was a noted linguist, conversant with Hebrew, German, Italian, French, Spanish, Turkish, Latin, Greek, and Arabic. His work is divided into eight parts, and its features include diagrams of human anatomy, a map of the world showing Europe and America, illustrations of astronomical and mathematical instruments, and a Turkish-Latin-Spanish vocabulary.[67]

The first Hebrew grammar, by the Hebraist and polemicist Alfonso de Zamora (1474–1544), was printed in Spain in 1526. Its author was converted to Christianity in 1492 and was engaged by Cardinal Ximenes (1436–1517) in the preparation of the Complutensian Bible. The text of the Hebrew grammar appeared at the end of the sixth volume of this work. The Hebrew type faces used are exceptionally beautiful, unequaled in sixteenth-century printing. In a letter to Pope Paul III, dated April 1, 1544, Alfonso de Zamora speaks of himself as being seventy years old and the last of the Hebrew scholars in Spain.[68]

In addition to many first editions, 2,000 volumes of rabbinic *responsa,* and miscellaneous items on Jewish sects, the library has valuable material on Biblical archaeology. Special attention is devoted to books referring to America and to early books published there.

Outstanding in this section is *Iggeret Orchot Olam,* a cosmographic and geographic work in thirty chapters by the Italian scholar Abraham ben Mordecai Farissol (1451–1525), printed at Venice in 1587; this is one of the earliest Hebrew accounts of the "distant American Islands recently discovered by Portuguese ships." Farissol utilized Jacopo Filippo Foresti da Bergamo's *Supplementum,* which contains the first attempt in Hebrew to present a Map of the New World.

Another noteworthy possession is the first American publication dealing with Hebrew grammar. It was written by the Franciscan monk Martin del Castillo (d. 1680) in Mexico, and published in Madrid in 1676. Also on record is the first sermon printed in America. It was preached in Newport, Rhode Island, on May 28, 1773 (6th day of *Sivan* 5533) by a visitor from the Holy Land, Rabbi Chayyim Isaac Karigal of the city of Hebron. Originally delivered in Spanish, it was translated into English by Abraham Lopez.

Room 217 is well stocked with liturgical works. It has the *Prayers for Shabbaths, Rosh Hashanah and Kippur,* translated by Isaac Pinto of New York and printed by J. Holt in 1766, as well as *The Form of Daily Prayers, according to the custom of the Spanish and Portuguese Jews. As read in their Synagogues, and used in their families.* These prayers were translated from the Hebrew into English by Solomon Henry Jackson and printed at New York in 1826. The first Passover Haggadah printed on the American continent, dated 1837, was a reprint of the Hebrew text with an English translation by David Levi which was originally published in London in 1794. Also of interest is an edition for German-Jewish settlers of the prayer book for the Day of Atonement, the *Gebetbuch für Israelitische Reform-Gemeinden,* published in New York in 1856.

The Jewish Division possesses thousands of pamphlets acquired over the last three decades. It also had a collection of unusual books in Aramaic, Yiddish, Judeo-Spanish, Judeo-French, and Judeo-Italian, using the Roman alphabet instead of the Hebrew.

The library is well stocked with Bibles. It has Johann Gutenberg's Bible, and the Polyglot Bible of 1514–17 (known as the Complutensian Polyglot or Ximenes' Polyglot because it was produced under the patronage of Cardinal Ximenes, founder of the University of Alcala). A particularly notorious edition is the "Wicked Bible" printed by Robert Barker in 1631, in which the negative was inadvertently omitted from the Seventh Commandment, so that it reads with startling permissiveness, "Thou shalt commit adultery." The printers are said to have been fined £300 for their carelessness. The edition was suppressed by Archbishop William Laud (1573–1645), with the result that only four copies have survived. The first book to be published in the English settlements in America was the Bay Psalm Book, printed in Cambridge in 1640 and so called because its authors—Richard Mather, Thomas Welde, and John Eliot—were ministers of the Massachusetts Bay Colony. Since there was as yet no font of Hebrew type in America, the Hebrew characters were specially cast for the printing of the 119th Psalm, and it was here that the Hebrew alphabet appeared for the first time in the New World.

The library was well served by the successors of Freidus, its first librarian. Joshua Bloch (1890–1957) left a collection of cards in a catalogue which include half a million entries. Today scholarly Abraham Bėrger, a true friend of Jewish books and book lovers, presides over Room 217.

Chapter XIII

The Columbia University Library

A few minutes' walk from the Jewish Theological Seminary of America stands its distinguished neighbor, Columbia University. A city within a city, the Columbia campus occupies nine buildings, and its libraries hold 2,875,815 volumes and nearly 300 homogeneous manuscript collections. On the sixth floor of the Nicholas Murray Butler Library is the Hebrew collection, containing over 20,000 books of Judaica, 28 incunabula, 300 sixteenth-century books, and more than 1,000 Hebrew manuscripts.

The University was founded in 1754, during the reign of George II of England, and was then known as King's College. The minutes of a meeting of the trustees on May 12, 1761, record that books "were given to the College by the late Rev. Dr. Doncombe Bristowe of London." Dr. Samuel Johnson (1696–1772), the first president of King's College (1754–1763), regarded Hebrew as "essential to a gentleman's education." He himself had studied Hebrew at Guilford Grammar School in Connecticut, and had compiled an English and Hebrew grammar. However, there were few Hebrew books to be found at the University during the first hundred years of its existence.

It was in 1887, with the appointment of Richard James Horatio Gottheil as professor of Semitic languages at Columbia University, that the foundation was laid for today's magnificent Hebrew collection. His father, Gustav Gottheil (1827–1903), was rabbi for thirteen years at the Reform Synagogue in Manchester, England, and from 1875 was rabbi at Temple Emanu-El, the famous Moorish Romanesque edifice in New York. In 1868 Temple Emanu-El bought from an Amsterdam book dealer, Frederick Müller, a collection of forty-three manuscripts and 2,500 printed books. Many of these originated from the libraries of famous Jewish scholars, such as Joseph Almanzi of Padua, Talmudist Jacob Emden of Altona (1697–1776), and others. On May 10, 1892 the trustees of Temple Emanu-El, "by a sense of obligation for the free tuition which a number of Jewish students have received at the College and as appreciation of the important service rendered by the Trustees of the College in placing upon a permanent basis the chair of Rabbinical literature which members of Temple Emanu-El originated five years ago", presented this significant collection to Columbia.

A new stimulus to the Hebraic expansion came from the appointment in 1930 of Dr. Salo Wittmayer Baron (b. 1895), author of the *Social and Religious History of the Jews,* as professor of Jewish history, literature, and institutions. In the course of the next two years, six hundred manuscripts were acquired from the famous bookdealer Rabbi David Frankel of Vienna, and several thousands of books of Hebraica were purchased from the Amtorg Corporation (the Soviet Russian trading corporation in New York). In 1939 the library of Richard Gottheil was presented to Columbia University by his widow Emma. It comprised 10,000 volumes, a third of them in Hebrew, as well as pamphlets and newspaper clippings relating to nineteenth-century American Jewry.

During the past decade Columbia has acquired an additional 10,000 books, many dealing with modern Hebrew literature and contemporary Jewish problems.

Columbia's manuscript collection is second in New York only to that of the Jewish Theological Seminary. It contains Bibles and Biblical commentaries, works on Midrash, Halakhah, history, liturgy, philosophy, kabbalah, and theology, as well as *responsa,* minute books, illuminated marriage contracts, Persian Geniza fragments, and Oriental poems from North Africa, Turkey, Syria, Iraq, and Italy.

Of particular importance are manuscripts in the collection on history and sociology. In a petition addressed to Doge Aloysio Mocenico in Venice by the community of Corfu, on September 14, 1572, six Christian councilors ask for the repeal of the Venetian decree ordering the expulsion of the Jewish community. In statutes of the community of Larissa, the rabbis and leaders who are the signatories complain of the extravagances displayed by wealthy Jewish townsmen and of how the poor were left in destitution. To redress the scale it was decreed that festivities be conducted with restraint and a certain percentage of each business transaction be donated for the support of the poor.

Another interesting manuscript in the possession of the library is *Olam Hapuch,* an account of a plague in the Ghetto of Padua in 1630–31, written in 1631, by the physician Abraham Catalano (d. 1642). The chronicle relates in detail the precautions taken for the safety of the Ghetto, arrangements for the disposal of the dead, and relief measures for the needy.

A find for the historiographer is *Divre Yemei Napoleon,* a history of Napoleon (1769–1821) by a contemporary German Jew. The manuscript is prefaced by an account of the French Revolution (1789), before Napoleon's meteoric rise to power. There are also items of specifically Jewish interest relating, for example, to Maximilien Robespierre's attitude to the Jewish religion, the Assembly of Notables which met in Paris on May 26, 1806, and to the Paris Sanhedrin which met on February 9, 1807. An autobiographical note records the author's arrest in Frankfurt-on-Main on a charge of espionage.

The student of religious development will be interested in six *responsa* and a ban promulgated by rabbis of Hamburg in the second decade of the nineteenth century against the use of any language other than Hebrew in religious services, and against the playing of the organ in the synagogue. Lovers of art will find delight in a late seventeenth-century manuscript on calendar computations, colorfully illuminated in colored inks. Many of the drawings, however, have no bearing on the text, but are merely decorative; there are, for example, pictures of Adam and Eve and of the execution of Agag, king of the Amalekites, by the prophet Samuel.

In the departments of archaeology and philosophy there are five hundred cuneiform tablets dating from 2300 B.C. to 800 B.C. and referring to the Sumerian, Babylonian, and Neo-Babylonian periods, legal documents from the reigns of Nebuchadnezzar, king of Babylon (604–562 B.C.), who destroyed the Temple in 586 B.C., and Cyrus (d. 529), founder of the Persian Empire, who allowed the Jewish exiles to return to Judea in 538 B.C.

A descriptive catalogue of the Hebrew manuscripts was prepared before the outbreak of World War II by Richard J.H. Gottheil, Abraham S. Halkin, Salo W. Baron, and Isaac Mendelsohn. It still awaits publication.

Chapter XIV

The Yeshiva University Library

"A space-age educational point to meet space-age educational needs" is Dr. Samuel Belkin's description of the Yeshiva University, which is currently celebrating its seventy-fifth anniversary. The largest Jewish university in the Diaspora, it is an extraordinary educational edifice, an unparalleled fusion of *yeshiva* and university. It sprang from a fragile seed planted by a tiny group of East European immigrants on New York's Lower East Side. This little day school *Yeshiva Etz Chayyim,* was born in 1886. The second major component of Yeshiva University was the *yeshiva* of Rabbi Isaac Elchanan, founded in 1896 for advanced study of the Talmud. A year later, on March 20, 1897, it was incorporated under the laws of the State of New York as the Rabbi Isaac Elchanan Theological Seminary.

In 1915 it merged with the *Yeshiva Etz Chayyim* and the first President, Dr. Bernard Revel (1885–1940), laid the foundations for a structure combining a high school, teacher's institute, and graduate school. Thirteen years later America's first Jewish liberal arts college was established, and thereafter developments were incredibly fast. In syllabus, in status, in physical scope, Yeshiva University continued to grow, its growth fostered by an education-conscious community. In 1954 Stern College for Women was opened, the first women's college of liberal arts and sciences under Jewish auspices. A year later the Yeshiva opened the Albert Einstein College of Medicine, America's first Jewish-sponsored medical school. In 1960 the Yeshiva University inaugurated a ten-year, thirty-million-dollar development plan, while the medical school began a similar expansion program. The Yeshiva University has 4,000 students and 850 teachers, and consists of seventeen schools and divisions. It is concentrated in six teaching centers, offering specialized courses in Bible, Talmud, physics, organic chemistry, and psychology. These necessarily bare facts outline the most extraordinary achievement on the Jewish-American scene.

The Albert Einstein College of Medicine and Stern College each has its own library. The Pollack Library holds 45,000 books dealing with the arts, sciences, psychology, history, and economics. The Edward L. Bernays Library, established in 1958 at the Graduate Center, specializes in educational public relations.

However, the main library of Judaica is that named after Mendel Gottesman (1859–1942), a treasurer of the Yeshiva University. It consists of 125,000 volumes and 600 manuscripts, and is located in the heart of Yeshiva University, at Amsterdam Avenue and 187th Street, in a building erected at a cost of $250,000 and dedicated on December 9, 1928.

Of unusual historical interest are the manuscripts of Rabbi Joseph David Sinzheim (1745–1812), first rabbi of Strasbourg and the most learned member of the Assembly of Notables convened by Napoleon. Sinzheim became chairman (*nasi*) of the Great Sanhedrin, and on March 17, 1808, he was appointed chairman of the Central Consistory. He was a prolific writer but only one of his writings, his commentary on tractate *Berakhot, Yad David,* was ever published (Offenbach, 1799). All the other manuscripts are now in the possession of the Yeshiva University Library. Among them are a 570-page autographed commentary, *Daat David,* on the *Yoreh Deah;* a volume of homiletics and dissertations on Halakhic subjects; a commentary on almost the entire Babylonian Talmud divided into four parts; *Minchat Ani,* consisting of *novellae* on Talmudic problems, written in Paris in 1810; and a 280-page book of sermons.

Many rabbinic writings rest upon the library's shelves, proof that the New World was not entirely devoid of Jewish learning in the last decades of the nineteenth century. It possesses a *hadran* (a haggadic and pilpulistic discourse delivered at the formal conclusion of a tractate) by Rabbi Eliezer Graff of Chicago, and also a work on homiletics by Rabbi Joseph Kran of Königsberg, later of Hartford, Connecticut. Another scholarly rabbi was Nechemiah Gitteleson. Born in 1851, he studdied at the *yeshivot* of Kovno and Slobodka, and came to New York in 1890. Among the twenty Gittleson manuscripts, written while he was rabbi in Cleveland, Ohio, are commentaries on the liturgy, the *Ethics of the Fathers,* the Song of Songs, and the Haphtarot.

Particularly valuable are *novellae* of Akiba ben Moses Eger (1761–1837), rabbi of Posen from 1814 until his death and the greatest Halakhic authority of his generation. The library has twenty letters written to his son Solomon (1786–1852), an opponent of Reform Judaism, and correspondence addressed to various other prominent rabbis. Another item of interest is a 42-page compilation of the eighteenth century giving the sections of the Torah according to a triennial cycle, as practiced by the Neue Synagogue in Breslau. Notes on the various Biblical passages are followed by a rota of the householders who had undertaken to provide meals for a needy *yeshiva* student one day of the week in keeping with the age-old Jewish tradition of supplying practical support to scholarship.

The library possesses some forty *pinkasim* (registers in which community events are recorded) from Posen, Waltsch (1758–1768), and Strasbourg (1879–1886), as well as a record book of the butchers' guild of Kempin, dated 1844.

A total of twenty-five collections, large and small, were merged over the years into the Yeshiva University Library. Hundreds of volumes of *responsa* originally in the library of Chayyim Fishel Epstein, at one time rabbi in St. Louis, and Moses Chayyim Rabinowicz, for many years rabbi in Brooklyn, New York, founded a fine collection on Rabbinics. Peter Wiernik (1865–1936), editor of the Yiddish daily *Morgen Journal* and author of the first comprehensive *History of the Jews in America,* published in 1912, enriched the library with historiographical books in Hebrew, English, Yiddish, German, Russian, and Polish. He was noted for his daily question-and-answer column, *Der Brief Kasten* ("The Letter Box")—hence the device of a mailbox on his bookplate.

A gift from patrons enabled the library to purchase for $3,500 the collection of Dr. Samuel Krauss (1866–1948), scholar, philologist, former lecturer at the Budapest Rabbinical Seminary (1894–1905) and the Vienna Rabbinical Seminary (1906–1938), and author of *The Archeology of the Talmud* and many other scholarly works.

From Dr. Chayyim Tchernowitz (1871–1949) the library acquired 2,000 volumes of Judaica. Tchernowitz, who wrote under the pseudonym Rav Tzair ("Young Rabbi") was professor of Talmud at the Jewish Institute of Religion in New York beginning in 1923, and became widely known as a progressive Hebrew writer. In 1939 he founded the Hebrew monthly *Bitzaron.*

Books were bought from all sources. The library acquired most of the Yiddish library of Morris Odoner (1868–1957). Born in Warsaw, Odoner was a member of the General Federation of Jewish Workers, known as the Bund, and in 1916 came to America where he found employment as an upholsterer. He saved his pennies to build up one of the greatest Yiddish collections in America. He had access to Yiddish literature produced in the Soviet Union between the two world wars. Valuable collections of Hebraica and Judaica forming the nucleus of the University Library's valuable collection of *responsa* were obtained from Rabbi Dr. Hillel (Phillip) Klein, a Hungarian scholar who was for many years rabbi of the Ohel Zeddek Synagogue in New York.

The library also benefited from gifts by its own faculty members. Among them were Nathan Klotz, professor of Bible, and Jacob Bachursky, Hebrew educator and library assistant from 1931 to 1958, both of whom contributed works of Biblical exegesis. From Jewish Cultural Reconstruction, Inc., which distributed unclaimed books salvaged in Europe after World War II, the library received 9,407 volumes, including many new books published in Poland on the eve of the war, as well as the infamous anti-Semitic collection of the virulent racist Julius Streicher.

"I want a poor student to have the same means of indulging his learned curiosity, of following his rational pursuits, of consulting the same authorities, of fathoming the most intricate enquiry, as the richest man in the kingdom," said Sir Anthony Panizzi, keeper of the British Museum, to the Royal Commission in 1836. The Yeshiva University has followed this dictum. It is fitting that the religious Jewish student, the traditional Talmid *chakham,* should find the libraries within the walls of his own Alma mater on a par with those provided by the other theological colleges. In the words of the president, Dr. Samuel Belkin, "A student who pursues his education at Yeshiva University becomes both a better Jew and a better American. He is more deeply rooted in the rich soil of his faith and he blossoms in the shining light of modern knowledge. He becomes better able to grapple with his people's problems and finds himself in a more advantageous position for serving his nation."

Chapter XV

The New York University Jewish Culture Foundation

Bordering the Greenwich Village "Bohemia" is New York University, located on Washington Square. The Jewish Culture Foundation Library is housed at the New York University's adjoining Religious Center. Though the Jewish Culture Foundation is one of the youngest institutions of its kind, it already has a library of 20,000 volumes, 140 manuscripts, and 12 incunabula, with an estimated value of over a million dollars.

Hebrew has been taught at the University since 1831, and in 1934 courses in modern Hebrew were first introduced. In 1937 the Jewish Culture Foundation was established and seven years later the chair of Hebrew culture and education was instituted, the first such faculty in any teachers' college in America. The University Bulletin announced that "the Professorship, with the University's special library of Hebraica and Judaica presented through the Jewish Culture Foundation, will provide adequate facilities for the education of teachers of modern Hebrew, the stimulation of research in Jewish Culture, and the encouragement of student interest in the field of Hebrew Culture and Education."

In 1893 John D. Prince (b. 1868), dean of the Graduate School and professor of Semitics since 1882, purchased the Oriental library of Paul Lagarde (1827–1891). This German scholar and notorious anti-Semite had achieved further notoriety by his critical researches into the Septuagint text. His library formed a unique collection of Semitics. In 1942 William Rosenthal (1881–1958) presented his father's collection of five hundred books on Hebrew language and literature, and also established an annual fund to be used for the development of the library. In the same year Mitchell M. Kaplan presented a collection of manuscripts, incunabula, and rare editions, totaling 4,000 items. A noted author and poet, Kaplan spent his life savings in collecting this library, and himself compiled and edited a *Panorama of Ancient Letters—Four and a Half Centuries of Hebraica and Judaica.* Among ancient Kaplan manuscripts is *The Wisdom of Kabbalah and Astronomy,* which begins enigmatically with the words "This is the work of a great righteous man, unknown to us," [69] and attempts to penetrate the mysteries of heaven and earth, the manifestation of God and His relation to the visible world. "Man is a type of Divinity and all parts of the human body have a symbolical significance, representing the reality of the Upper Kingdoms." There is also a fragment of a grammar (*mikhlol*) written by David Kimchi a century before the first edition was printed in Constantinople in 1532. "For the history of paper manufacture," Kaplan noted, "this fragment is of considerable interest. It is still in a primitive state on which one can notice the unbeaten interlaced fibres of the rags out of which the paper was made. The ink was of the primitive kind which contained sharp acid (vitriol) hence the burning through the paper." [70]

One of the library's documents is a letter written in 1773 by Rabbi Elijah Greiditz in a reply to a certain Jacob Pick who had asked for a rabbinical diploma. Rabbi Elijah explained that his own teacher, Rabbi Akiba Eger, had vowed not to grant rabbinical diplomas because this privilege had been abused or misused by even the best of his many disciples. Greiditz followed his master's footsteps and was not in the habit of granting diplomas. He even declined to recommend petitioners, since such recommendations would be unfair to other candidates.

Among the incunabula is *Aurea Biblica,* the Golden Bible or Repertory of Golden Books, printed at Venice in 1496. The fourteenth-century author Antonius Rumpigolis, an Augustinian monk, was lecturer on sacred theology at the universities of Genoa and Naples. His work is a dictionary on ethics and theology, treating in alphabetical sequence such qualities as abstinence, avariciousness, beatitude, chastity, confession, hypocrisy, and luxury. There are only two copies of this edition in America.

From Sidney Matz (1899–1946) New York University received a collection of Yiddish books and 2,000 Yiddish newspapers, as well as an assortment of Hebrew textbooks and dictionaries used in the schools of modern Israel.

THE RUSSIAN GENIZA

The Russian Revolution had isolated Russian Jewry long before the Iron Curtain divided the East from the West, yet Czarist Russia had rich repositories of Hebrew books and manuscripts. To that era belongs the controversial figure Abraham B. Samuel (Aben Reshef) Firkowitch. Born in the Crimean peninsula, he was obsessed with the notion that the Karaites were descended from the Ten Lost Tribes of Israel. Though his motives were above reproach, his methods certainly were reprehensible. He unearthed inscriptions in the ancient cemetery of Chufut-Kale which many authorities condemned as spurious. However, he received wide acclaim for the remarkable books and manuscripts which he collected in his wanderings through Egypt, Palestine, Turkey, and other countries.

On the recommendation of the Orientalist Daniel Chwolson (1819–1911), professor of Oriental languages at St. Petersburg, Firkowitch's first collection was purchased in 1859 by the Imperial Library of St. Petersburg, which subsequently acquired his second collection in 1876. The latter consisted of 159 scrolls on parchment, 4,933 Hebrew and 1,243 Arabic manuscripts, 344 non-Biblical manuscripts, and fourteen Hebrew Bibles whose dates range between 929 and 1121. Firkowitch was one of many notable Russian bibliophiles.

Contemporary with him was Antonin, the Russian Archimandrite who in 1860 lived at Jerusalem. One of the Geniza pathfinders, Antonin gathered 1,200 of these historic fragments. The book-loving Rothschild of Russia was David Guenzburg (1857–1910), Orientalist and civic leader whose father Horace (1833–1909) was decorated by the Czar for philanthropic work. Moses Aryeh Lob Friedland (1826–1899), for thirty years general army contractor for the Russian Government, collected 300 valuable manuscripts and 10,000 printed books, which were partially listed by Samuel Weiner in his catalogue, *Kehilat Moshe*. In 1890 he presented this library, rich in Biblical, philological, and Karaite literature, to the Asiatic Museum of the Imperial Academy of Sciences. David Maggid, author of *Toledot Mishpat*, also assembled a valuable library. His father, Noah Maggid (1829–1903), was the author of *Gan Perachim*, a biography of David Oppenheimer.

For almost four decades (1917–1956) these momentous collections, totaling 50,000 items, were completely inaccessible to scholars outside the Soviet Union. In August 1956 Dr. (Abraham I.) Katsh, chairman of the New York University's Department of Hebrew Culture and Education, visited the Soviet Union with his colleague Christian O. Arndt. Katsh, born in Poland in 1908 and son of the Chief Rabbi of Petach Tikvah in Israel, is an ardent advocate of the teaching of Hebrew in American universities.

In Leningrad he examined the Firkowitch and Antonin antiquities, and at the Oriental Institute of the Academy of Science he found the Friedland collection. In the Lenin State Library of the U.S.S.R. at Moscow, which possesses between eighteen and nineteen million volumes, he came upon the collections of Guenzburg, Maggid, and other notable collectors.

Financed by the American Council of Learned Societies and the Rockefeller Foundation, Katsh made no fewer than three return visits to Russia, in 1958, 1959, and 1960, and succeeded in recording five hundred items on microfilm. A two-part catalogue of Hebrew manuscripts preserved in the U.S.S.R., *Ginze Russiyah*, has already been published. Part I of the catalogue lists 165 microfilms and 200 selected items, and Part II lists 60 manuscripts and 335 facsimile reproductions. Many of the microfilmed manuscripts are over 1,000 years old, and among them is a twelfth- or thirteenth-century parchment of Genesis IX:2–13—a text without vowels or accents, written twelve lines to a leaf. Even older—perhaps dating to the tenth or eleventh century—is a Geniza fragment, a Tannaitic Midrash attributed to Simon ben Yochai (*fl. ca.* 130–160), one of the most prominent of the *tannaim,* reputed author of the Zohar. There are also *responsa* and kabbalistic sermons by Samuel Portaleone, physician in Mantua (d. July 29, 1612), who was licensed by Pope Gregory XIV to attend Christian patients.

Particularly noteworthy are manuscripts throwing light on Shabbethai Zevi. There is also a manuscript by Nathan Benjamin Ha-Levi Ghazzati, a Shabbethaian prophet, entitled *Apology for the Conversion of Shabbetai Zevi,* his *Messiah ben Ephraim,* and other interesting studies of Shabbethaism.

From the Oriental library of the Hungarian Academy of Science in 1961, Katsh acquired microfilm copies of the entire collection of 594 rare manuscripts gathered by David Kaufmann (1852–1899), which includes scholarly works in Arabic and Hebrew from the thirteenth and fourteenth centuries. Dr. Katsh also microfilmed the manuscript collection of the Jewish Historical Museum in Warsaw.

"Perseverance prevails even against heaven," says Rabbi Nachman in the Talmud.[71] Certainly it prevailed against the Iron Curtain, enabling Dr. Katsh to open rich new realms of research to scholars—"enough material," to use the professor's own words, "for a thousand Ph.D. theses."

Chapter XVI

The Jewish Institute of Religion

A charter granted by a special act of the legislature of the State of New York in 1922 authorized the creation of the Jewish Institute of Religion, "for the purpose of establishing and maintaining an institution to train, in liberal spirit, men and women for the Jewish ministry, research and community service . . . to advance Jewish scholarship, to establish and maintain a library and to educate and train rabbis and teachers."

The Institute opened in 1922 with fifteen students, in temporary quarters at the Community Center of Temple Israel. Shortly afterwards, it moved to its present building on West 68th Street in New York City.

The founder of the Institute, Dr. Stephen Samuel Wise, was born in Budapest on March 17, 1874. His father, Rabbi Aaron Wise, son of the Chief Rabbi of Hungary, Joseph Hirsch Weiss, emigrated to the United States in 1875 and became the spiritual leader of Temple Rodeph Shalom in New York City. Stephen Wise was educated at Oxford University in England and at Columbia University in New York. He studied under Dr. Alexander Kohut and Rabbi Gustav Gottheil, and was ordained in Vienna by Chief Rabbi Adolf Jellinek who was rabbi and preacher in Vienna.

Wise was no weathervane, to be turned this way and that way at the will and whim of lay leaders. "The pulpit must be free," was his clarion call, a conviction which disqualified him from becoming the rabbi of Temple Emanu-El, then "under Marshall Law," in the witty words of a contemporary. It was Louis Marshall (1865–1929), founder and president of the American Jewish Committee, who declared in uncompromising terms: "Dr. Wise, I must say to you at once, that the pulpit of Temple Emanu-El has always been under and is subject to the control of the Board of Trustees."

A dedicated reformer, Dr. Wise was an equally fervent Zionist and one of the early architects of the State of Israel. On July 4, 1897 he founded the first Zionist Federation in New York and a year later he journeyed to the second Zionist Congress at Basel. The militant anti-Zionist spirit of Cincinnati, the phenomenal growth of New York as the greatest Jewish center in the world, the need to provide facilities for students who found the Jewish Theological Seminary too conservative and the Yeshiva University too orthodox—these were factors that led to the establishment of the Jewish Institute of Religion.

The Jewish Institute was gradually shaped by renowned scholars from both the New and the Old World, who were members of its faculty from time to time. From England came Dr. Israel Abrahams, Schechter's successor at Cambridge and a joint editor of twenty volumes of the *Jewish Quarterly Review*. Another Englishman was the sociologist, Rabbi Harry Samuel Lewis (1863–1940), of Toynbee Hall in London. From Berlin came the liturgical historian Ismar Elbogen, lecturer at the Berlin *Lehranstalt für die Wissenschaft des Judenthums* (1902–1938) and one of the editors of *Lehren des Judenthums,* "Doctrines of Judaism," (1920–1929) of the *Jüdisches Lexikon* (1927–1930), of the *Encyclopedia Judaica* (1923–1934), and of Moses Mendelssohn's collected works (1929). Other faculty members included the American theologian and Orientalist George Foot Moore (1851–1931), the German Biblical scholar Felix Perles (1874–1933), the American Semitic scholar Charles Cutler Torrey (b. 1863) of Yale (1900–1932), and the professor of mysticism Gershon Scholem (b. 1897).

To Stephen Wise, Jewishness "meant and means a sense of oneness with our brothers in all lands and times whatever their circumstances, their faith or unfaith. Jewishness meant loyalty to historic ideas, spiritual, moral and intellectual." [72] In less than four decades the library of the Jewish Institute accumulated 77,000 books, 2,000 pamphlets, 7 incunabula, 200 manuscripts, 200 sixteenth-century printed works, and most of the tractates of the first edition of the Bomberg Talmud. Wise himself provided a nucleus of 5,000 volumes, many of which had belonged to his father. His own collection specialized in theology, homiletics, biography, psychology, and Zionism, and contained also a number of books on hellenistic literature and many of the early editions of the works of Josephus.

The Jewish Institute was strongly Hebrew-oriented. Graduate courses were conducted in modern Hebrew, and for a time one of the lecturers was David Yellin (1864–1941), founder of the Hebrew Teachers' Seminary of Palestine and the first teacher of secular Hebrew in his native Jerusalem. It is not surprising that the Institute should have built up one of the finest modern Hebrew collections in the country, whose very comprehensive array of current Israeli publications includes all the works issued by the Hebrew University of Jerusalem.

In 1923, a year after its establishment, the Institute acquired part of the library of Marcus Brann (1840–1920), the German-Jewish historian who succeeded Graetz as professor of Jewish history at the Jewish Theological Seminary in Breslau.

The fate of the Brann library hung in the balance for a considerable time. In an editorial entitled "Wanted: £400," the London *Jewish Chronicle* on June 3, 1921 made an impassioned appeal to its readers: "There is an opportunity, which the community should not let slip by, of acquiring the valuable Library of the late Professor Brann. It is a collection of books which would be of good value to Jews' College, and for that matter would be of no small use, whatever institution possessed it. Mrs. Brann asks M.100,000 for the Library of her late husband and this sum at present exchange works out at about £400. It is a trifling amount which ought easily to be forthcoming. We imagine there must be say twenty people among us who would give £20 each in order to secure for Anglo-Jewry a really important addition to its all too scanty collections of books."

Three weeks later, on June 24, 1921, the organ of Anglo-Jewry renewed its plea: "We evidently over-estimated the zeal of the community in the cause of education, but we hope that the amount needed will yet be made up by smaller sums. For it would be something of a shame if Anglo-Jewry, rich and prosperous and always boasting of its keenness in the cause of education, should allow this valuable Library to slip from its hands because our co-religionists are too indolent, or too mean, to find the paltry amount needed for its purchase. Apart from all else, it does seem to show besides that the essentially Jewish sense of securing a good bargain has in some way become dulled in our community, when a Library which, in normal circumstances, is worth some £5,000 can be obtained in consequence of the exigencies of the exchange for £400, is not at once purchased —maybe to be eagerly bought up by some German bookseller, or transferred to America."

These gloomy forebodings were soon fulfilled, and on September 9, 1921, the *Jewish Chronicle* recorded the outcome:

It is with profound regret that we have to announce that the Brann Library which we have endeavoured to secure for Jews' College has been lost to this country. That is because so many of those to whom we appealed neglected to place us into the position for availing ourselves in time of the option we had secured. Rabbi Stephen Wise of the "Free" Synagogue in New York, doubtless ascertaining that the term of our option had gone by, promptly made an offer for its purchase which was accepted. It perhaps will be an equally grievous thought to many that it has gone to an Institution designed for the propagation and maintaining that particular sort of Judaism with which Rabbi Wise is so prominently associated. To those who do not know him, we would explain that his "Judaism" is so "advanced" that its adherents look upon the teachings of

Rabbi Mattuck [Israel Isidor Mattuck, 1883–1954, leader of Liberal Judaism in England] and Mr. Claude J. G. Montefiore as reactionary."

In 1923 Dr. George Alexander Kohut moved a portion of the library of his father, Alexander Kohut, to the Jewish Institute. Through the Alexander Kohut Memorial Foundation, the Jewish Institute received a share of this literary bounty, along with Yale and the rabbinical colleges of Vienna and Budapest.

The library received a valuable collection, particularly noteworthy for its material section on Steinschneider, from the Reverend Dr. Gerson B. Levi of Chicago, who also presented the library of his father-in-law, Dr. Emil Gustav Hirsch (1852–1923). The latter was the scion of a distinguished family. His father, Samuel Hirsch, was Chief Rabbi of the grand duchy of Luxemburg. His father-in-law, David Einhorn (1809–1879), a former *illui* (prodigy of Talmudic learning) of the orthodox *yeshiva* at Fürth, Bavaria, was a pioneer of the Reform movement and rabbi of Har Sinai Temple in Baltimore. His brother-in-law was the American rabbi and Reform leader Kaufmann Kohler (1843–1926), rabbi of Temple Beth-El in New York (1879–1903) and president of the Hebrew Union College (1904–1920). Born in Luxemburg, Hirsch had come to America with his father in 1866, when the latter became rabbi of the Reform congregation Knesset Israel in Philadelphia. In 1872 he returned to Europe, where he studied at the universities of Berlin and Leipzig. He was appointed professor of rabbinic literature at the University of Chicago by William Rainey Harper, its first president (1856–1906). Hirsch was editor of the *Reform Advocate* and of the Bible section of the *Jewish Encyclopedia.* His library of 15,000 volumes was a valuable addition to the library.

Three years later the library acquired the book collection of Dr. Nechemiah Mossessohn (1853–1926), founder and editor of the *Jewish Tribune* of New York. Dr. Mossessohn was educated at the rabbinical academy of Zhitomir and also at Odessa. He emigrated to the United States in 1887 and served several congregations as Orthodox rabbi. He took his law degree at the University of Oregon and later practiced in various courts.

Among the noteworthy manuscripts are early Halakhic fragments. They include the oldest known fragments of the Midrash Hagadol on Genesis and Exodus, written in Yemen by an unknown author; a manuscript of the *novellae* of Rabbi Akiba ben Moses Eger (1761–1837) which differs considerably from the text in the published version and is probably an autograph copy; a manuscript of the Talmudical commentary of Rabbenu Gershon ben Judah of Mayence "The Light of the Exile," (960–1040) and Rabbenu Chananeel ben Chushiel (990–1050), as well as an autograph poem by Mordecai Samuel Ghirondi, Chief Rabbi of Padua. The library is the proud possessor of a musical manual by the cantor Isaac Offenbach which includes compositions sung by his son Jacques (1819–1880), composer of *The Tales of Hoffmann,* of whom Wagner wrote: "Offenbach can do what the divine Mozart did. Offenbach could have been a Mozart." The original typescript of Israel Zangwill's classic *The Children of the Ghetto* carries notes and comments in the author's hand. There is also an autographed essay on Jesus by Dr. Samuel Krauss.

In 1948, twenty-six years after its establishment, the Jewish Institute of Religion entered a new era. As a result of the work of Ralph Mack, chairman of the Hebrew Union College Board of Governors, and Rabbi James G. Heller of Cincinnati, the Institute merged with the Hebrew Union College, although the library is maintained as a separate unit with its own specialized character.

Throughout the years the Jewish Institute of Religion remained, as its founder desired, "liberal in spirit, wherein its teachers and students are not committed to any special interpretation of Judaism, and wherein the different interpretations of the literature, history and religion, the different constructions of Judaism, and of Jewish life, orthodox, liberal, radical, Zionist and non-Zionist, will be expounded to the students in courses given by men, representing these different points of view." [73]

Chapter XVII

The Hebrew Union College Library

The oldest Jewish seminary in the United States is the Hebrew Union College, and it possesses the second largest Jewish library in the country. The foremost training ground for American Reform rabbis, it is located in Cincinnati, Ohio, 755 miles southwest of New York City. Founded in 1875, its library in almost ninety years of existence has amassed over forty private collections by purchase, bequest, and donation. It now numbers approximately 160,000 books, 5,000 manuscripts, 140 incunabula, and 1,500 sixteenth-century Hebrew books (almost three-quarters of all Hebrew books known to have been printed in the sixteenth century), as well as the largest collection of Samaritan manuscripts in America. The manuscripts and the new Dalsheimer Rare Book Wing are the particular pride of the library.

In the original Hebrew Union College building the library occupied one small room. The first library building, erected through a fifty-thousand-dollar donation by the industrialist and philanthropist Isaac Wolfe Bernheim (1848–1945) of Louisville, Kentucky, was planned to hold 40,000 volumes, and was dedicated on January 22, 1913. In an address entitled "His Majesty's Opposition," Dr. Solomon Schechter, president of the Jewish Theological Seminary, spoke of his joy in "this great edifice with its commodious halls, its well-equipped library, its fine classrooms, erected to the glory of God." [74]

Eighteen years later, on May 31, 1931, the library acquired a new home, a two-story, Tudor-style structure erected at a cost of $300,000. It has a shelf capacity of 160,000 books and complete bookbinding, recording, and microfilming facilities. The library continued to expand and has since overflowed into a new building, the Klau Library, which was dedicated June 3, 1961.

THE HEBREW UNION COLLEGE

"Fate has always forced me from one fight to another, from one task to another, it never granted me any hours of recreation." These were the words of Isaac M. Wise—his own assessment of his life work. He was born at Steingrub, Bohemia in 1819, and studied under Solomon Judah Loeb Rapoport (1790–1867), from whom he received his rabbinical diploma. At the age of twenty-seven he decided to make a new life for himself in the New World, and after a voyage lasting sixty-three days he arrived in New York on July 23, 1846, with a wife, a child, and two dollars. His philosophy was already established. "To be sure, I am a reformer, as much as our age requires; because I am convinced that none can stop the stream of time nor can check the swift wheels of the age; but I have always the Halakhah for my basis and I never sanction reform against the *Din*." [75]

Wise became rabbi of the Congregation Beth-El in Albany at a salary of $250 a year. Quickly he adapted himself to the American way of life, and America became "my country," its people "my people." He once said that he was "already an American in Bohemia," for he had always had "the American fever."

When one of his members opened his store on the Sabbath, Wise was uncompromising in his attitude and harshly condemned the offender. As a result, on the eve of Rosh Hashanah the forthright rabbi was dismissed. The synagogue president forbade him to officiate, and when the rabbi proceeded to take the Torah scroll from the Ark, President Spanier struck him and knocked off his headgear. But Albany's loss was Cincinnati's gain. Wise was elected rabbi of the B'nai Jeshurun congregation of Cincinnati in April 1854, and stayed there for the remaining forty-six years of his life.

In Cincinnati Wise "Occidentalized" Jewish worship and organized the Union of American Hebrew Congregations. Wise's father had conducted a school (*cheder*) for Jewish children in Bohemia. The son's ambition was to found a college in the New World for the training of rabbis. At a meeting on July 8, 1873, presided over by Julius Freiberg, it was decided "to establish a Hebrew Theological Institute to preserve Judaism intact; to bequeath it in its purity and sublimity to posterity." Fifty-five congregations unanimously decided to establish such a college, with Wise as its first president. It opened with seventeen students on October 3, 1875, in the school room of B'nai Yisrael, at Eighth and Mound streets. In his opening address Wise, who was to guide the College for twenty-five years, declared: "The student ought to acquaint himself with science and Talmud alike, and like Rabbi Meir of old, enjoy the kernel and reject the shell."

THE ORIGIN OF THE LIBRARY

In 1875 the library consisted simply of a set of the Babylonian Talmud and Midrash *Rabbah*. Strangely enough, Sir Moses Montefiore, staunch upholder of orthodoxy in Anglo-Jewry, was one of the earliest benefactors of this temple of Reform. Like the British statesman Lord Palmerston, Sir Moses was in this instance a conservative at home and a revolutionary abroad. From London Montefiore dispatched a set of the Warsaw edition of the rabbinic Bible, *Mikraot Gedolot* (1860–1868) and in a dedication dated December 30, 1875, he wrote: "Allow me the pleasure of depositing in the library of the College to be established by the Union of American Hebrew Congregations, a copy of the Bible in five folio volumes, containing thirty-two commentaries of our most ancient and most celebrated authors, accompanied by a copy of the statutes of the regulations of the College *Ohel Moshe We' Yehoodit* in Hebrew and English, which I beg the Council of the Union will be pleased to accept and regard as a manifestation of the high esteem in which I hold the zealous exertions of our brethren in America for upholding and vindicating our holy law, as revealed on Sinai and expounded by revered Sages of the Mishnah and the Talmud." [76]

In 1879 Isaac Rubenstein published a 64-page catalogue of the books, periodicals, and pamphlets of the library. Nevertheless its scope was circumscribed and its budget limited. The Annual Report of 1881 recorded that "the sum of 50 dollars had been appropriated for books purchased by the president of the College." Apparently library management was not in very qualified hands. "In consideration of services to be rendered by the janitor in arranging the Library etc., his salary of (additional) ten dollars per month is ordered to be continued during vacation." Six months later the situation was remedied, and it was resolved "that the committee on Course of Study, Text-Books and Library, select, if necessary a competent person to arrange the Library in the new College building, and also an assistant to the Librarian, and that sixty dollars be appropriated for that purpose."

Events then began to move rapidly. In 1881, through the good offices of the Reverend A.S. Bettelheim (1830–1890), the library acquired 2,000 volumes in Hebrew, Latin, Greek, German, and English from the Reverend Henry A. Henry (1800–1879) of San Francisco, whose collection had been forty years in the making. In the same year Dr. Wise presented books that had belonged to his father-in-law, the Reverend Jonas Bondi (1804–1874) of New York.

A decade later, in 1891, the library received the collection of Dr. Samuel Adler (1809–1891), father of Felix Adler (1851–1933), professor of Hebrew and Oriental literature at Cornell University. Adler's collection consisted of 1,600 bound volumes and 300 pamphlets, and is still maintained as a separate unit. The library, at that time the only great Hebrew repository in America, received bequests with gratifying regularity. Many echoed the sentiment expressed by Jacob Ezekiel of Cincinnati, Ohio, in a letter dated May 3, 1892: "It is my desire that whatever books I may be possessed of, which are not specially wanted by my family, should be given to the Hebrew Union College."

In 1893 the trustees of Temple Emanu-El of New York presented three hundred books and two incunabula to the library. These were from the famous Almanzi collection, most of which had been donated to Columbia University and the Jewish Theological Seminary. In 1904 the library acquired 3,000 volumes and 6,000 pamphlets of great historical significance from Meyer Kayserling (1829–1905), historian and fighter for Jewish equality. It was somehow fitting that Kayserling, who had been a rabbi in Budapest and was the author of a monograph on Columbus and the Jewish participation in his voyage, should have transmitted his library to America.

Wise had once described the United States as a country where "ignorance held sway." This slur soon lost its sting. The first two decades of the twentieth century saw the publication of the *Jewish Encyclopedia* and its Hebrew counterpart, *Ozar Yisrael.* The number of scholars increased greatly, and many of them accumulated fine book collections. The Hebrew Union College Library later benefited greatly from a number of such collections. It received five hundred volumes from David Einhorn (1809–1879), the leader of Reform Judaism in Baltimore, who was known as the "abolitionist rabbi." It acquired the collection of Moses Mielziner (1828–1903), professor of Talmud at the Hebrew Union College and its acting president from 1900 to 1903. It gained books from Dr. Kaufman Kohler 1843–1926), rabbi of Temple Beth-El in New York (1879–1903), and "the most powerful intellectual force in Reform Judaism," who contributed in the neighborhood of three hundred articles to the *Jewish Encyclopedia.*

"The pilot of a ship is worth as much as all the crew," says Philo.[77] The appointment of Adolph Oko as librarian was a landmark in the library's development. Like Alexander Marx of the Jewish Theological Seminary, Oko was constantly on the watch for possible new acquisitions, and like Marx he was able to enlist the men who could make his dream come true.

"No great seat of learning has ever been established without a library," Oko maintained. He was far from satisfied with the library at his disposal and in his report of 1909 he demanded rhetorically: "Shall we lack in the apparatus of Biblical research such indispensable works for the textual criticism as Brian Walton's *Polyglot,* De Rossi's *Variae Lectiones*? I would recommend that a sum of $200 to $300 annually out of appropriations be set aside solely for the purchase of such works as those mentioned above." His plans were ambitious, and to a large extent they were realized.

TREASURES

Only a Steinschneider could do justice to the treasures of the Hebrew Union College Library. Manuscripts range over a thousand years, from the tenth century to the present day, and include Biblical codices, legal documents, communal records, scientific and pseudo-scientific tracts, and illuminated manuscripts of great artistic value.

Elaborate illuminations refute the often repeated accusation that Jews ignored the arts in the Middle Ages. A fourteenth- or fifteenth-century manuscript of the *Hagiographa,* in square characters on vellum, has the initial letter of each chapter lavishly wrought in Spanish style. At the tops and bottoms of the pages, exquisitely written in miniature Hebrew letters, is the text of the Hebrew translation by Moses ben Samuel Ibn Tibbon (1240–1283) of the *Guide of the Perplexed* by Moses Maimonides.

Many of the Haggadot are elaborate productions. The Cincinnati Haggadah, a fifteenth-century manuscript by Meir ben Jaffe consists of sixty folio pages. The Hebrew word *yaknehaz,* is a mnemonic device for the sequence of blessings to be recited when Seder night coincides with the termination of the Sabbath. The sound of the word *yaknehaz* has a remarkable similarity to that of the German words *er jagt den Has*[*en*], "he chases the hare." One illustration in the Haggadah shows a hunter brandishing a large lance while running behind his dogs over the hilly landscape in pursuit of two hares. The hunter runs, the hounds jump, and the hare tries to escape. The "wise son" is portrayed as an old man and the "wicked son" as a soldier grasping a large sword. The colophon reads: "I, Meir, the copyist, son of Israel Jaffe (honored be his repose), of Heidelberg, have produced this work, in token of esteem for R. Enechen, the Levite, of Schiffermuehl, son of Aaron the Levite. May his be long life and happiness. God grant unto him the grace to narrate herefrom the story of the Exodus from Egypt. And praise be to God in Heaven."

Particularly noteworthy is the library's collection of incunabula. Among them is a Bible printed in Naples in 1487 with a commentary by Kimchi, in which manuscript notes of exegetical character run through the entire book. The burning of the Talmud which occurred in September 1453 is mentioned as a recent event. Among the non-Hebrew incunabula is a remarkable work by Isaac ben Solomon Israeli (*ca.* 830–923), physician and philosopher. This rare book by one of the greatest physicians of the Middle Ages was one of the first medical treatises to be printed in any language.

There are miniature Hebrew books printed on vellum and many books distinguished by their highly ornate bindings. Of special interest is a first edition of the Babylonian Talmud printed by Daniel Bomberg in Venice in 1520–23. The book had at one time belonged to David Alexander Edward, Earl of Crawford (1871–1940). Clearly the nobleman was no

Talmudist, for the pages remained uncut while in his possession. Yet he refused to exchange this work for a valuable stamp collection which Elkan Adler offered in its stead. Another important book in the library's possession is *Consolations for the Tribulations of Israel,* by Samuel Usque. This sixteenth-century poet and historian, who lived first in Ferrara and then in Safed, traces the course of Jewish history over a thousand years and draws on the Bible for comfort and inspiration.

A sizable section consists of archives of the Portuguese Inquisitions from 1612 to 1748, including sermons preached at the fearful *autos da fé*. In meticulously kept ledgers, the Holy Inquisitors listed the name of each victim together with his crime and his punishment. Among these documents is a letter signed by the Archbishop of Seville in 1497, granting absolution to parishioners for the sin of eating meat or drinking wine with Jews or Moors and for attending Jewish or Moorish weddings.

Representative of some four hundred years of religious controversy is an assortment of tracts written between the fifteenth and nineteenth centuries. It contains arguments advanced by both sides of the controversy (1509–1521) in which the non-Jewish German humanist and friend of the Jews, Johann von Reuchlin (1455–1522), vigorously defended the Hebrew books which the apostate and persecutor of Jews, Johann Pfefferkorn (1469–1521), had urged the Emperor Maximilian to destroy.

Several celebrated Israelis have contributed to the library, which holds the books of storyteller Samuel Joseph Agnon (b. 1888), as well as the stamp collection of the Jewish labor leader David Remez (1886–1951), first Minister of Communications (1948–1950) and later Minister of Education (1950–1951) in the State of Israel. It received 9,753 volumes from Jewish Cultural Reconstruction, Inc., and also collection of books confiscated by the Nazis and kept at the non-Jewish library of Mannheim. After the war the authorities returned the books to the ninety survivors of this once flourishing community, and at the suggestion of Rabbi Henry Tavel, U.S. Army chaplain and graduate of the Hebrew Union College, the collection was transferred to Cincinnati.

Today, the farsighted and far-reaching words of Adolph Oko have a prophetic ring: "There shall be gathered in the Library of the Hebrew Union College collections as complete as possible of books and manuscripts and perhaps also of archaeological material of Biblical as well as of a general Jewish interest, to illustrate the life, history, and custom of the Jewish people all over the world. Indeed nothing short of this program is worthy of our institution." [78] To a high degree that hopeful prophecy has been realized.

Chapter XVIII

The Hebrew Union College Library: Special Collections

The Hebrew Union College possesses one of the greatest Spinoza collections in the world. This comprises 3,200 volumes, and in fact, is second only to that of the library at the Hague. The librarian of the Hebrew Union College, Adolph Oko, agreed with Nachum Sokolow [79] that "a man does not become a Jew by a blast of the shophar and he does not cease to be one by a blast of the shophar. Jewish existence is a matter of nature, of birth. Spinoza was a Jewish genius and only Jewish. Spinoza belongs to us and the excommunicators belong to us." Although the excommunication (*cherem*) of July 27, 1656 was never officially annulled, Baruch Spinoza (1632–1677) has long been recognized as one of the major planets in the Jewish philosophic firmament. One of the greatest poets of Germany, Heinrich Heine (1797–1856), declared with a pun on Spinoza's trade as an optical worker, that "all our modern philosophers, though often unconsciously, see through the glasses that Baruch Spinoza ground." The world has indeed endorsed that verdict.

Here, in the Spinoza collection, every aspect of the philosopher's life and literary activities is represented. Many editions of his work all available, including reprints, reissues, and translations into Latin, Dutch, English, French, Polish, and Spanish. The Galician Hebrew author, Solomon Rubin (1823–1910) whote a compendium of Spinoza's writings entitled *Moreh Nebuchim ha-Chadosh* (Vienna, 1856–1857) as well as *Cheker Eloah im Torat ha-Adam,* a Hebrew translation of Spinoza's "Ethics". The collection has first editions of the *Tractatus,* which appeared anonymously during Spinoza's lifetime, and which was placed on the *Index Librorum Prohibitorum* by the Catholic Church, and of the "Ethics" (*Ethica ordine geometrica demonstrata*), published posthumously in 1677.

In addition to biographies in many language: there is the first Hebrew work on Spinoza. *Yesod ha-Torah* by Mordecai Gumpel Leive Levisohn (d. 1797), published in Altona in 1792. The "maker of lenses" attracted not only philosophers and thinkers but also painters and sculptors. There are thus many works of art, drama, fiction, and poetry, together with periodicals and portraits, with Spinoza as their subject. Oko was not able to acquire the famous Freudenthal collection of Spinoziana, but in the course of two decades he accumulated a collection which almost surpassed it.

A DECADE OF EXPANSION

After World War I had devastated Europe, rescue operations were launched by American Jews to salvage the cultural treasures of European Jewry. Oko collected tens of thousands of dollars for this purpose, and one of his significant purchases was the Birnbaum collection. Acquired in 1918, this assembledge of 12,000 books and 3,000 manuscripts is one of the most important of its kind.

Cantor Eduard Birnbaum (1855–1920) was born in Cracow and studied music under Solomon Sulzer (1804–1890), the Austrian cantor and composer who is known as the "father of the modern cantorate." Sulzer was a professor at the Imperial Conservatorium of Vienna, a knight of the Order of Francis Joseph I, and a maestro of the Reale Accademia di St. Cecilia in Rome. His two-volume work *Shir Ziyyon* (Vienna, 1840–1865), became a source book of synagogical music. Birnbaum pursued his Jewish studies under Jellinek and under Heinrich Graetz (1817–1891), the "father of modern Jewish history." At the age of sixteen Birnbaum was asked by Graetz to serve as a *chazan* at the Breslau Jewish Theological Seminary. He held a number of cantorial positions before finally settling down in Königsberg, Prussia.

Between 1880 and 1909, the cantor wrote twenty-nine studies and articles. His *Briefe aus Königsberg, Der Jüdische Cantor* (1883-4) was written at the request of Francis Lyon Cohen of London (1862–1943), rabbi and writer on Hebrew music. It was Birnbaum's ambition to compile as his *magnum opus,* a history of Jewish music, and with this object in mind he devoted forty-five years to the acquisition of the "most copious and authentic material extant both in manuscript and in print on the development of Synagogue Music." His collection consisted of general Hebraica, books and periodicals on synagogue music, and music manuscripts. A particularly valuable work is an index of 10,000 handwritten cards listing the melodies of all synagogue songs printed or written in Europe between 1700 and 1910. It is truly a thematic thesaurus.

From a survey of the manuscripts (some of them autographed) of *chazanim* of Russia, Poland, France, and England, it is possible to piece together a picture of liturgical development in Central Europe. There is enough material here for an encyclopedia on Jewish music. Among items of interest is a book, *De Accentibus et Orthographia Linguae Hebraicae* (Hagenau, 1518), by Johann von Reuchlin, in which Hebrew musical notations are recorded. Of historical interest is the story of the Italian scholar, poet, and rabbi Leon (Judah Aryeh) of Modena (1571–1648). Leon engaged in no less that twenty-six professions (preacher, teacher, proofreader, notary, and bookseller, among others) and was also addicted to gambling. Acting on the principle that attack is the best form of defense, he wrote a learned polemic rebuking the community for censuring him. On *Shemini Azeret* and *Simchat Torah* in the year 1628 Leon officiated with two choirs, singing figural music accompanied by an organ.

Another notable manuscript is one written in 1791 by the cantor and musician Aaron Baer. It includes 447 numbers, arranged for fifty-three Sabbaths of the year and for the festivals. Baer explains on the title page: "If a person hear a tune but once a year, it will be impossible for him to sing with the Cantor during the Service and therefore he will not be able to confuse the *chazanim*. It has become a plague to the *chazanim* to have the members of the Congregation join the song."

The library was certainly fortunate in its acquisitions of musical works. Before the advent of the Birnbaum collection it had received from Hugo Steiner of Baltimore some six hundred books and sheets of synagogue music collected by Alois Kaiser, cantor of Eutaw Place Temple in Baltimore.

"The Temple of Music is adjacent to the Temple of Learning": in this mystic belief the library apparently shared. Through the generosity of Marcus Aaron of Pittsburgh, who gave $10,000 in memory of his father Louis Aaron, it acquired the magnificent Library of Dr. Aron Freimann of Frankfurt-on-Main. Freimann (1871–1933), grandson of one of the leaders of modern Orthodoxy, Jacob Ettinger (1798–1871), Chief Rabbi of Altona and teacher of Rabbi Samson Raphael Hirsch, was heir to a great tradition. He himself studied archival and library administration, as well as history and Oriental languages. In 1897 he was appointed to the *Stadtbibliotek* in Frankfurt-on-Main, and three years later became one of the editors of the *Zeitschrift für Hebraische Bibliographie*. His personal library consisted of 7,000 volumes and pamphlets, 33 Hebrew incunabula, and copies of more than half of all Hebrew books printed in the sixteenth century, as well as monographs of *Jüdische Wissenschaft* in Hebrew, Latin, French and German privately printed between 1890 and 1920.

Like the Jewish Theological Seminary of America, the Hebrew Union College is indebted to Anglo-Jewish bibliophiles for many of its acquisitions. In 1913 the Reverend Isidor Lewinthal of Nashville presented thirty-two volumes of the London *Jewish Chronicle* (1880–1912), a gift which was highly prized. In his annual report for 1913 the librarian said: "Had they been offered for sale, we should not have hesitated to pay five dollars per volume."

Although Israel Solomons had sold his main collection to the Jewish Theological Seminary, his home was never bare of books. After his death in 1923, the residue of his library was acquired by the Hebrew Union College. Though this collection cannot either qualitatively or quantitatively match the Seminary's acquisitions, it contains a number of items particularly interesting to the student of Anglo-Jewry. Among these are the original minute books of the Jews' Hospital in London, established by the Spanish and Portuguese in 1747. The minutes cover the period 1758 to 1779 and list the names of Sephardi families who have long since disappeared from the Anglo-Jewish scene. There are many autographed letters, including one from Isaac D'Israeli (1776–1848), father of Lord Beaconsfield, who had his children baptized at the church of St. Andrew, Holborn in London. There are also series of caricatures of English Jews of the eighteenth and nineteenth centuries and of bookplates owned by Anglo-Jewish bibliophiles. Solomons was deeply interested in historical research. In an alphabetical box file he indexed the family tree of most of the Anglo-Jewish families who had come to England in the seventeenth century.

Among important manuscripts acquired by the library was that of the *Pachad Yizchak* (an encyclopedia covering the entire field of rabbinic scholarship) by Isaac ben Samuel Lampronti (1679–1756), which had once belonged to Samuel Hirsch Margulies (1858–1922), Chief Rabbi of Florence, principal of the Collegio Rabbinico Italiano, and founder of the periodical *Revista Israelitica.* The library also acquired many important books and manuscripts from Elkan Adler, and a 300-volume collection of the Mishnah *Ethics of the Fathers* from S. Rehfisch (d. 1924), the official interpreter of Yiddish at the Whitechapel County Court in London.

THE CHINESE MANUSCRIPTS

Of unusual significance are fifty-nine manuscripts which relate to the ancient Jewish community of China. The origin of this community is veiled in obscurity. An *Account Written by Two Mohammedan Travelers Through India and China* in 851 states that the "Jews have been settled in China from time immemorial . . . and many of them for the sake of riches and preferment have abjured their own religion." The Jewish settlement has been associated not only with the Ten Lost Tribes but even with the Babylonian captivity of 586 B.C. The allusion in Isaiah XLIX: 12—"Behold, these shall come from far: and lo, these from the north and from the west and these from the land of Sinim"—probably pointed to China.

The Chinese called the Jews *Tiao-chin chiao* "a religious group that removes the sinew"—a reference to the Biblical prohibition in Genesis XXXII:33. At the time of the Emperor Hias-Tsung (1163–1190) seventy Jewish families were settled in China. Marco Polo at the end of the thirteenth century testified to the important role of the Jews in Cathay.

Kai-Fung-Foo is one of the ancient cities of China. Built on the Hoang (The Yellow River), it is the capital of the central province of Honan. The synagogue in Kai-Fung-Foo was erected in 1163 and was rebuilt on a larger scale in 1279. Its construction was after the fashion of King Solomon's Temple. It was 400 feet long and 154 feet wide. An inscription on one of the stiles, dated 1512, refers to the Most High as *Toa.* On another stile the inscription reads in part: "Our first ancestor was Adam, our religion was founded by Abraham, afterwards Moses came who was the mediator of the Holy Scripture. At the time of the Han Dynasty (200 B.C. to 200 C.E.) this religion was introduced in China." But "China's Sorrow," as the Yellow River was commonly called, continuously overflowed its banks and the synagogue was destroyed three times.

Christian missionaries, among them Matteo Ricci of Peking (1552–1610) and Jules Aleni (1582–1649), who was "so uncommonly wise that the Chinese called him 'the Confucius of Europe,'" were the first to describe this small, scattered, and distinctive community.[80] A century later Jean-Paul Gozani (1647–1732) of the Society of Jesus made a brief study of the community and left an illuminating report.

> I visited them in their *Li-pai-ssu* or Synagogue, [he writes]. I saw their inscriptions, some of which are in Chinese, and the rest in their own language. They showed me their *Ching,* or religious books, and permitted me to go into the most sacred place of their synagogue, which they themselves are not allowed to enter. This place is reserved solely for their *Chang Chiao* or Ruler of the Synagogue, who never goes into it but with the most profound reverence.
>
> These books were written on long pieces of parchment and rolled round sticks. I prevailed with the Ruler of the synagogue to let the curtains of one of the tabernacles be undrawn, and get one of the parchment books unfolded. It seemed to be written in a very clear and distinct character. . . . It is not surprising that whenever they read the Bible in their synagogues, they cover their faces with a transparent veil, in memory of Moses who came down from the mountain with his face covered and thus promulgated the Decalogue and the Laws of God to his people.[81]

There is a letter in the British Museum[82] written in 1760 by the *Chakham*

David Nieto, to the Chinese Jewish community, imploring them to give information on their origin and their needs. In 1842, when the Treaty of Nanking was concluded, James Finn, afterwards British consul in Jerusalem, and a student of Jewish history, addressed a letter to the Chinese Jews. By a series of accidents the reply was delayed for twenty-six years. In his book *The Orphan Colony of Jews in China* (1872) he gives the text of his letter and of the reply: "Daily with tears in our eyes we call on the Holy Name; if we could but again procure Ministers to put our house of prayer in order, our religion would have a firm support."

A new chapter was added to this story in 1849, when George Smith was appointed bishop of Victoria, in Hong Kong, and was requested by the London Society for Promoting Christianity amongst the Jews to enquire into the conditions of the Jews at Kai-Fung-Foo. On November 15, 1850, armed with a letter in Hebrew, written by an employee of Sassoon and Company at Canton, two Chinese missionaries, Chiu Tion Sheng from Batavia and Chiang Jung Chi, set out from Shanghai, and after a journey of twenty-one days they finally reached the community. They found the Jews greatly reduced in numbers and circumstances—probably there were no more than two hundred individuals in all. They had had no rabbi for fifty years and "there is not one of the profession of Judaism in the present day in Kai-Fung-Foo who can read one word of Hebrew." In the words of the Bishop, "Here in the midst of the surrounding population, two-thirds of whom were Mohammedans, close to a heathen temple dedicated to the god of fire, were found a few Jewish families, sunk in the lowest poverty and destitution—their religion scarcely more than a name and yet sufficient to separate them from the multitude around. Exposed to reproach and the pain of long deferred hope, they remained the anxious repository of the oracle of God. They were hoping that the Emperor would have pity on them and build up their Synagogue." [83]

Out of a subsidy amounting to three hundred and fifty pounds which has been provided by Miss Jane Cook of Cheltenham, England, the missionaries bought a number of manuscripts, which were preserved at the Museum of the London Society for Promoting Christianity amongst the Jews at Lincoln's Inn Fields. In January 1924 Adolph Oko, the librarian of the Hebrew Union College, purchased fifty-nine of these for that institution at a price of one thousand pounds.

These manuscripts were written in large, clear Hebrew characters in the blackest of ink. Evidently they had been damaged in floods, for in many places the writing was washed away and the pages still show water stains. They consist of passages from the Torah prescribed for weekly readings in the synagogue, and strangely enough are supplied with vowels. Individuals of the community paid for the writing of some of these manuscripts. "So-and-so has donated it" is a notation that occurs frequently. The names on the manuscripts are partly in Hebrew and partly in late Judeo-Persian. The Sabbath prayers are partly vocalized. Other prayers for the Sabbath give the formula for announcing the new moon, with the days of the week in Syriac and the names of the months in Hebrew. Part of a colophon reads, "From an offering of Abraham, the son of Gamaliel."

There are also prayers for the Ninth of Av, for the New Year, and for the Day of Atonement. Another manuscript, entitled "The Hundred Blessings," lists all the benedictions which it is possible to recite in the course of one day. There are Haggadot with translations and directions in Persian, an indication that the Chinese Jews were probably indebted for their liturgy to the Jews of Persia.

The Genealogical Register, a 106-page codex in Hebrew and Chinese scripts, covering the period from 1660 to 1676, lists the names of 453 men and 259 women in both Hebrew and Chinese. It is noteworthy that the terms *shelliach* (messenger), *sopher* (scribe), and *melamed* (teacher) are found, but not *rabbi* or *chazan*.

"I asked the *shamash* whether I could obtain a volume of the Mishnah," wrote Isaac M. Wise, founder of the Hebrew Union College, describing his experiences in a New York synagogue in 1846. "That individual laughed so mockingly that I readily perceived what a sign of 'greenness' it was on my part to ask for an ancient Hebrew book in the New World." Today it is no longer a sign of greenness. Enlightened principles and assiduous librarians have made the library of the Hebrew Union College one of the largest and most important of its kind in the United States.

"We are a liberal institution of higher learning in Judaism," said its president, Dr. Nelson Glueck. "Nothing in the Jewish past or present is alien to our interests . . . It is a Judaism rooted in history, buttressed by tradition, freely interpretable by the fully informed, rich in promise to the faithful, dedicated to the blessed unity of the all embracing love of one God, the God, of Israel, the God of mankind, the God of the Universe."

Chapter XIX

Dropsie College

In his last will and testament, dated September 17, 1895, Moses Aaron Dropsie provided for the establishment and maintenance in the city of Philadelphia of "a college for the promotion of and instruction in the Hebrew and Cognate languages and their respective literatures". He stipulated that the college was to be open to all students without restriction as to creed, color, or sex. The entire Dropsie estate, valued at nearly one million dollars, was devoted to this institution.

Moses Dropsie (1821–1905) was one of the pioneers of the Street Railway of Philadelphia and head of the engineering company which built one of the bridges across the Schuylkill River. Child of a Jewish father and a Christian mother, young Moses decided at the age of fourteen to live a Jewish life. He became a devout Jew who castigated Reform Judaism as "Deform Judaism". When Maimonides College was founded in Philadelphia in 1867 for the training of rabbis, teachers and educated laymen, Dropsie was appointed its president, a position he filled until it closed in 1873.

The first meeting of Dropsie's executors took place in Washington, in the office of Oscar Solomon Strauss (1850–1926), who in 1909–10 was United States Secretary of Commerce and Labor. Possibly this was the first time that the initial steps towards the organization of a college had been taken in the office of a member of the Presidential Cabinet. The College was designed and built by William Tachin in an adaptation of the style of the period of Louis XVI. And so the new college became a neighbor of Mikveh Israel Synagogue and Gratz College at the junction of Broad and York streets.

Dropsie College was opened in 1909 under the presidency of Cyrus Adler (1863–1940), who had been the first student to receive a Ph.D. degree in Semitics from The Johns Hopkins University. Adler had a background of scholarly achievement. In 1887 he was assistant curator in the Department of Oriental Antiquities of the U.S. National Museum in Washington, and in 1889 he became custodian of its Division of Historic

Religious Ceremonials. The Smithsonian Institution had sponsored his travels to the Near East to prepare the Oriental exhibits for the World's Columbian Exhibition at Chicago in 1893. Up until 1908 Adler was engaged in developing the departments of Historic Archaeology and Historic Religion at the National Museum. From then on for thirty formative years, he devoted himself wholeheartedly to Dropsie College.

Philadelphia, "the city of brotherly love," with a community of 331,000 Jews, is only ninety-six miles from New York. In this home of a hundred synagogues and of the Jewish Publication Society of America, Dropsie College soon began to play a leading role. It has received acclaim for its School of Education, its Institute for Israel and the Middle East (founded in October 1948), its New York Branch, its *Jewish Quarterly Review,* and its fine library.

Today its collection numbers almost 70,000 books of Hebraica, Biblical literature, philosophy, theology, Kabbalah, and Jewish history; 256 manuscripts in Arabic, Ethiopic, Hebrew, Samaritan, Coptic, Persian, Sanscrit, and Turkish; 32 incunabula, 450 Geniza fragments, and 290 sixteenth-century printed books.

The development of a good library was one of Adler's major projects. He declared in 1913, "The Library we hope to make the most important upon the Biblical side. We recognize the great importance of rabbinical studies, Oriental philosophy, history and other contributing subjects, but it is the Bible, its text, its translations, its meaning, its study from every point of view that it is our natural duty to promote."

During his tenure of office he extended these carefully defined boundaries and himself presented 2,000 volumes of diversified content, as well as a number of Geniza fragments. Though Philadelphia is extraordinarily rich in libraries (especially notable being those of Gratz College, and the University of Pennsylvania, and the Free Library of Philadelphia), Adler felt that his college would be incomplete without adequate literary resources of its own.

On December 23, 1912, Dropsie received the library of Isaac Leeser (1806–1868). Leeser, born at Neuenkirchen in the Prussian province of Westphalia, emigrated to America at the age of eighteen and worked as a clerk in his uncle's counting room at Richmond, Virginia. An article in an obscure paper, the *Richmond Whig,* made his reputation as an educationalist. He became *chazan* of the Mixveh Israel Congregation in Philadelphia. In a letter to Chief Rabbi Solomon Hirschell of London, Leeser wrote with humility, "Knowing my own want of proper qualification, I would never have consented to serve, if others more fitting in point of standing, information, or other qualities had been there; but this is not being the case (as is proved by there being yet two congregations at least in this country without a regular *chazan*), I consented to serve."

Leeser's influence made itself felt outside his own community. In 1838 he issued *The Hebrew Reader; Hebrew and English, Designed as an Easy Guide to the Hebrew Tongue for Jewish Children and Self Instruction.* This book was inspired by Miss Rebecca Gratz (1781–1869), founder of the American Jewish Sunday school movement, and the prototype for Sir Walter Scott's Rebecca, heroine of *Ivanhoe.* "This little book owes its origin", acknowledges the author, "to the promise I made to a valued friend to print for the sake of the school which she has lately commenced, a Hebrew spelling book, in order to contribute the little that lies within my power to aid her in the laudable endeavors of disseminating knowledge of the ancient language of Israel among the youth of our people." A year later, in 1839, Leeser printed at his own expense his *Catechism for Younger Children. Designed as a Familiar Exposition of the Jewish Religion which ye shall command your children to observe to do all the words of this law.*

In 1843 he became the editor of a monthly magazine, *The Occident,* the first Anglo-Jewish periodical in America. When Maimonides College was opened on October 28, 1867, Leeser became its provost and professor of homiletics. He bequeathed his library to Maimonides College, and later it was used by the Young Men's Hebrew Educational Association. Eventually the executors of Leeser's will, Mayer Sulzberger and William B. Hackenburg, deposited the library with Dropsie College, and Syrus Adler compiled a catalogue.

"He who gives and wishes others to give is a saint," says the Mishnah.[84] Sulzberger fulfilled both qualifications. When he died on April 20, 1923, he bequeathed to Dropsie a small fortune in money as well as a major fortune in bibliographic items—7,000 volumes and 20 incunabula from his library. A collection of cuneiform tablets and Assyrian seals, secured by Dr. Ephraim Avigdor Speiser (b. 1902) in the excavations of Tepe Gawra near Baghdad, was the donor's share of the findings of an archaeological expedition sponsored jointly by Dropsie and the University of Pennsylvania. Later this collection was augmented by the brothers Howard and Lionel Levy, who presented a stone block from the third wall of Jerusalem. In 1923 Dropsie College acquired one thousand Himyaritic and Sabean books collected by Eduard Glaser (1855–1908), the well known Arabian traveler during an expedition to Arabia in 1883–1894.

Many scholarly benefactors left their mark upon the library. Among them was Henry Malter (1867–1925). He was born in Banse near Zabno, Galicia, and studied at Heidelberg. In 1899, on the suggestion of Steinschneider, he catalogued the rare books and manuscripts of the well-known book collector Fischel Hirsch. A year later Malter became the librarian of the Communal Library in Berlin. In 1900 he accepted the position of instructor of Mediaeval philosophy and Arabic at the Hebrew Union College. However, he found the atmosphere in Cincinnati uncongenial, for he could tolerate neither anti-Zionist nor Reformist doctrines. In 1909 he became professor of rabbinic literature at Dropsie, a post which he held until his death, and some of his cherished books were bequeathed to the library.

Another benefactor was Solomon Leon Skoss (1844–1953), professor of Arabic at Dropsie from 1925 to 1953. Skoss, a native of Chosovaya, Russia, spent the years 1922–1925 in Egypt on a Dropsie Fellowship. He also obtained photostatic copies of Judeo-Arabic manuscripts in the Soviet Union.

The Biblical Lecture Room was enriched by the books of Max Leopold Margolis (1866–1932), whom William Foxwell Albright, professor of semitic languages at The Johns Hopkins University, called "the world's greatest living authority on Biblical texts." Margolis, author of *The Book of Joshua in Greek, The Hebrew Scriptures in the Making,* and *The Story of Bible Translations,* collaborated with Alexander Marx in the writing of *A History of the Jewish People.* Born in Meretz, Vilna, Margolis was a descendant of the Talmudist Yom-Tov Lipmann Heller (1579–1654). He studied first in Berlin, and then at Columbia University under Professor Gottheil. In 1892 he joined the staff of the Hebrew Union College.

As early as 1903 Margolis had declared that Zionism was essential to counteract "the dangers of assimilation, the absolute cosmopolitanism of denationalized Judaism and the belated imitation of Christianizing sects." [85] In a sermon entitled "The Message of Moses" he expressed the view that Judaism would languish and die without a center of its own. "*The Lord, God of Israel,* and *Israel, the people of the Lord,* are", he explained, "correlative terms." These views were constantly reiterated and underscored. "There have been at all times Palestinian Jews and Dispersion Jews, National Jews and International Jews," wrote Margolis. "Just because everywhere else the Jews must form a minority, we Zionists clamor for the one land where the Jews may constitute the majority and where alone a full national life becomes possible." [86]

It is not surprising that such doctrines aroused the ire of Kaufmann Kohler, president of the Hebrew Union College, who believed that "Zionism perverts history and rejects divine providence, can claim no share in the working out of a theological system of Judaism, certainly not of Reform Judaism in America." [87] Margolis followed the Malter pattern. He, too, left the Hebrew Union College, and from 1909 to 1925 served as professor of Biblical philosophy at Dropsie. The library inherited some of his books.

Many valuable volumes were received in 1954: a rich assortment of *responsa* from M. L. Gittelson for the establishment of the Nechemiah Gittelson Library of Rabbinics, as well as 1,000 volumes of rare items of rabbinics and Haskalah from the Jewish Reconstruction, Inc., including one incunabulum, David Kimchi's commentary on the later Prophets, printed in 1486.

GENIZA FRAGMENTS

Dropsie owns a unique array of Geniza fragments. Their nucleus was the collection acquired by Cyrus Adler when he visited Egypt in 1891, five years before Schechter. This was augmented by Dr. Henry Friedenwald (1870–1944), first secretary of the American Jewish Historical Society (1892–1914) and editor of *The American Jewish Year Book* (1903–1913). Dropsie then purchased the collections of Professors David Werner Amram and Camden M. Cobern. In 1924 Benzion Halper (1884–1924) compiled his *Descriptive Catalogue of the Geniza fragments in Philadelphia,* which shows that the Dropsie fragments are particularly rich in Halakhah and Liturgy, and in which 150 *piyyutim* are minutely described.

Of special interest are six *responsa* in Arabic and part of Chefes ben Yasliach's *Book of Precepts.* In one *responsum* the questioner asks whether it is permissible to rescue from prison a Jew who has confessed to murder and has been sentenced to death by a non-Jewish court. The affirmative reply stresses that it is the duty of every Jew to rescue such a man by all possible means. An autographed *responsum* of Abraham ben Moses Maimuni (1186–1237), son of Maimonides, answers a complex question. A man named Reuben had a wife who owned half a dwelling valued at six dinars, but Reuben had pledged it to a creditor. Should the wife pay the debt after the demise of her husband?

Of even greater antiquity is part of a Hebrew letter addressed by Saadia Gaon to three of his students in Fustat concerning the calendar of the year 233 of the Moslem era. The Gaon yearned for his disciples and complained that he had received no word from them for six and a half years, although he had written them a letter of condolence on the death of their grandfather.

A number of legal documents in Judeo-Arabic throw light on twelfth-century legislation in the court of Masliach ha-Kohen (Fustat, 1127–1148). One such document from Fustat is dated *Tammuz* 1475, then under the jurisdiction of the Great Prince Daniel, Exilarch of all Israel, who is probably the Exilarch of Baghdad mentioned by the famous twelfth-century traveler Benjamin of Tudela.

On May 22, 1959, Dropsie College celebrated its semi-centennial. President Abraham Aaron Neumann (b. 1890) declared: "As we gaze back upon the fifty years of existence of the College, we behold Dropsie's faith gloriously vindicated. The record of our alumni drawn literally from all parts of the world . . . the faith which inspired the founders of the *Jüdische Wissenschaft* is the basic philosophy of the work of Dropsie College."

Chapter XX

The Hebraic Traditions at Cambridge, Massachusetts

"Hebraic mortar cemented the foundations of American democracy," is an aphorism that might well be applied to the oldest university in the United States, Harvard, at Cambridge, Massachusetts. Its library consists of some ninety special collections with an aggregate of 6,900,000 books. Among them is a fine division of Hebraica and Judaica numbering 25,000 volumes and 28 incunabula.

In the seventeenth century the soil of Massachusetts, "the Jerusalem of this land," was a fertile one for Hebrew studies. The foundations of the Harvard Library were laid in 1638 by a legacy from the Reverend John Harvard (1607–1638), Master of Arts of Emmanuel College, Cambridge, England. Harvard, who settled in Charlestown, Massachusetts, in 1637, left his library and half of his estate, valued at about £800, to the newly founded college at "New Towne," later to be called Cambridge. Nearly three-quarters of Harvard's collection consisted of Biblical commentaries.

The Code of Laws drawn up by the first president of the College, Henry Dunster (1609–1659), decreed that "every scholar that on proof is found able to read the original of the Old and the New Testament and Latin tongue, being of honest life and conversation may be invested with his first degree." The college rules of 1655 stated "that all students shall read the Old Testament in some part of it out of Hebrew into Greek except the freshmen who shall read it out of English into Greek." [88]

Dunster himself was a distinguished Hebraist. At eight o'clock in the morning he lectured to freshmen on Hebrew grammar; at nine he lectured to second-year students on Aramaic, and at ten he lectured to third-year men on Syriac. A Hebrew Bible with Dunster's name inscribed in Hebrew characters is now a treasured possession of the Harvard Library.

Harvard's Hebrew tradition remained unbroken. John Lightfoot (1602–1675), an English Hebraist and rabbinical scholar, Vice-Chancellor of Cambridge University in England, and author of *Horae Hebraicae et Talmudicae* (five volumes, 1658–1674), who died in 1675, left his Oriental books to Harvard. Equally learned was Cotton Mather (1663–1728), who in 1689 wrote a thesis entitled *All the Hebrew letters may be found in one verse of Isaiah, Chapter V:25*. Mather, who frequently quoted rabbinical sayings in his diaries, maintained that the vowel points of the Bible were of divine origin.

Yet despite this keen interest in Hebraic studies, the growth of the Library's Hebraica was slow. The first printed catalogue, issued in 1723, listed a total of 3,516 books, of which 99 were in Hebrew and Oriental languages. This collection was so inadequate that at a meeting on May 7, 1746, the treasurers decided to obtain from England "50 Hebrew Psalters of Dr. Jan Leusden, *viz.* Hebrew and Latin, a good edition, well bound but plain."

It was in Harvard that the star of Judah Monis (1683–1764) rose. He was born either in Algiers or in Italy, and studied in Leghorn and Amsterdam. When he came to the United States in 1715 he made his living in a variety of ways, which included selling nails, iron, leather, pipes, tobacco, and hinges to Harvard. In 1720 Monis became the first student of Jewish birth to receive a degree at Harvard. On March 22, 1722, he converted to Christianity, in the College Hall at Cambridge, although he continued throughout his lifetime to observe the Seventh Day as the Sabbath. "God has not only taken Moses' veil from me," Monis maintained, "but has placed me in his Service, i.e. to teach and promote the knowledge of the Hebrew tongue at Harvard College, in New England especially for the advantage of those that will dedicate themselves to the Service of the Sanctuary." [89] For nearly four decades (1722–1760) Monis taught Hebrew to Harvard collegiates, and the annual salary of £50 voted him on April 30, 1722, rose in 1739 to £120. In 1735 he published *Dickdoog leshon gnebreet. (A Grammar of the Hebrew tongue, being an essay to bring the Hebrew Grammar into English, to facilitate the instruction of all those who are desirous of acquiring a clear idea of this primitive tongue by their own studies).*

Monis was truly well read and learned in Kabbalah and Rabbinics, and when in 1760 he resigned his office, he was to be remembered in the annals of American History as the first Hebrew teacher and grammarian in the United States. From Monis the Library received a number of Hebrew and Kabbalistic works, many of which he used for the preparation of his grammar.

The year 1764 was a dual milestone in the history of Harvard; it marked the establishment of the Hancock professorship of Hebrew and Oriental languages by Thomas Hancock (1703–1764), and the destruction by fire, on January 24, of the major part of the library. All but 404 of the books that had been accumulated for 125 years were destroyed. Of John Harvard's own books only one was saved. The whole library of Dr. Lightfoot, which at his death he bequeathed to the College and contained "Targumim, Talmudim, Polyglots and other valuable tracts relating to Oriental literature" —all went up in flames.

The nineteenth century was a period of prolonged inactivity so far as the restoration of the Hebrew collection was concerned. In 1911 the Harvard Library absorbed the Andover Theological Seminary Library, which included a large number of Hebrew books. In November 1898 Leo Wiener (1862–1939), philologist and professor of Slavic languages, presented 325 books and 1,100 pamphlets, which had served as source material for his *History of Yiddish Literature in the 19th Century.* Wiener had visited Russia and Poland in search of material, and Albert Harkavy (1839–1919), chief of the Semitic department of the Imperial Public Library of St. Petersburg, had given him many items. "Who wants such rubbish?" said Harkavy to Wiener, who was quick to accept the costly gifts so casually bestowed.

Later, through the *Jewish Daily Forward,* the New York Yiddish newspaper, and the Harvard Yiddish Book Fund Committee, as well as through the efforts of Dr. A.A. Roback (b. 1890), a psychologist and author, who was a Harvard instructor, a fine collection of Yiddish books was developed. Among them is a Yiddish version of parts of the Prophets, printed at Constance in 1544, only twenty years after Martin Luther's translation of the Bible into German. There is also a little book by the writer Levitan, published in Vilna in 1892, which tells of queer constructions and events. It describes a building erected in Minneapolis consisting of twenty-eight stories "built on top of one another," with "two steam machines" to go up and down and two staircases in the event of the "steam machines" ' getting out of order. A translation into Yiddish of Sir Walter Scott's *Ivanhoe* was made by Balbine Klattschke, wife of a pious rabbi at Yanipol on the Dniester. The Yiddish version of Shakespeare's *Othello,* published in 1895, bears an interesting introduction to "the admirable performance which the world-famous philosopher [*sic*] Shakespeare wrote with his wonderful pen. There is no modern language in which the wonderful tale has not been translated and now we have translated it with many improvements in jargon. We saw how their eyes became red from tears. A great chill had penetrated their bones. One scientific lady languished listening to it."

The twentieth century saw new developments in the growth of Harvard's Hebraic collection. In 1926 Leon N. Alberts presented 350 Hebrew books left by his father, Z. Alberts (1850–1925), a Hebrew teacher in Boston. Three years later the merchant and philanthropist Julius Rosenwald (1862–1932), head of Sears, Roebuck & Co., in New York, bought 3,000 books consisting of Rabbinica, works in modern Hebrew, and rare periodicals, which he presented to Harvard in honor of Julian William Mack (1866–1943), the jurist and Zionist leader.

In 1929 The Harvard Library had its *annus mirabilis*. In November of that year the glove manufacturer Lucius Littauer (1859–1944) came to Cambridge to attend the Yale–Harvard football match. A graduate of Harvard himself, he had endowed a chair of Jewish literature and philosophy under Dr. Harry Austryn Wolfson (b. 1887). Wolfson told Littauer that Deinard's library was for sale—a collection comprising 12,200 books, 29 manuscripts, and 15 incunabula, as well as 368 books printed in the sixteenth century. Accompanied by Alexander Marx, librarian of the Jewish Theological Seminary of America, Littauer at once set out for New Orleans, where he speedily concluded the purchase. In January 1930 the Deinard collection arrived at Harvard, packed in seventy-four cartons.

Littauer continued to serve as Harvard's benefactor. In 1935 he donated two million dollars for a graduate school of public administration, and two years later, when he presented $10,000 to the Jewish Theological Seminary, he stipulated that all duplicates of the books in Rabbi H.G. Enelow's collection should be presented to Harvard. Thus Harvard acquired another 3,000 volumes of Hebraica.

Attorney Lee M. Friedman (1871–1957), another Harvard graduate, collected donations from 287 people and bought the valuable library of Felix Friedman of Amsterdam. It consisted of 4,000 books, 7 incunabula, 37 manuscripts, and 800 books printed before 1800. A Heine collection consisting of over 1,000 items accumulated by Salli Kirschstein (1869–1934), was presented on May 28, 1935 by James Loeb (1867–1933), brother-in-law of Jacob Schiff and founder of the Loeb Classical Library.

Harvard's Semitic Museum was opened on February 5, 1903, as a direct result of Schiff's donation of $273,000. "The standards of life which I have laid down for myself tell me that the satisfaction one gets from the endeavors to be helpful to one's fellow through altruistic action should be a sufficient reward," wrote Schiff. The Museum contains tiles used by the Tenth Legion stationed in Jerusalem in 70 C.E., as well as skin bottles dating to the first century.

On the gates at the entrance to Harvard Yard are engraved the aims that Harvard has pursued for three hundred years: "To advance learning and perpetuate it to Posterity, dreading to leave an illiterate Ministry to the Churches when our present Ministers shall lie in the Dust." Harvard's Hebraica have richly contributed to this advancement and perpetuation of learning.

Chapter XXI

The Yale University Library, New Haven

Urim VeTummim ("The Lights and the Perfections") were objects used by the High Priest for divination until the destruction of the First Temple. These Hebrew words together with a free translation into Latin *Lux et Veritas,* jointly form the motto in the emblem of Yale University, third oldest institution of higher learning in the United States.

New Haven, Connecticut, seventy-three miles northeast of New York, a city noted for its diversified industry, is the setting for this "Ivy League" university, highly reminiscent in its atmosphere and its gothic architecture of Oxford and Cambridge. The main library, designed by James Gamble Rogers, culminates in a stack tower 150 feet high, "a combination of sky-scraper and a cathedral cloister," and houses 4,205,000 books. The Hebrew collection totals 19,000 volumes, 145 manuscripts, and 31 incunabula.

In 1701, in the house of the Reverend Samuel Russell at Branford near New Haven, a total of forty folio volumes were placed on a table by eleven ministers of religion, each of whom in return declared: "I give these books for the founding of a college in this colony." This was the birth of Yale. One of these natal gifts was a book by the historian and Jewish apologist Flavius Josephus.

In 1733 George Berkeley (1685–1757), dean of Derry and later bishop of Cloyne, presented a thousand volumes which were at that time, in the words of Thomas Clap (1703–1767), president of Yale from 1739 to 1766, "the finest that ever came together at one time in America." The eight cases in which the collection was packed contained a number of volumes of Judaica, including, in addition to Bibles and lexicons, *The History of the Jews* (London, 1708) by Jacques Basnage de Beauval, and Humphrey Prideaux's *The Old and the New Testament connected in the History of the Jews and Neighboring Nations,* published in 1716–18.

In 1743 Yale's Orientalia were listed in a printed catalogue under such headings as "Hebraica and Chaldea," "Jewish Histories," "Bible," "Grammar and Dictionaries." The library's progress was slow, although in 1766

President Clap recorded with a degree of satisfaction: "We have a good library of about 4,000 volumes well furnished with ancient authors."

A new era opened with the advent of Ezra Stiles (1725–1795), president of the college from 1778 to 1795. A Hebraist, Stiles believed that America was "God's America," and that George Washington was "Joshua leading his people to freedom." At his induction as Yale's president he delivered a Hebrew oration. It had long been his practice to read one chapter of the Bible in Hebrew together with some passage of its Aramaic version every morning before breakfast, and on July 27, 1778, he volunteered to teach Semitics at the University. Two years later he inaugurated a daily Bible reading in Hebrew; this was subsequently increased to two readings. Stiles was convinced that one of the Psalms he taught his students would be the first they would hear chanted in Heaven. At one time he met a rabbi, Saul Cohen, who came from Jerusalem, and concerning whom the president noted in his diary: "This afternoon I spent with the Rabbi. I asked him when he expected the Messiah. He said daily, probably within forty years." Stiles bought a copy of the Zohar, the Bible of the Kabbalah, for his own studies, and later presented it to the library, with other volumes of Hebraica.

In view of this emphasis on Hebrew it is not surprising that in 1781 the Reverend Richard Salter, D.D., of Mansfield, Connecticut, established a special fund of £22 per annum, accruing from two hundred acres of land, for a professorship of Hebrew and other Oriental languages.

At Yale as at Harvard, the eighteenth-century enthusiasm for Hebrew subsided and remained dormant for a hundred years or so. Still, the Day Missions Library, established late in the nineteenth century by Professor George E. Day as part of the Divinity School Library, adopted the words *Yehi Or* ("Let there be light"), from Genesis 1:3 as the motto on its bookplate. It was indeed the dawn of a Hebraic renaissance.

What Sulzberger accomplished for the Jewish Theological Seminary, George Alexander Kohut accomplished for Yale. Kohut (1874–1933), "devoted servant of Judaism and dauntless protagonist of the Universal Power of Enlightenment," was born in Stuhlweissenburg, Hungary, the heir to a great literary tradition. His father, Alexander Kohut, who died in 1894 at the age of fifty-two, had spent twenty-five years of his life working on an edition of the *Aruch*—a comprehensive dictionary of the Talmud and Midrash compiled in Rome by Nathan ben Jechiel during the eleventh century—which consisted of 8,000 columns and took fourteen years to be printed. Kohut's work was described by Schechter as "the greatest and finest specimen of Hebrew learning ever produced by any Jew on this continent." [90] George Kohut, the son, was educated in Berlin at the *Hochschule für die Wissenschaft des Judentums,* and studied under Moritz Steinschneider.

In filial tribute the younger Kohut published at Berlin in 1897 *Semitic Studies in Memory of the Rev. Dr. Alexander Kohut,* in which forty-three distinguished Jewish and gentile scholars participated. Always deeply concerned with perpetuating the memory of scholars, he edited *Jewish Studies in memory of Israel Abrahams* (New York, 1927), and provided the inspiration for *Studies in Jewish Bibliography and Related Subjects in Memory of A.S. Freidus* (1867–1923) (New York, 1929), as well as *Abhandlungen zur Erinnerung an Hirsch Perez Chajes* (Vienna, 1933) and a special *Festschrift* to commemorate the eightieth birthday of the Orientalist Immanuel Löw (1854–1944) of Szeged, Hungary.

When Albert Tobias Clay (1866–1925), who was Laffan Professor of Assyriology and Babylonian Literature at Yale and the author of *A Hebrew Deluge Story in Cuneiform,* suggested that Kohut might consider Yale University as a repository for his father's books, the scholarly son, author of *Ezra Stiles and the Jews,* readily responded. In 1915 he presented 5,000 volumes of his father's library, a rich assortment of history, philosophy, Midrash, Halakhah, *responsa,* ethics, theology, and liturgy together with complete sets of several important Hebrew periodicals.

Books of special interest include the first edition of Muscato's *Nephutzot Yehudah* (Venice, 1588), one of the earliest collections of Jewish sermons; and the Yiddish translation of *Yossipon* ("Pseudo-Josephus") by Michael Adam, dated 1546, which is "one of the earliest Jewish books printed in Zurich, one of the few early Jewish illustrated books and one of the most beautiful specimens of Jewish printing in general." [91] It contains sixty-five woodcuts and was printed by Christoph Froschauer, who came to Zurich from Germany. Between 1521 and 1564 Froschauer printed 620 works, but *Yossipon* is his only Jewish production.

A fund of $5,000 provided by George Alexander Kohut for the library's upkeep was later considerably increased by a bequest from his devoted stepmother, Mrs. Rebekah Kohut. In 1919 Kohut established at Yale a fellowship for the advancement of studies in Semitics as well as a publication fund, and he showed constant concern for the library's growth. In 1929 he made this promise in a letter to Dr. Andrew Keogh, the Yale librarian: "One of these days I shall give you my Heine Collection, which is becoming really valuable. I have not much, but I believe there are something like 75 or 100 items among them, many precious autograph letters, parts of his published works in holograph." The following year he substantially increased the value of his Heine collection by purchasing four hundred volumes from Dr. Rutra in Munich.

The remarkable Heine library which he presented to Yale contains first and early editions, French translations, scholarly monographs, critical studies, biographies, a series of pamphlets of an anti-Semitic nature, and even some correspondence concerning the Heine monument in Düsseldorf. It has a perfect copy of the first edition of *Buch der Lieder* and a copy of the *Hamburg Waechter* of 1817 in which Heine made his debut as a poet. There are examples, too, of literary censorship. When Heine in somewhat unbridled terms describes Napoleon as "the revolutionary incarnate who booted and spurred and spattered with the blood of the battlefields, had mounted the bed of an Imperial blonde", the censor substituted "had married an imperial princess."

In 1913, in accordance with Kohut's will, his library was apportioned to the Jewish Institute of Religion, the American Jewish Historical Society, and Yale. The last received 950 volumes, including two Hebrew and three Latin incunabula, together with a copy of the Book of Numbers in Hebrew bearing the autograph of Isaac Touro, who served as a Jewish minister in Newport and was a close friend of Ezra Stiles.

THE ASCH COLLECTION

Through the philanthropist Louis M. Rabinowitz (1887–1957), Yale acquired the library of Sholem Asch (1880–1957), a native of Kutno, Poland who had emigrated to America in 1910, and was the foremost Yiddish novelist of all time. His library included 150 rare volumes, 30 manuscripts, and 7 incunabula acquired from the collector David Frankel. There were also eighty editions of his own works. This collection was acquired for Yale in 1944, and a catalogue was compiled and published by Leo Nemoy.

Asch's home was in Stamford, Connecticut, and both Dr. Nemoy, curator of Hebrew and Arabic literature, and Yale's librarian, James T. Babb, helped him in his literary work. Asch wrote in the introduction to the catalogue [92]: "I must confess that I have sought a home for my collection not in a Jewish institution, but in a general American one. America is no longer a temporary home, it is our permanent home, and we must plant our tree in its soil. Our contribution to human civilization through our contribution to the Jewish Christian idea must be represented in the general American Institutions of Learning."

The Asch collection includes numerous Bibles, rare editions of the Haggadah, scrolls of the Book of Esther, illuminated marriage contracts, and dowry lists. One of the printed books, the *Sepher Ziyyoni* by Menachem Ziyyoni, was condemned to be burnt—even though it had been revised by Vittorio Eliano, a convert of Jewish birth, and licensed by the Inquisition—and only a few copies escaped destruction.

The collection also provides illuminating glimpses of Asch himself. Among his own autographed manuscripts are those of the novels *Beim Opgrunt* ("The War Goes on"), *Farn Mabul* ("Three Cities"), *Got fun*

Nekomoh ("God of Vengeance"), *Gots Gefangene* ("God's Prisoners"), and *Der Sheliach* ("The Apostle"), as well as of *Was ich glaub* ("What I Believe"). Among personal papers are 277 communications, including letters, postcards, and telegrams, from many great contemporaries, among them the Hebrew poet Chayyim Nachman Bialik (1873–1934), Albert Einstein (1879–1955), Stefan Zweig (1881–1942), and Chaim Weitzmann (1874–1952). A letter, dated 1933, from the Yiddish P.E.N. Club in Warsaw, urges Asch not to decline the insignia of the Order of *Polonia Restituta* awarded to him by the government of Poland, which he was reluctant to accept because of its oppressive policy towards Polish Jews.

Ezra Stiles had regarded Hebrew "as a glorious language which throws more light on the Old Testament than all the commentators." In the 183 years since he made this statement, Hebrew has played a great and growing role in the academic life of Yale.

Chapter XXII

The Library of Congress, Washington, D. C.

"The Library of Congress is a people's library which provides for the people . . . the written record of their civilization." In these words Archibald Macleish, former Librarian of Congress and winner of the Pulitzer Prize for poetry, capsules the function of the largest library in the world.

Today the Library of Congress comprises 250 rooms, 35 acres of floor space, and 270 miles of bookshelves. It has approximately 40,000,000 items, 12,075,000 of which are classified as books and pamphlets; 5,600 are incunabula, 16,531,000 are manuscripts, and 167,000 are bound volumes of newspapers. In addition to nearly 150,000 books dealing with the Bible, Judaica, Palestine, and Zionism, there are a total of 68,470 books and 120 manuscripts in Hebrew and Yiddish.

The Library was established by an Act of Congress in 1880. In 1814 the British troops set fire to the Capitol and the collection was destroyed. It made a very slow recovery. After fifty years, in 1864, as onetime chief assistant librarian Frederick W. Ashley was later to declare, "The Library of Congress was nothing more than the name implied—a legislative collection, numbering 82,000 volumes. . . . It was nationalist in no sense but ownership." [93] Librarian Herbert Putnam put the Library on the bibliographic map. By another Act of Congress, the Division of Semitics and Oriental Languages was established on July, 1913, under Israel Schapiro (b. 1882), professor of Semitics at George Washington University from 1916 to 1927. He was followed by Dr. Theodor Herzl Gaster (b. 1906), son of the Sephardi *Chakkham* of England, Dr. Moses Gaster. Like so many collections in the United States, the Library of Congress owes a major part of its Hebraic possessions to benefactors Deinard and Schiff. The former collected the books; the latter purchased and donated them. The Jewish Theological Seminary of America, Yale, and Harvard are all indebted to Ephraim Deinard (1846–1930). Born in Sosmaken, Russia, Deinard traveled widely in Asia and Africa in search of hidden treasures. Eventually he established himself as a bookseller in Odessa. In 1888 he emigrated to the United States. A prolific writer Deinard was the author of fifty-two Hebrew books and edited the Hebrew weekly *Heleummi,* which ran to twenty-three issues. Putnam, "a progressive, original, practical and tactful commander, with a positive genius for creating enthusiasm and interest among his subordinates," forged the link between Deinard and Jacob Henry Schiff, banker and philanthropist.

In 1897 Schiff reorganized the Union Pacific Railroad, which was "battered, bankrupt and decrepit", and on his seventieth birthday he gave $100,000 to the Jewish Theological Seminary of America, especially earmarking this sum for the increase in faculty salaries. In response to an appeal from Putnam in 1912, Schiff purchased from Deinard a total of 9,936 volumes and 15 incunabula, for which he paid $30,000. Two years later he bought an additional 4,200 volumes. In 1917 and 1921 the Library of Congress bought 2,500 and 3,000 volumes from this same source. In all Deinard was responsible for the acquisition of nearly 26,000 volumes, over a third of the Library's entire collection of Hebraica.

"Such a collection," Putnam wrote, "ensures to the Library a fundamental beginning in a field in which it had as yet done practically nothing. We may justly expect that its presence here will invite additions which will not merely reinforce it in Jewish literature but expand it into a significant department embracing all semitics." His optimism was justified. The Library received three hundred Yiddish books from Dina Feingold in memory of her husband Max, and another 5,708 items from Jewish Cultural Reconstruction, Inc. The Committee of Sponsors for the Acquisition of the Rare Frankel Hebraica for the Library of Congress achieved its goal and purchased a complete collection of rarities brought to the United States by David Frankel of Vienna, well-known collector of Hebrew books and manuscripts.

The Library of Congress possesses a fine collection of Hebrew Bibles both with and without commentaries, including translations in ancient and modern languages from the sixteenth century to the present time. It has thirty-eight complete editions of the Mishnah and twenty-five different editions of the Talmud. It is particularly rich in liturgical works, among which are such treasures as the first Hebrew prayer book composed by Gaon Amram ben Sheshna, head of the Academy in Sura in Babylon, the prayer book of Saadia Gaon, and the *siddur* of Rashi. Also in the collection are synagogue rituals developed in individual communities, among them *Minhag Romi* (Rome), *Minhag Temen* (Yemen), and *Minhag Fez* (Morocco). There is a first edition of the Karaite prayer book (Venice, 1528–9), and also a copy of the *Tephilot ha-Falashi,* prayers of the Falasha Jews in Abyssinia, in which the Ethiopian text is accompanied by a Hebrew translation by Joseph Halevy, published in Paris in 1876.

As early as 1901 Samuel Wiener, the librarian of the Friedlaender Collection in the Asiatic Museum of the Russian Academy of Sciences, listed 909 editions of the Haggadah, and in 1960 Abraham Yaari listed 2,717 such items.[94] Today the Library of Congress has 530 different editions of Haggadot. A significant collection of American Hebraica is reinforced by thousands of Yiddish monographs and periodicals from Soviet Russia and a good representation of modern Hebrew literature.

Highly relevant to American Jewish history is *La Découverte des Sources du Mississippi* by J.C. Beltrami, dated 1824, from the press of Benjamin Levy, the first Jewish printer in New Orleans. Another book of importance is *The Republican Bank 1839 being an essay on the Present System of Banking: showing its evil tendency and developing an Entirely New Method of establishing a currency, which will not be at all subject to the various ill effects of our present paper money* (Madison, 1839). In a covering letter dated June 15, 1841, addressed to "His Excellency John Tyler, President of the United States," the author, E. Levy explained his patriotic motivation: "Respected Sir, Feeling deeply anxious about our beloved country I have thought a great deal about the tendency of our Monetary System. The enclosed pamphlet embodies the result of my investigation," etc. etc.

Twenty manuscript books and a number of receipts relate to the activities of the Inquisition in Spanish America (mainly Mexico) between 1611 and 1796. One document, dated April 30, 1611, attests that the ancestry of a certain Don Antonio Ziminez de Torres is "free from Jewish or Moorish blood."

As far as Jewish interests are concerned, the Library was of great service during the period of the Nazis and at the time of the establishment of the State of Israel. It supplied legislators and investigators with all manner of up-to-the-minute information regarding aspects of Jewish life and details of Nazi aggression. A Hebrew Union Catalogue containing 218,000 cards serves as a register for the holdings of the College of Jewish Studies in Chicago, the New York Public Library, Columbia University, YIVO, the Hebrew Union College, Dropsie College, Yale, and other major collections in the United States.

As one walks through the stately structure, built at a cost of seven million dollars, which is the setting for the most costly and elaborate library in the world, the words of British statesman James Ramsay MacDonald (1866–1937) aptly come to mind. At the laying of the cornerstone of the Manchester Public Library in 1930 he declared: "I do not want you to consider a library as a collection of books. A library is a dwelling place of great genius and powerful minds and spirits. Walk into a library . . . there will be some sentiment that will come into your mind. . . . You will feel that you ought to take your shoes off your feet, because the ground you are treading upon is holy ground."

The noble aspirations and great achievements of the Library of Congress are captured by such dicta as these, inscribed upon its marble walls: "Too low they build who build beneath the stars", and "The true *Shekinah* is man." It is fitting that the literary treasures of the Jews should be receiving growing attention in the capital of the United States of America.

Notes

1. *Megillah,* 29b.
2. Job VIII:7.
3. G. R. De Beer, *Sir Hans Sloane and the British Museum,* p. 139.
4. British Museum, Oriental Add. 4710. Edwards, *Memoirs of Libraries* (London, 1859), Vol. I, pp. 453–4; *Gentleman's Magazine,* February 1859; *Jewish Chronicle,* November 25, 1859.
5. *Jewish Chronicle,* July 29, 1881, p. 4.
6. On the Shapira case see *Times* for August 3, 17, 21, 25 and 27, 1883; *Jewish Chronicle* for August 3, 10, 24 and 31, 1883, and also for December 28, 1956 and February 15, 1957; British Museum Add. Mss. 41294; *Academy,* August 25, 1883, p. 131. Oscar K. Rabinowicz, "The Shapira Forgery Mystery" in *The Jewish Quarterly Review,* Vol. XLVII, No. 2, pp. 170–183.
7. S. Schechter, "The British Museum Hebrew Collection" in *Studies in Judaism,* p. 321.
8. Vol. XXX: p. 217b (1849).
9. Thomas Winton, *Documents from the Old Testament Times,* p. 187.
10. G. W. Wheeler, *Letters to James,* p. 187.
11. *The Bodleian Quarterly Record,* Vol. I, p. 228.
12. W. D. Macray, *Annals of the Bodleian Library,* p. 68 (note).
13. Cecil Roth, "Edward Pococke and the First Hebrew Printing in Oxford" in *The Bodleian Library Record.* Vol. II n. 27, p. 216.
14. Macray, *op. cit.,* p. 134.
15. Bodleian Library, MS. 28337, Western Add. C. 766.
16. I. Epstein, "Contribution of Jews' College to Jewish Learning" in *104th Annual Report of Jews' College* (1961), p. 91.
17. Bodleian MS. C. 47 fol. 135.
18. *Jewish World,* March 15, 1889.
19. *Oxford University Gazette,* May 15, 1960, p. 547.
20. Norman Bentwich, *Solomon Schechter,* p. 58.
21. *Menachot,* 29b.
22. Bentwich, *op. cit.,* p. 140.
23. Bentwich, *op. cit.,* p. 130.
24. P.E. Kahle, *The Cairo Geniza,* p. 11.
25. *Jewish Chronicle,* December 30, 1898, p. 12.
26. *Jewish Chronicle,* April 1, 1898.
27. Kahle, *op. cit.,* p. 12.
28. I Samuel XXVIII:8–25.
29. *Catalogue of the Pamphlets,* p. VI.
30. I. Abrahams and C.E. Sayle, "The Purchase of Hebrew Books by the English Parliament in 1647," p. 67.
31. J.E. Blunt, *A History of the Establishment and Residence of the Jews in England,* p. 71.

32. Claudius Buchanan Works, p. 193.
33. Cambridge University Add. MS 2581.
34. G.W. Prothero, *A Memoir of Henry Bradshaw,* p. 128.
35. Cambridge University Add. 2592.873.
36. *Ibid.*
37. *Jewish Chronicle,* May 20, 1886, p. 6.
38. Vol. 4–6. 1892–4.
39. *Cambridge University Reporter,* October 2, 1926.
40. *Abot* IV:3.
41. R. Lehmann, *History of Jews' College Library,* p. 1.
42. Ecclesiastes I:5.
43. *Jewish Chronicle,* December 15, 1905, p. 26.
44. Cecil Roth, *History of the Great Synagogue,* p. 270.
45. *Jewish Chronicle,* August 25, 1876.
46. *Ibid.,* October 17, 1845, p. 8.
47. Philip Ornstein, *Historical Sketch of the Beth Hamidrash,* p. 6.
48. Jewish Historical Society Transactions, X:150.
49. Norman Cohen, "Dayan B. Spiers," p. 590.
50. *Jewish Chronicle,* September 8, 1876.
51. *Hagadah for Passover,* p. VII.
52. Ornstein, *op. cit.,* p. 11.
53. A. Marx, *The Library of the Jewish Theological Seminary of America: Semi-centennial volume,* p. 88.
54. Bentwich, *op. cit.,* p. 97.
55. Solomon Schechter, *Seminary Addresses,* p. 19.
56. A. Marx, *op. cit.,* p. 90.
57. *Ibid.,* p. 91.
58. *Jewish Chronicle,* May 4, 1923.
59. E. Levine, "Essays in Memory of E.N. Adler," p. 119.
60. Mark Dvozhetsky, *Yerushalayim Delite in Kamf un Umkum,* p. 222.
61. *Catalogue of the Exhibition, The Shtell 1900–1939.*
62. *Jewish Chronicle,* August 26, 1932.
63. *Ibid.*
64. Leonard Stein, *The Balfour Declaration,* p. 218.
65. *Jewish Quarterly Review,* II (n.s.):256–276.
66. Aron Freimann, *A Gazetteer of Hebrew Printing.*
67. Joshua Bloch, *The People and The Book,* pp. 96–97 and Zedner's *Catalogue,* p. 758.
68. Bloch, *op. cit.,* p. 82, and A. Neubauer, "Alfonso de Zamora," in *Jewish Quarterly Review,* VII:398–417.
69. Mitchell M. Kaplan, *Panorama,* p. 237.
70. *Ibid.,* p. 239.
71. *Sanhedrin,* 105b.
72. Stephen S. Wise, *Challenging Years,* p. 72.
73. *American Jewish Year Book,* Vol. 49, p. 32.
74. Schechter, *op. cit.,* pp. 239–244.
75. Israel Knox, *Rabbi in America,* p. 51.
76. *Hebrew Union College Jubilee Volume,* p. 51.
77. *Virtue,* p. 74.
78. *Hebrew Union College Monthly,* Feb. 1918, p. 152.
79. N. Sokolow, *Baruch Spinoza Uzmano,* p. 6.
80. W.C. White, *Chinese Jews,* p. 31.
81. *Ibid.,* p. 44.
82. British Museum MSS. 29868.
83. *Report of the London Society,* p. 75.

84. *Abot* V:16.
85. Robert Gordis, "The Life of Professor Max Leopold Margolis," p. 8; also *The Maccabean,* Vol. XII, n. 3, 1907, pp. 93–9.
86. *Ibid.,* Vol. XXI, n. 2, pp. 41–6.
87. Kaufmann Kohler, "Reform Judaism and Zionism," in *Reform Advocate,* Vol. XXXIII, No. 7 (April 6, 1907) p. 198ff; also Gordis, *op. cit.,* p. 10.
88. *American Jewish Historical Society of America,* XXXIII:155.
89. G.A. Kohut, "Judah Monis," in *The American Journal of Semitic Languages and Literature,* p. 219; also Lee M. Friedman, "Judah Monis, First Instructor in Hebrew at Harvard University," in Publications of the *American Jewish Historical Society,* n. XXII:1–24.
90. Schechter, *op. cit.,* p. 12.
91. L. Nemoy in *Yale University Library Gazette,* IV:3.
92. L. Nemoy, *Catalogue,* p. XVI.
93. Frederick W. Ashley, "Three Eras in the Library of Congress," in *Essays offered to Herbert Putnam,* p. 57.
94. Abraham Yaari, *Bibliography of the Passover Haggadah.*

Glossary

Abot—Literally, "Fathers"; tractate of the *Mishnah Nezikin*. It contains the sayings and religio-ethical teachings of the sages from the third century B.C. to the third century C.E.

Adar—Twelfth month of the Jewish calendar.

Ashkenazim—Jews originating in Northern or Central Europe.

Av—Fifth month of the Jewish calendar.

Baal Shem—Master of God's Name, a Kabbalist.

Baba Batra—Name of a tractate of the Talmud.

Ben—Son of.

Berakhot—Literally, "Blessings"; first tractate of the *Mishnah* order of *Zeraim*. It deals with the recitation of the *Shema,* blessings, and prayer in general.

Bet Din—Literally, house of law; i.e., a gathering of three learned men acting as a Jewish court of law.

Bet Hamidrash—House of study.

Chakham—Sephardi Chief Rabbi.

Chalizah (pl. *Chalizot*) —The rite which enables a childless widow to remarry.

Chassidim—Pietists, followers of Rabbi Israel Baal Shem Tov (1700–1760).

Chazan—Reader.

Cheder—Literally, a room, i.e., a Hebrew elementary school.

Cherem—A form of excommunication.

Chevrah—Society, study circle.

Dayyan—Literally, "Judge"; a member of the *Bet Din*.

Elul—Sixth month of the Jewish calendar.

Gaon (pl. *Geonim*) —The title of the head of the rabbinical academies in Babylon.

Haggadah—(1) The Book containing the service read at the family table on the first two nights of Passover; (2) the portion of the Talmud containing homilies, as distinct from Halakhah.

Halakhah—Literally, guidance; (1) legal literature of Judaism; (2) final decision of the rabbis, whether based on tradition or on argument concerning disputed rules of conduct.

Haphtarah—Literally "conclusion"; selections from the prophetic books of the Bible read in the synagogue on Sabbaths, festivals, and afternoons of fast days, after the reading from the Pentateuch.

Haskalah—Literally, "enlightenment"; the movement for spreading modern European culture among Jews.

Hoshanah Rabbah—Seventh day of the Feast of Booths.

Illui—Literally, "exalted"; a title given to an exceptionally brilliant young student of the Talmud.

Kabbalah—Mysticism.

Karaites—Members of a sect that recognized only the literal interpretation of the Bible.

Ketubah—Literally, "writing"; the document embodying the obligations of the bridegroom towards his bride, which in rabbinic law is a prerequisite of marriage. The minimum settlement for a virgin is two hundred zuz and for a widow remarrying, one hundred zuz.

Kinot—Elegies recited on the 9th of *Av*.

Machzor—Prayer book for solemn days and festivals.

Marranos—Name given in Spain to the Jews who had been compelled to adopt Christianity.

Masorah—The body of tradition which concerns the correct spelling, writing, and reading of the Hebrew Bible.

Megillah—Literally, "scroll," a term commonly applied to the Book of Esther, which is read in the synagogue on the eve and morning of Purim.

Mekhiltah—Literally, "measure"; Midrash on Exodus.

Midrash (pl. *Midrashim*)—Literally, "expositions," books devoted to the homiletic exposition of the Scriptures.

Mishnah—The collection of the statements of the *Tannaim* edited by Rabbi Judah the Patriarch (*c.* 135–*c.* 220).

Mohel—A person qualified to perform ritual circumcision.

Nisan—First month of the Jewish calendar.

Passover—The festival commemorating the liberation of the Jews from their bondage in Egypt.

Piyyutim—Liturgical poems.

Purim—Literally, "lots"; the festival celebrating the story told in the Book of Esther.

Responsa—Written replies of the rabbis to question on Jewish Law.

Rosh Hashanah—Literally, "head of the year"; the Jewish New Year observed on the first and second days of *Tishri*.

Sanhedrin—The Council of State and supreme tribunal of the Jewish people.

Seder—Literally, "order"; the religious home service recounting the liberation from Egyptian bondage, celebrated on the first and second nights of passover.

Sephardim—Jews originating from Spain and Portugal.

Sepher Torah—Scroll of the Law.

Shamash—Beadle.

Shechitah—The ritual slaughter and preparation of meat for consumption by Jews.

Shekhinah—The Divine Presence.

Shema—Literally, "hear"; the Biblical verse "Hear O Israel," etc., Deut. VI:4.

Shemini Azeret—The eighth day of Tabernacles.

Shochet—Ritual slaughterer.

Shophar—Horn of a ram blown on Rosh Hashanah.

Siddur—The authorized daily Prayer Book of the Jews.

Sidra—The weekly portion read at the synagogues.

Simchat Torah—Literally, "Rejoicing of the Torah"; the festival immediately following Succot.

Siphra—Literally, "the book"; Midrash on Leviticus.

Succot—The Festival of the Ingathering, which commences on the 15th of *Tishri* and which also commemorates the divine protection given to the Israelites during their wanderings through the wilderness.

Takkanah (pl. *Takkanot*)—A communal ordinance.

Talmud—Literally, "learning." The general sense of the word is "study" of the Law. It is more common in the narrower sense of the comments and discussions (the *Gemara,* lit. "completion") on the text of the Mishnah by Palestinian and Babylonian scholars from the third to the fifth century C.E., which constitutes the Palestinian Talmud (*Talmud Yerushalmi*) and the Babylonian Talmud (*Talmud Babli*). The Babylonian Talmud contains nearly 3,000 pages and was edited by Rav Ashi (352–427 C.E.), whereas the Palestinian Talmud was finished in the fifth century and is only one-seventh as long as the Babylonian Talmud.

Tammuz—The fourth month of the Jewish calendar.

Tanna (pl. *Tannaim*)—A rabbi quoted in the Mishnah or Baraithas.

Targum (pl. *Targumim*)—Literally, "Translation." The word "Targum" may mean a translation into any language. However, beginning with the Talmudic period, it usually meant the Aramaic translation of the Bible.

Tevet—Tenth month of the Jewish calendar.

Torah—Literally, teaching; the whole body of Jewish religious literature.

Tosaphot—Critical glosses on the Talmud by French rabbis of the twelfth and thirteenth centuries.

Yeshiva—A college for talmudic studies.

Yom Kippur—The Day of Atonement.

Zohar—Literally, splendor; a mystical commentary on the Pentateuch attributed to Rabbi Simon bar Yochai.

Bibliography

ABRAHAMS ISRAEL and C.E. SAYLE. "The Purchase of Hebrew Books by the English Parliament in 1647," in *Transactions of the Jewish Historical Society of England,* VIII: 63–78. London. 1918.

Accounts & Papers printed by Order of the House of Commons. London, 1849.

ADLER, CYRUS. *I Have Considered the Days.* Philadelphia, 1941.

ADLER, ELKAN N. "The Hebrew Treasures in England," in *Transactions of the Jewish Historical Society of England,* VIII: 1–19. London, 1918.

American Jewish Year Book, The. Cyrus Adler, Harry Schneiderman, eds. Philadelphia, 1889—.

ASHLEY, FREDERICK, W. "Three Eras in the Library of Congress," in *Essays offered to Herbert Putnam by His Colleagues and Friends on His Thirtieth Anniversary as Librarian of Congress.* William Warner Bishop and Andrew Keogh, eds. New Haven, 1929.

BARWICK, G.F. *The Reading Room of the British Museum.* London, 1929.

BENTWICH, NORMAN. *Solomon Schechter.* Philadelphia, 1948.

BEN JACOB, ISAAC. *Otzar Hasepharim.* Vilna, 1880.

BLOCH, JOSHUA. *The People and the Book.* New York, 1954.

BLUNT, J.E. *A History of the Establishment and Residence of the Jews in England; With an Enquiry Into Their Civil Disabilities.* London, 1830.

Bodleian Quarterly Record, Oxford, 1917; and *The Bodleian Library Record.* Oxford, 1938.

BUCHANAN, CLAUDIUS. *Works.* New York, 1812.

Catalogue of the Exhibition, the Shtetl 1900–1939. YIVO, New York, 1959.

Catalogue Exhibition, Vilna—A Jewish Community in Times of Glory and in Time of Destruction. YIVO, New York, 1960.

Catalogue of the Exhibition, Jewish Life in Shanghai. September 1948–1949. YIVO, New York, 1949.

COHEN, BOAZ. "The Library of the Jewish Theological Seminary of America," in *Jewish Forum,* XVII, nos. 1 and 2, Jan. and Feb. New York, 1934.

COHEN, NORMAN. "Dayan B. Spiers" in *The Jewish Monthly,* pp. 588–598. London. January, 1952.

COWLEY, A.E. *A Concise Catalogue of the Hebrew Printed Books in the Bodleian Library.* Oxford, 1929.

DE BEER, G.R. *Sir Hans Sloane and the British Museum.* Oxford, 1953.

De Ricci, Seymour. *British Collectors of Books and Manuscripts 1830–1930.* Cambridge, 1936.

Dvozhetsny, Mark. *Yerushalayim Delite in Kamf un Umkum.* Paris, 1948.

Epstein, Isidore. "Contribution of Jews' College to Jewish Learning," in the *104th Annual Report of Jews College.* London, 1961.

Esdaile, Arundel. *The British Museum Library.* London, 1961.

——. *National Libraries of the World.* Rev. ed. by F.J. Hill. London, 1957.

Evans, Charles. *American Bibliography.* 12 vols. Chicago, 1903–34.

Freidus, A.S. *Studies in Jewish Bibliography and Related Subjects in Memory of Abraham Solomon Friedus (1867–1923) Late Chief of the Jewish Division, New York Public Library.* Alexander Kohut Memorial Foundation, New York, 1929.

Freimann, Aron. *A Gazetteer of Hebrew Printing.* New York, 1946.

Ginzberg, Louis. *Geonica.* 2 vols., New York 1909.

——. *Geniza Studies in Memory of Dr. Solomon Schechter.* 2 vols., New York, 1928–29.

Goitein, S.D. "Geniza papers of a Documentary character in the Gaster Collection of the British Museum" in *Jewish Quarterly Review,* LI:34–67. Philadelphia, 1960.

Golb, Norman. "Sixty Years of Geniza Research", in *Judaism,* VI:3–16. New York, 1957.

Goodman, Philip. "Love of books as revealed in Jewish Bookplates," in *Jewish Book Annual,* XII:84ff. New York, 1934.

Gordis, Robert (ed.). *Max Leopold Margolis, Scholar & Teacher.* Philadelphia, 1952.

Halberstamm, Solomon. *Kehillat Shlomoh* (a catalogue of his manuscripts). Vienna, 1890.

Halper, B. *Descriptive Catalogue of the Genizah Fragments in Philadelphia.* Philadelphia, 1924.

Harstein, Jacob I. "Yeshiva University," in *American Jewish Year Book* (5704), XLV:73–84.

Hebrew Union College. *Jubilee Volume.* Cincinnati, 1925.

Hirschfeld, Hartwig. *Descriptive catalogue of the Hebrew MSS. of the Montefiore Library.* London, 1904.

Jewish Quarterly Review, Oct. 1888–July 1908, London; and from July 1908, edited for the Dropsie College for Hebrew and Cognate Learning, Philadelphia.

Kahle, Paul E. *The Cairo Geniza.* Oxford, 1959.

Kaplan, Mitchell M. *Panorama of Ancient Letters: Four and a Half Centuries of Hebraica.* New York, 1942.

Katsh, Abraham I. *New York University, Chair of Hebrew Culture and Education.* A report, July, 1952. pp. 1–2.

——. *Ginze Russiyah.* New York, 1958.

Kerstein, Solomon. "Jewish Book Collections in American Libraries and Universities," in *Jewish Book Annual,* IV:104–120. New York, 1945–6.

KIEV, EDWARD I., and JOHN J. TEPFER. "Jewish Institute of Religion," in *American* Jewish Year Book, 5078 (pp. 91–100). New York, 1947.

———. "The Jewish Theological Seminaries and their Libraries", in *Library Trends,* Vol. 9, No. 2. University of Illinois, 1960.

KNOX, ISRAEL. *Rabbi in America.* Boston, 1957.

KOHUT, G.A. "Judah Monis", in *The American Journal of Semitic Languages and Literature,* Vol. XIV, No. 4. New York, 1898, pp. 217–226.

KOHUT, REBECCA. *His Father's House; The Story of George Alexander Kohut.* New Haven, 1938.

KRAELING, CARL H. "Yale's Collection of Judaica", in *The Yale University Li brary Gazette,* XIII:85–94. New Haven, 1939.

LEHMANN, RUTH P. *History of Jews' College Library 1860–1960.* London, 1960.

LEVEEN, JACOB. *The Hebrew Bible in Art* (The Schweich Lectures, 1939). London, 1944.

LEVINE, E. "Essays in Memory of E. N. Adler," in *Miscellanies of the Jewish Historical Society of England,* Part V. London, 1948.

LOEWE, HERBERT. *Catalogue of the printed books and of the Semitic and Jewish MSS. in the Mary Frere Hebrew Library at Girton College.* Cambridge, 1915.

———. *Catalogue of the MSS. in the Hebrew character collected and bequeathed to Trinity College Library by the late William Aldis Wright.* Cambridge, 1926.

MACRAY, W.D. *Annals of the Bodleian Library.* Oxford, 1890.

MARGOLIOUTH, G. *Descriptive list of the Hebrew and Samaritan Manuscripts.* London, 1893.

———. *Catalogue of the Hebrew and Samaritan MSS. in the British Museum.* 4 vols., London, 1899–1935 (Vol. IV by J. Leveen).

MARX, ALEXANDER. *The Library of the Jewish Theological Seminary of America: Semi-centennial Volume.* New York, 1939. pp. 87–120.

———. *Studies in Jewish History and Booklore.* New York, 1944.

———. *Essays in Jewish Biography.* Philadelphia, 1947.

———. "The Importance of the Geniza for Jewish History", *in Proceedings of the American Academy for Jewish Research,* XVI:183–204. (1947).

———. *The Polemical Manuscripts in the Library of the Jewish Theological Seminary. New York,* 1929.

MARWICK, LAWRENCE. *The Hebraic Section and the Collections of Hebraica in the Library of Congress.* Typescript sent to the author, 1961.

MENDELSOHN, ISAAC. "Near East Collection at Columbia", in *Columbia University Quarterly.* New York, 1940. pp. 289–295.

METCALF, KEYES D. "Jewish Collections in American Libraries." (Lecture delivered at the Boston Book Week, May 7, 1939).

MULLINGER, J.B. *The University of Cambridge.* 3 vols., Cambridge, 1873.

NEMOY, LEO. *Catalogue of Hebrew and Yiddish Manuscripts and Books from the Library of Sholem Asch presented to Yale University by Louis M. Rabinowitz.* New York, 1945.

———. "Hebrew and kindred Manuscripts in the Yale University Library" in *Journal of Jewish Bibliography,* I:07–110; III:44–47. New York, 1939, 1942.

———. "George Alexander Kohut," in *The Yale University Gazette,* IX:96–98. New Haven, April 1935.

———. *Check list of an exhibition of Judaica and Hebraica held at the Sterling Memorial Library, Yale University, April to June,* 1933. New Haven, 1933.

———. "Sholem Asch Library", in *The Yale University Library,* No. 4. April, 1944. pp. 54–63.

———. "Alexander Kohut Memorial Collection of Judaica", in *Yale University Library Gazette,* II:17–25. October 1927.

NEUBAUER, A. *Catalogue of the Hebrew MSS. in the Jews' College, London.* Oxford, 1886.

———. "Alfonso de Zamora," in *Jewish Quarterly Review.* Vol. VIII. London, 1894.

———. *Catalogue of the Hebrew manuscripts in the Bodleian Library* (Vol. II by A. Neubauer and A.E. Cowley) . Oxford, 1886–1906.

OATES, J.G.T. *A Catalogue of the 15th Century Books in the University Library.* Cambridge, 1954.

OKO, ADOLPH S. "The Jewish Book Collections in the United States," in *American Jewish Year Book,* 5704 (Vol. XLV) . New York, 1943.

ORNSTEIN, PHILIP. *Historical Sketch of the Beth Hamidrash.* London, 1905.

Oxford University Gazette. Oxford, 1960.

PALMER, E.H. *A Descriptive Catalogue of the Arabic, Persian and Turkish manuscripts in the Library of Trinity College, Cambridge. With an appendix containing a catalogue of the Hebrew and Samaritan MSS. in the same Library.* Cambridge, 1870.

PEARSON, J.D. *Oriental Manuscript Collections.* London, 1954.

PERILMAN, NATHAN A. *One Hundred Years of Congregation Emanu-El.* New York, 1945.

PROTHERO, G.W. *A Memoir of Henry Bradshaw.* London, 1888.

Publications of the American Jewish Historical Society. New York, 1893.

RABINOWICZ, H. "Undiscovered World at Cambridge," in *Jewish Chronicle,* Sept. 23, 1960.

———. "Treasures of the Bodleian," in *Jewish Life.* New York, June 1960.

———. "Hebrew Treasures", in *Jewish Chronicle,* January 15, 1960.

RABINOWICZ, OSCAR K. "The Shapira Forgery Mystery," in *The Jewish Quarterly Review,* XLVII:170–183. Philadelphia, 1956.

Report of the London Society for Promoting Christianity Amongst the Jews. London, 1851.

RIEU, CHARLES. *Catalogue of the Persian Manuscripts in the British Museum.* 3 vols. London, 1879–83.

ROBAK, A.A. "Rare Yiddish Books in the Library of the University of Harvard," in *Philologische Schriften,* II:381–400. Vilna, 1928.

ROTH, CECIL. *Magna Bibliotheca Anglo-Judaica.* London, 1937.

——— (ed.). *Jewish Art: an Illustrated History.* Tel-Aviv, 1961.

——. *History of the Great Synagogue,* London, 1950.

——. "Edward Pococke and the First Hebrew Printing in Oxford," in *The Bodleian Library Record,* Vol II. Oxford, 1948.

——. *The Kennicott Bible.* Bodlein Picture Books No. II. Oxford, 1957.

ROSENBACH, A.S.W. *An American Jewish Bibliography.* New York, 1926.

SAYLE, CHARLES. *Annals of the Cambridge University Library.* Cambridge, 1916.

SCHECHTER, SOLOMON. "Notes on the Hebrew MSS in the University Library of Cambridge," in *Jewish Quarterly Review,* IV–VI:90–101. London, 1892.

——. "British Museum Hebrew Collection" in *Studies in Judaism,* pp. 306–328. London, 1896.

——. *Seminary Addresses.* New York, 1959.

SCHILLER-SZINESSY, S.M. *Catalogue of the Hebrew manuscripts preserved in the University Library,* Vol. I. Cambridge, 1876.

SPIERS, BERNARD (ed.). *Hagadah for Passover.* London, 1954.

SOKOLOW, NACHUM. *Baruch Spinoza Uzmano* (Baruch Spinoza and His Times). Paris, 1929.

STEIN, LEONARD. *The Balfour Declaration.* London, 1961.

STEINSCHNEIDER, MORITZ. *Catalogus Librorum Hebraeorum in Bibliotheca Bodleiana.* Berlin, 1852–60.

TEICHER, J.L. "Hebrew printed Fragments" in *Bodleian Library Record.* I:234–36. Oxford, 1939–41.

THOMASON, G. *Catalogue of the Pamphlets, Books, Newspapers and Manuscripts Relating to the Civil War, The Commonwealth and Restoration, Collected by George Thomason, 1640–1661,* Vol. I. London, 1908.

VAN STRAALEN, SAMUEL. *Catalogue of the Hebrew Books in the British Museum Acquired During the Years 1868–1892.* London, 1894.

WHEELER, G.W. *Letters to James.* Oxford, 1926.

WHITE, WILLIAM CHARLE:. *Chinese Jews.* Toronto, 1942.

WINTON, THOMAS. *Documents from the Old Testament Times.* London, 1958.

WISE, STEPHEN SAMUEL. *Challenging Years.* London, 1951.

WOLF, EDWIN and JOHN F. FLEMING. *Rosenbach: A Biography.* New York, 1960.

WOLFSON, HARRY. "Hebrew Books in Harvard," in *Harvard Alumni Bulletin* XXXIX:886–897. New Haven, 1932.

WORMALD, F., and WRIGHT, C.E. *The English Library before 1700.* London, 1958.

ZAFREN, HERBERT C. "Printed Rarities in the Hebrew Union College Library," in *Studies in Bibliography and Booklore,* V:137–156. Cincinnati, 1961.

ZEDNER, JOSEPH. *Catalogue of the Hebrew Books in the Library of the British Museum.* London, 1867.

Index